A unique new framework for industry

STORM
the NORM

PRAISE FOR THE BOOK

'Disrupting what you do today will be a key capability to win tomorrow. Anisha Motwani has put together a lovely collection of brand stories that 'storm the norm'. The future will belong to leaders and marketers who have the benefit of the experience, wisdom and pointers from this wonderful book. Carry it, read it, annotate it. This book will be the norm!'
—D. Shivakumar, Chairman and CEO,
PepsiCo India Holdings Pvt. Ltd

'Brands are the most valued and prized possessions in today's world. Creation of brands is both an art and a science; and a treatise like this that analyses how successful brands have been built in India—seen through the lens of an experienced and successful marketer like Anisha Motwani—is an invaluable read for anyone who has anything to do with business, branding, marketing, advertising or media.'
—Sam Balsara,
Chairman, Madison World

'Carry this book in your bag and refer to it often if you are looking at storming the norms in your industry. Each story has insights you won't find anywhere else.'
—Ajay Bijli,
Chairman and Managing Director, PVR Ltd

'In today's world everyone seems to be "over-promising and under-delivering". Lofty claims, promotions and advertising often mislead people. Anisha's book compiles brands that are examples of true excellence. She helps you understand and learn "how they did it".'
—Analjit Singh,
Founder and Chairman, Max India Group

'Developing a successful brand is a challenging but significant process. Anisha Motwani has researched and presented twenty successful brands that show us the value and power of innovative brands in India. As a professor of marketing, I know how important such a work can be for the business world. We can all learn from this timely and worthwhile book.'
—Professor Dipak C. Jain, Director, Sasin Graduate Institute of Business
Administration of Chulalongkorn University, Bangkok, Thailand

A unique new framework for industry

STORM the NORM

UNTOLD STORIES OF 20 BRANDS THAT DID IT BEST

Conceptualized and Edited by

ANISHA MOTWANI

Foreword by
SANTOSH DESAI

Afterword by
RANJAN MALIK

MAVEN
RUPA

Published in Maven by
Rupa Publications India Pvt. Ltd 2016
7/16, Ansari Road, Daryaganj
New Delhi 110002

Sales Centres:

Allahabad Bengaluru Chennai
Hyderabad Jaipur Kathmandu
Kolkata Mumbai

ISBN: 978-81-291-3702-9

First impression 2016

10 9 8 7 6 5 4 3 2 1

Printed by Replika Press Pvt. Ltd., India

To my father, who left imprints of
knowledge and wisdom in my life.
Wherever you are, you'll always be in my heart.

Success is the consequence of courage,
commitment, and competence.
You cannot seek a consequence—it has to be created.
—Sadhguru Jaggi Vasudev

CONTENTS

FOREWORD

That we live in a world of brands is now a statement of fact and not hyperbole. Brands are all around us, and indeed we have begun to look upon almost everything as a brand. In spite of the undeniable fact that we find the idea of a brand so useful in our everyday lives, and that brands have been around for such a long time in this country, we know little about what makes these brands tick, who the people behind these brands are, and what goes into their making and, sometimes, unmaking. Brands are the building blocks of modern business, intangible assets often more valuable than those of the brick-and-mortar variety, ideas that live on even as products and companies that were once their vehicles pass on.

We read the biographies of great men and women, we devour the stories of business empires and create folk heroes out of figures in popular culture. When we do hear about brands, it is either by way of highly structured case studies or by way of anecdote or sketchy journalistic coverage. When business talks about brands, it displays a peculiar knack for taking a highly interesting subject and burying it knee deep in clichés. What suffers is genuine learning, a process that requires data and past experience, filtered through the lens of nuanced analysis. What is needed is a new way of talking about brands and learning from those who have built something powerful and essential out of the raw material of ideas, insight and rigorous practice.

It is time for us to hear the stories behind brands, for building brands is not merely about business. Brand stories are like detective stories of ideas—they involve a deep understanding of some human truths, they slice open implicit cultural impulses, create products and services that make us experience the world in new ways, act in ways clever and wise, bold and inspired, fail in ways stupid and spectacular, communicate in a dazzling array of forms. In short they tell us about themselves, the people behind them and, above all, about ourselves, those who interact with these brands.

Building brands in India presents challenges of many kinds. An ancient culture with its own codes, an unevenly developed market, a bursting-with-aspiration consumer, diverse competitors and a fragmented media landscape, all add up to complexity of a formidable kind. Growing categories and building leadership positions require a combination of many abilities and doing so consistently is a daunting enterprise.

The stories that follow are handpicked accounts of what went into building some of the most powerful and innovative brands in the country. Given that business in India has tended to look Westwards when it comes to case studies involving brands, indeed there is greater familiarity among Indian practitioners with brands like Apple, Microsoft, Nike, Dove and Virgin than with local success stories. This book is a treasure trove of stories about Indian brands that have succeeded in the face of great challenges. Like all good stories, they carry nuggets of wisdom and learning, and, like the truly great stories, they sometimes leave the extraction of this learning to the reader. Covering a diverse range of categories and contexts, they are designed to stimulate thought and promote reflection. The learning lies in stories of both similarity and difference; in some cases readers will find situations that are analogous to the ones they encounter, while in others they will find ideas that help imagine their own context very differently.

Under the able handling of Anisha Motwani, who is both an experienced marketer and an engaged thinker, the book that you are about to read will make it easy to learn from the experience of successful brands; more importantly, it will open new doors in your mind.

Santosh Desai

INTRODUCTION

As human beings, we are born to be curious. We are wired to search for knowledge, ideas and patterns and see how we can use them to better our own world and the world of those around us. As someone passionate about consumer insights and behaviour, I was always intrigued by companies that managed to create strong consumer connections by thinking ahead of their time, by not following the beaten path. As I grew in my career, so did the urge to find out what went on behind the scenes in these organizations. This book is an outcome of harnessing my long journey of curiosity to create a reservoir of success stories that can benefit others who are equally hungry for knowledge.

The idea for the book began with a simple thought. In a diverse, challenging and often unpredictable market like India, a handful of companies are doing an excellent job of attracting consumers and meeting their needs as well as creating business value for themselves. Digging deeper, I realized that most of these companies have done something out of the ordinary and, in the process, they have stormed and shaken up the market, transforming stale categories into vibrant ones.

Some of these are also companies talked about in the media, but most often, the details are sketchy and sporadic. A marketing campaign here, a quote from a senior official there or, sometimes, an interview with the head of the company to seemingly get a preview of what's cooking inside. But what emerges most often is a snapshot of their market performance or the new launches that are on the way. The whole gamut of thinking and work that is feeding their success engine is seldom examined— what challenges they faced; what internal and external obstacles became stumbling blocks; what decisions were made at key junctures; and what the execution roadmap that paved the way for actual performance was.

It is out of the need to address these very gaps that this book has emerged. I felt that if the wisdom of this handful of companies could be made available to a wider public, it would help many more people, in turn, become winners in their own spheres.

The stories in this book belong to leading businesses and the people that run them. On the face of it, we already recognize them as markers of success in their categories. However, my real interest lay in uncovering the strategies that have been undertaken to help them achieve continuous success. What did they do that was against the expected? How did they storm the norm to create fresh new categories or business models or change consumer habits permanently? And did they do that right from the word go, or did they have to sweat it out to become the powerful influencers they are today?

Interestingly, while going through the chosen businesses, along with Ranjan Malik, an innovation specialist, I discovered that it is possible to put a method on how to learn from these brands, how one can actually storm the norm. We have synthesized this in the form of a framework which you can find in the Afterword. You could go through it after you have read some or all the stories and feel free to use it as a template to storm the norm and succeed in your next big challenge.

Coming back to the book. The first step in the creation of *Storm the Norm* was to decide which businesses to cover. A structured, rigorous and multi-phased process was adopted to arrive at the set of brands that you see featured in this book. The process began by scanning the marketplace for companies that are successful in India. These could be home grown, multinational or global, but the focus was their operations in India. This turned out to be a huge list. It was then pruned after assessing these companies along various parameters like market share, brand popularity, consumer trust and how action-oriented they had been. Another round followed to eliminate those organizations about which a lot has already been written and whose strategies are widely known. This shortlist was then evaluated to ensure that a diverse mix of industries was represented.

But it was not enough to simply have brands represented across a variety of sectors. I wanted to get stories from businesses operating at differing life stages and with different mindsets. This led to developing a segmentation approach in order to classify businesses based on these aspects. The result? The following three segments emerged:

a) Legacy Businesses: Companies that have been in the country for several years, often decades, and have continued to stay on top of their game by storming the norm and by reinventing and innovating themselves.

b) Challenger Businesses: Companies that have made a significant mark by challenging the leader in their category through innovative products, services and marketing.

c) Entrepreneurial Businesses: Companies that may be big or small, standalone or part of a large corporate, but which stand out for their entrepreneurial spirit—their ability to unlock hidden opportunities, take bold steps and create entirely new categories by themselves.

Each of the final set of brands that made the cut falls into one of these segments. For instance, *The Times of India*, Saffola, Cadbury Dairy Milk, Raymond, Kissan and MTR Foods are all legacy businesses. On the other hand, Sprite, Axis Bank, Ford EcoSport, Fiama Di Wills, Honda Motors, Idea, Mahindra XUV500, Tata Tea, Sensodyne and Kurkure are all challengers; while PVR, MakeMyTrip, Dabur Real and Radio Mirchi fall under the entrepreneurial segment.

Once the final list was complete, the next step was to contact the businesses and seek permissions for their participation. I have to admit here that I was delighted to have every single company I approached say a resounding yes to joining me in being part of this book.

In order to get the story out, a master framework was designed, that could trigger all the information necessary for stitching up a story. The framework was not a prescriptive template, but rather a guidepost comprising a series of questions to get the teams thinking in the appropriate direction. To elaborate, the framework had questions around how the brand's journey began, impediments faced during the most critical times for the business, principles and philosophy of the brand, key strategies adopted to beat the competition, innovations that helped leapfrog the business and finally, the results of the all the sweat, toil and hard work.

This framework was then customized based on the segment the brand belonged to. For instance, businesses belonging to the legacy segment were specifically asked to dwell upon how they have managed to reinvent and stay relevant with changing consumer needs and evolving social and cultural norms. Businesses belonging to the challenger segment were asked to share how they took on the established brands in their category. Details on how they thought differently, what disruptive strategies they implemented and how they positioned their brands in order to carve out their own niche were sought from them. Businesses belonging to the entrepreneurial segment were asked to describe how they spotted new opportunities and made the most of them. In other words, what risky decisions they undertook that at that time seemed very bold and perhaps even foolish and how they got consumers to re-evaluate the entire category.

In addition to this, some more customization was done to include questions based on the nature of the industry the particular business was in and some questions exclusive to the brand as well. Only then was the final framework, unique to each brand, shared with the respective brand custodians. Often, this guidepost served as a great discussion tool that led to more ideas and more information territories that would make the story compelling and insightful.

All through this phase, I was supported by Pragya Khanna, a creative thinker, hands-on marketer and an expert on branding herself. She contributed wholeheartedly and brought in a lot of insightful perspectives on the approach and methodology for selection of brands and in arriving at the three business segments.

The next critical step was to decide upon how these stories would get written. I was clear that each brand story had to be authored by the people who were behind the wheels of the business, the people who conceptualized and executed game-changing strategies. Only those in the thick of the action would know the inner workings, the events that unfolded, the highs and lows experienced and the interlinkages across various functions in their organization. Only they, and not an outsider, would be able to create a holistic picture of what took place. Each story that you read here is thus a true reflection of the personal experiences of an individual or a team.

This decision has led to a couple of very interesting outcomes. First, what you see in this book are clearly people and business stories and not sterile case studies. There are strategies and tactics outlined for sure, but equally there are anecdotes, experiences and even blunders because that is the reality that precedes success. And like in life, the flow of events is sometimes non-linear and discontinuous.

Second, the narrative is not templated and typecast in some rigid format. Since the individual stories have been crafted by different people, it was felt that the flavour needed to be retained in the final output. Hence each business story has deliberately not been standardized for tone of voice or style of narration. So you will see plenty of writing styles. You will find some to be formal while some a little less so, some written from the point of view of a business team while others written almost as personal experiences. There are also differences in the time span. Some have chosen to sketch their whole journey from inception to date while others have chosen to put their focus on recent efforts only.

Third, how brands have chosen to define their success metrics is itself not a universal format. So across the rich spectrum of companies covered, you will read versatile definitions of success. Growth, share, behaviour change, external recognition, consumer take-up rate are just a few of the ways different brands have expressed their accomplishments. And rightly so, given that each organization is unique and so is its culture, stage of life and character, so how can success be one-dimensional?

However, the lessons one can learn from each account as well as the key strategies that made achievements possible have uniformly been highlighted across the stories. Often, when a story is being told chronologically, it is possible that the big picture gets missed or the critical decisions and ideas seem obvious in retrospect. But that is where the real lessons lie for others. Hence the effort has been made to bring those out very clearly.

The result? A diverse assortment of stories that give insight into what kind of levers can be used to create a winner brand. Take for example chocolate maker and market leader, Cadbury. Everyone has savoured the taste of Cadbury Dairy Milk, and nearly every marketer worth his/her salt would be aware of the brand's successful integration into the traditional sweet-eating habit of Indians. But what strategies and actions went into achieving this? The Cadbury story documents how it all began with a big shift in thinking about business and growth. It is a lesson at many

xvi • *Storm the Norm*

levels: a lesson on how a large and potent target audience can slowly become a roadblock for future business; a reminder that the path to growth need not always be through growing market share; a story of how it is possible for a foreign brand to become part of the cultural fabric without localizing the product too much. Equally the story showcases the magic that ensued when the brand adapted itself and created new codes that fitted more seamlessly with category and culture.

Another example of a legacy brand is *The Times of India* (TOI), a brand that has been around more than 175 years. The TOI is a shining example of thriving and not just surviving in the marketplace. Its story documents a remarkable journey from being a marker of news and change to becoming an influencer of change for the nation. By taking bold bets and initiatives that were first of their kind, the brand not only helped its own business but also positively impacted and grew the entire sector. It is also a fascinating story of the much-less-talked-about business lever—pricing. The TOI's continuous innovation on pricing helped boost its profitability in a cost-loaded business. There are other important lessons to be learnt such as how to refresh the product to attract new consumers without alienating existing ones in a category that is strongly habit-driven. The TOI story depicts how razor-sharp identification of target audience and subsequent ways of connecting with it ensure that the brand is and will remain an indispensible part of millions of Indian lives.

Let's change gears to a challenger brand now. When you think of great products, bathing soap is hardly the first thing that comes to mind. However, that is exactly what the Indian Tobacco Company (ITC) aimed to do, when it decided to penetrate the category with Fiama Di Wills. A really late entrant into one of the oldest categories in the country, the brand was clear that its foremost intent was to challenge the typical soap and create a sensational new product—one that was differentiated not merely by form, colour or fragrance, but also a concoction of ingredients and technology that Indians had never witnessed before. The Fiama Di Wills story illustrates how some companies are clear that first it is critical to create a hero product. The bells and whistles and propositions and campaigns can come much later. In its endeavour to deliver a new, unmatched experience to consumers, there were so many stumbling blocks that the Fiama team had to face, so many occasions when it could have given up and created a me-too product and just used the ITC muscle to push sales. But it didn't. It persisted every time it was tested, to ultimately emerge with a winner.

Moving to another league of brands altogether—the young entrepreneurial businesses. While there are plenty of such success stories in India today, I have selected a few that have made a mark in more ways than one. These are businesses whose success is not simply measured in terms of business valuation or the fact that they are media darlings, but those whose start-to-date journeys hold vital lessons in doing business for everyone. For instance, MakeMyTrip. This is an extraordinary story of pursuing the dream of forever changing the way Indians researched, planned and booked their travel. From the days where vacation planning was a tedious project and life without travel agents and long ticketing queues unthinkable, to now, when online travel planning and purchasing is common practice, this brand has had a pioneering role in shaping the change. By riding emerging trends, taking sensible decisions when a large bulk of the market was not ready for their dream and fostering deep relationships with allied partners, Deep Kalra and his team strategized their way to success. Like a great movie, the journey had several twists and turns and a few occasions when the founder was tempted to sell or shut shop but chose to keep faith instead. What adds to the excitement is that the MakeMyTrip story is packed with not one or two but so many innovations across product offerings, service standards, technology, marketing and operations that one is constantly looking out for what next they did differently!

Such remarkable lessons continue across other entrepreneurial brands as well. What these kinds of brands do best is to open up refreshing ways of thinking and going about their business, so they naturally offer many valuable lessons along the way. Like PVR, where Ajay Bijli turned the whole expectation from cinema theatre upside down. Until the 1990s, cinema theatres were mostly just a destination, and movies were the real deal. The theatre itself was just a venue for stories to unfold. But he changed all that. Not only did he introduce the country to the multiplex, he created a new era in movie watching, where choice, comfort, luxury and entertainment all came together to take the movie-goer's experience to a new high.

There are several more examples of such category transformation. Radio Mirchi, for instance, is a story of a turnaround of the radio medium itself; of how a boring medium from which expectations had remained unchanged for decades, turned cool and irreverent; and how entertainment found a new source. It is also a great lesson on how you can win many fans by experimenting all the way through.

Many of you may not know this, but Raymond's 'The Complete Man' broke the conventions of fashion advertising in its time. Then there is Honda two wheelers—a fabulous story of storming the norm in scooters and making Activa a resounding success, and then of how it carried with it its winning strategies post its joint venture with Hero coming to an end. On a completely different note is the story of Sprite, a brand built on communication, on strongly marrying youth insights with product truth, of turning an absolutely niche lime category into a mass brand.

Similarly there are Ford EcoSport, Axis Bank, Kissan, MTR Foods, Saffola, Dabur Real, Sensodyne, Tata Tea and Mahindra XUV500. Each of their growth stories provides insights into creating a storm in their respective categories and achieving outstanding results. Some successes are based on distribution, some on product, some on communication, while others are based on core business models. There are stories of reinvention, of strategies on market expansion, and some even of using weaker siblings in the brand portfolio to fortify overall business.

So choose what interests you and make your start. I hope you will find something of value to help put your brand or business on fast track. It does not matter what stage your business or the organization that you work for is at—nascent, young, middle-aged or old. You will find a strategy and lesson that could help you storm the norm. On the way, you might pick up ideas for strengthening relationships with your customers and prospects, gather some insights on decision-making and become aware of strategies that are bound to fail and those that have high potential for succeeding. You will also see how consumers reject you when you go unprepared and try to market yourself as the best they have ever seen. You will learn about the consequences that the strongest of brands faced when they moved too far from their brand's core. Last, but certainly not the least, you will see how some companies identified hidden opportunities while others leveraged the most obvious of consumer trends to great advantage.

Whatever approach you choose to take, I hope that *Storm the Norm* proves useful and the thoughts presented in the book trigger ideas to help strengthen your own way of working and lead to you creating or boosting a winning business. Happy reading, happy storming.

Anisha Motwani

Entrepreneur

THE MULTIPLEX
REVOLUTION

One of the earliest and most enduring success stories of Indian liberalization is that of brand PVR, powered by its multi-talented Chairman and Managing Director (MD) Ajay Bijli. Ajay Bijli is a Harvard Business School alumnus and has been named in the World Economic Forum's list of young global leaders besides being awarded the EY Entrepreneur of the Year in Business Transformation in 2013.

From introducing the first multiplex experience in India, to becoming the undisputed leader in the space, the PVR Group is one of India's most successful entrepreneurial ventures. The inspiring story of brand PVR—crafted by the forward thinking and vision of Ajay Bijli—is recounted here.

One of the key traits of a visionary leader is their ability to spot opportunity and take calculated risks and that's exactly what Ajay Bijli did. Way back in 1997, he launched India's first multiplex and the rest, as they say, is history. Over a million people visited the multiplex within the first year of its opening. Today, the over ₹1000 crore PVR Group is the largest player in the Indian cinema exhibition space.

Act 1
Scene 1: Flashback

After completing his graduation from Delhi University, Ajay knew his calling was the family business. He joined the transport business set up by his grandfather (Lala Sain Das alias Bijli Pehelwan) in 1939. It was an old company, set in its ways, which may have been the reason he struggled in the business. The Amritsar Transport Company had its office near Rivoli cinema and Ajay would see it every day, little realizing that he would one day be the agent of its transformation. The Amritsar Transport Company also owned Priya Cinema in Vasant Vihar, a single-screen cinema at that time. It had been acquired by Ajay's father Krishan Mohan Bijli way back in 1976. Ajay frequented Priya often and very soon, triggered by his entrepreneurial itch, he got involved in the single-screen cinema business.

Scene 2: The idea takes seed

On a visit to Orlando, Florida, after his marriage in 1990, Ajay had his first experience of world-class cinemas and was fascinated by the new-age facilities of multiplexes. On returning, he renovated and transformed the old and dilapidated Priya cinema, until then screening only Hollywood movies largely for college-going audiences, into a modern, up-market, youth-centric hall. It became the first in India with a Dolby sound system.

Visionary leaders have a commitment to doing something big and a passion to make it happen. With the support of his mother, who was also his mentor, Ajay decided to pursue his dream and the marketplace was ripe with opportunity. Ajay brought in the next level of film entertainment with choice, comfort and convenience to viewers. In Ajay's own words: 'I was passionate about the desire to provide millions of people with impeccable cinema viewing and a wholesome entertainment experience. That was my early evolution as an entrepreneur.'

Scene 3: A new beginning

The technical transformation was just the beginning at Priya cinema. The facility experienced innovations and installations which further enhanced viewer comfort. Screening all big-budget Hindi films and Hollywood blockbusters, Priya became a hot destination for cinemagoers and acquired almost cult status.

This phase was Ajay's early evolution as an entrepreneur and the hands-on experience helped him develop clarity on the business segments he would focus upon.

It was the dawn of a new era in cine-viewing in the country—it was time for the country to embrace multiplexes.

Act 2
Scene 1: Winning through

The hurdle was that nobody in the country, including architects, knew how to make multiplexes. Every step was fraught with challenges which required tenacity and courage to overcome. Government permissions were needed to sell tickets and candy bars through computerized operations. Building bylaws were draconian.

It was at this point that Ajay decided to enter into a joint venture with a technology partner. In April 1995, brand PVR was created with a 60:40 share for Priya Exhibitors Pvt. Ltd and Village Roadshow Ltd of Australia.

About Village Roadshow Ltd: Based in Melbourne, Australia, Village Roadshow is a leading international entertainment and media company with operations spread across multiple countries. Its core businesses include theme parks, film distribution, cinema exhibition and film production. Village Roadshow has been listed on the Australian Securities Exchange (ASX) since 1988.

However, the challenges continued. Attracting talent was yet another hurdle that PVR faced. It was the desire to do something big and relevant that kept the momentum going.

PVR Anupam, which at that time belonged to old Delhi builders, was transformed into the first multiscreen cinema in 1997 and became a runaway success.

Scene 2: Building a property, building a brand

Ajay looked at the business through the customer's prism: what does the customer need and what is the market offering it? This took precedence over the typical emphasis on returns on investment or net profit margins. This shift in focus, backed by market studies, research and interactions with market players led to PVR embarking on its brand building journey.

Ajay understood that one of the important building blocks of a successful film entertainment and retail business was location. When it came to building multiplexes, PVR chose the *location* of its properties very carefully. Target market segment, socio-economic strata and catchment area were examined in granular detail.

Quality of experience was the next critical building block. Right from construction to fittings and styling—everything was fashioned to provide a plush viewing experience. Rich ambient lighting set the perfect mood and ideal temperature controls ensured total comfort. The auditoriums were designed to captivate cine goers with different ambiences and the highest quality of sound engineering made the entertainment experience thoroughly immersive. Special care was taken at every step to ensure that even common areas manifested the chic and premium PVR experience, thus providing all the ingredients that went into making PVR the benchmark for cine viewing.

PVR also brought in *transparency* into the system by introducing computerized bookings. Earlier film distributors would open films but were not sure of collections. However, they now had more money in their hands and wholeheartedly welcomed the new concept. It enabled producers to make better productions with good quality content.

There was significant focus on building a happy professional *work environment* for all employees with clear mandate to design out-of-the box solutions, so as to allow abundant creativity in key functions. That communicated the essence of what PVR was trying to do.

There have been tangible results and the brand has been able to garner higher seat occupancy levels in cinemas irrespective of average ticket prices. At the same time, movie goers have utilized the varied services offered by PVR including food and beverages. The intangible benefits have lain in PVR being seen as a thought leader—a company that respects innovation and is at the forefront of new ideas. PVR's large risk-taking appetite has also resulted in more opportunities coming its way. Its brand equity is also a competitive advantage and has helped PVR attract smarter talent.

Scene 3: Evolution of the brand and the big acquisition

Growth is imperative for any business. PVR, too, has systematically scaled up film-exhibition activities through an organic process for nearly seventeen years—be it in product, positioning, promotions or pricing.

After the 9/11 terror attacks in the United States, Village Roadshow Ltd curtailed its global operations and exited the joint venture. ICICI Venture picked up its entire 40 per cent stake for about 10 million dollars. Other private equity firms pumped in money as PVR branched into film production in 2007 with *Taare Zameen Par*, made in collaboration with Aamir Khan Productions.

Ajay's younger brother Sanjeev Kumar Bijli was instrumental in establishing key relationships with many Hollywood studios including Miramax, Newline, IEG and Zee MGM. He managed the film acquisition and distribution business and programming activities, and identified new business opportunities in areas like digital and franchise operations. A perfectionist and a pragmatic thinker, Sanjeev complemented Ajay's entrepreneurial streak to create the right balance in the business.

In November 2012, PVR acquired the entire 69 per cent stake of promoters in Cinemax India Ltd. At that time, Cinemax India was the No. 4 chain in the movie theatre business, with 138 screens across 39 properties all over India. The acquisition was made through PVR's wholly owned subsidiary Cine Hospitality Pvt. Ltd and made PVR the leader in the Indian cinema-exhibition business.

This multi-crore deal came with its own share of problems. The Cinemax acquisition was much more than the market cap of PVR Ltd and established PVR as the clear leader in the cinema exhibition business. While the PVR brand had always been committed to providing people excellence in this space, it now had the scale to achieve its goals.

This acquisition was one of the fastest-paced takeover deals in India's corporate history. The objective was to create India's largest movie

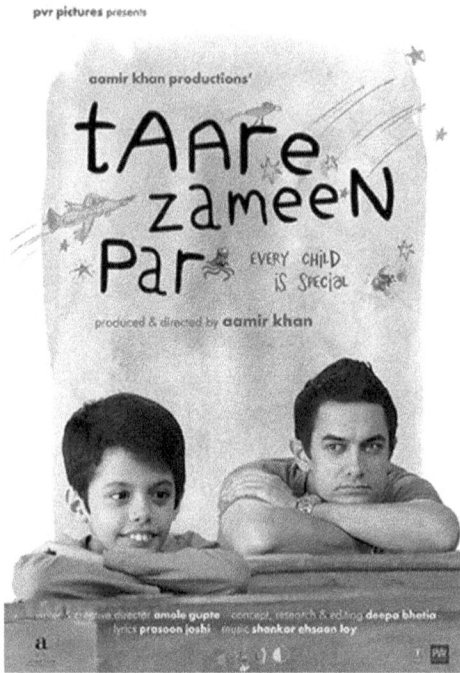

PVR Pictures Production:
Taare Zameen Par

exhibition chain and also to effectively utilize the synergy potential and cost benefits that would accrue from the larger scale of operations of the combined network, thereby creating value for all stakeholders.

In 2013, PVR multiplied in size and operations. The company expanded its presence from 27 cities to 41 and its market capitalization was reported to be ₹2,204 crore (as on 1 February 2014). It now owned just under a third of India's 1,500 odd multiplex screens. While it had long been the undisputed leader in the north, the Cinemax acquisition gave the company an edge in the west and a launching pad in the south.

By 2014, PVR, operating a network of 454 screens in 102 properties in 43 cities across the country, had emerged as the largest cinema exhibition company in India. The company plans to add 70 to 80 screens every year and have 1,000 screens across India by 2018 through organic and inorganic growth.

In 2015, PVR currently operates a cinema circuit comprising 474 screens spread over 106 properties in 43 cities across India. As a result of the acquisition of DT Cinemas, PVR will have a presence in 44 cities with 115 multiplexes and 506 screens. Currently amongst the top ten cinema companies in the world with respect to admissions per screen, PVR has entered the World Economic Forum's list of fastest-growing 'Global Growth Companies'.

Act 3
Scene 1: The PVR experience

India's leading film entertainment company came to be ranked among the top ten cinema companies in the world in terms of admissions per screen by the World Economic Forum (WEF) in 2014. Despite the advent of online consumption of film entertainment, PVR maintained its relevance and was not necessarily in conflict with it. With its long-term vision of excelling in the retail entertainment domain and maintaining a leadership position, PVR redefined the cinema-viewing experience for movie connoisseurs by providing world-class immersive viewing. PVR offered its patrons good and diversified content from Hollywood, Bollywood and regional film centres.

Scene 2: A calibrated portfolio strategy

The 100-year-old Hindi film industry still sets style and fashion trends in the country. With the benefits of economic liberalization percolating down, disposable income had risen and so had middle class aspirations and lifestyles.

Various independent market research surveys showed that the young sought a totality of experience which was a mix of wholesomeness and flaunting value. As a result, they saw movies as part of a bigger experience. Not being careful with their money, like earlier generations, they kept coming back to PVR which had turned theatres into classy, stylish luxury spaces and quasi-community centres. As Ajay Bijli stated, 'When people enter a PVR cinema, it should assure absolute escapism. I can't control the movies. But the environment that you see the movie in is something that we can assure will be perfect.'

While PVR remained the parent brand, it developed and positioned sub-brands to cater to specific customer segments through a range of properties. It set new benchmarks in the cinema exhibition business by building the first eleven-screen multiplex in the country, and by introducing Gold Class cinema, Director's Cut luxury cinema, IMAX technology theatres and Enhanced Cinema Experience (ECX).

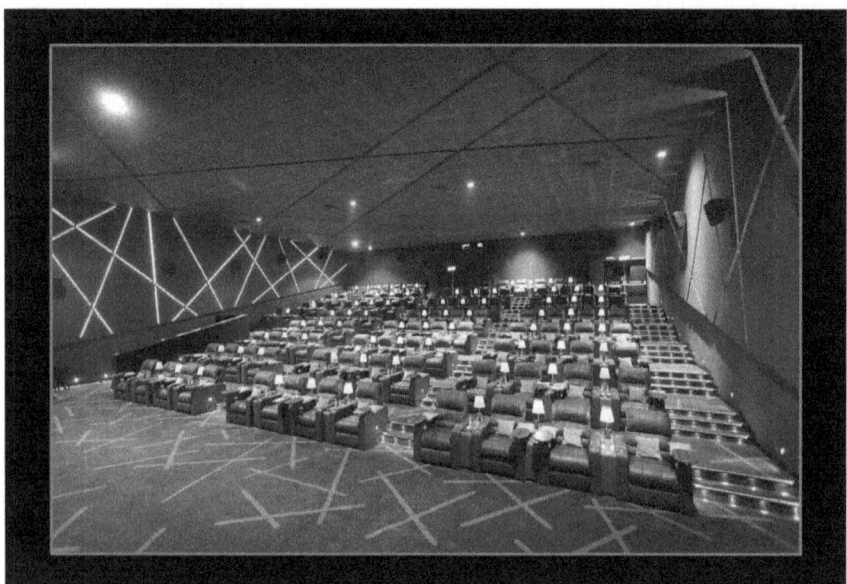

Director's Cut

The Director's Cut property is the ultimate in luxury cinema-viewing. This niche location is home to four luxury movie halls, a café and a book and souvenir store.

The Gold Class property offers its patrons comfortable, reclining, leather-upholstered seats, a personalized menu overseen by a maître d' and exclusive lounge areas with bookshelves and original art by renowned artists.

Gold Class

PVR Premier caters to the upper middle class in metros with distinctively styled new-age cinema halls for a world-class cinema experience.

PVR Mainstream is the popular brand catering to the middle class with regular but comfortable seating.

Scene 3: PVR Pictures: Bringing you the movies

PVR Pictures is the flagship motion-pictures arm of the PVR Group and has released many Hindi, Hollywood and regional films across genres. As a company, PVR Pictures keeps a tight watch on developments in the Hollywood market space, especially the films being recognized at various festivals—Cannes, Berlinale and American Film Market. Over the years, it has built a robust network of relationships with producers, sales agents and sales companies.

PVR Pictures was involved in the distribution of all the major 2013–14 Oscar-nominated films—*The Wolf of Wall Street, American Hustle, 12 Years a Slave, Her, Lone Survivor, Nebraska, Dallas Buyers Club* and *August: Osage County*—in the country.

In addition to distribution of Indian and international films, PVR Pictures also supported independent filmmakers by releasing their films under the PVR Director's Rare banner and introduced the concept of alternate content to India by launching a brand new platform—PVR LIVE—showcasing live and recorded events. It emerged as the dominant player with 90 per cent of the market share in this category.

Also, PVR Director's Rare had been instrumental in bringing about a paradigm shift from star-driven cinema to content-driven cinema. Most film production corporations were making films that were high on star value and entertained smaller town audiences more than chic urban audiences.

Director's Rare case study: The film *Lucia*

PVR Director's Rare discovered a small Kanadda independent film, *Lucia*, which was made for ₹52 lakh, raised through crowd funding. We provided the filmmaker and the film the much needed springboard for it to get noticed.

Lucia played for thirteen weeks at our theatres and had net box office earnings of ₹96 lakh at PVR Group theatres. The satellite rights of the film were bought by Udaya TV for ₹95 lakh. Fox Star India bought the Hindi remake rights and all other rights of the film have similarly been monetized.

Thus PVR Director's Rare provided an obscure documentary a theatrical release in commercial multiplexes in India. PVR Director's Rare has released six documentaries in two years' time and is behind the success story of documentaries like *Supermen of Malegaon* and *Fire in the Blood*.

FOOTFALLS (in crore)		SALES TURNOVER (in ₹crore)	
2008–09	1.7	2008–09	363
2009–10	1.62	2009–10	344
2010–11	1.96	2010–11	470
2011–12	2.47	2011–12	522
2012–13	5.49	2012–13	815
2013–14	5.98	2013–14	1,359
2014–15	5.91	2014–15	1,486

Act 4
Going beyond the cinema business

In Ajay Bijli's own words:

If you were to ask Howard Schultz what else he wants to do, he would say 'I want to open more Starbucks' and the same is the case with McDonald's. So while everybody wants me to vertically integrate, I ask why I should only be making cinemas. Like an entrepreneur tries various business models, pre-acquisition we too tried our hands at a few ventures. But post acquisition I have realized that I want to work only in cinema space, as this our core strength. India right now is very under-screened, and I want to expand everywhere I can. However pre-acquisition, we have invested in a few ventures from restaurants to bowling centres.

Scene 1: PVR and its subsidiaries: Bowling and more

The idea behind setting up bluO was to provide a one-stop entertainment destination to all and to promote bowling in India. Bowling is promoted as an indoor sport and as leisure and entertainment for patrons at PVR bluO. PVR bluO was the retail-entertainment arm of the PVR Group and was a 51:49 joint venture between PVR and Major Cineplex Group of Thailand, a leading film exhibition and retail entertainment company that operates 480 bowling centres in Thailand.

PVR bluO is a one-of-its-kind entertainment concept in India. Simply speaking, what T-20 has done for cricket in India, bluO has done for bowling. In other words, bluO is a mix of fun and bowling—world cuisine, music, sport—coming together. It has been able to redefine bowling as a popular lifestyle and entertainment sport in the country.

BluO Bangalore

BluO is a unique concept and some of the elements that go into giving it that extra edge are an exceptional rhythmic interior design with a sensual play of light and form and a ceiling that emanates as a ripple wave. It is energetic, stylish and in sync with the lifestyle and ideology of today's youth.

As of 2014, PVR bluO had six centres, two in Delhi NCR, two in Bangalore, one in Pune and one in Chandigarh. BluO offers some exceptional services to its patrons like playstation lounges, private karaoke lounges, exclusive platinum lounges, India's first international standard pro shop, stylish merchandise, a pulsating music den, a tattoo studio and well-equipped bars that serve a dazzling array of the finest liquor, beverages and wines.

Scene 2: PVR and its restaurants

PVR's other new subsidiary PVR Leisure Ltd, a joint venture between PVR Ltd and Mauritius-based L Capital Eco Ltd, focuses on rolling out food and beverages (F&B) at fine dining restaurants Mistral in New Delhi and Mr Hong in Bangalore. Apart from these, it also deals with retail entertainment concepts including hospitality, leisure and gaming. Nearly 24 per cent of the group revenues come from the F&B segment.

Mistral is a fusion of Mediterranean grill with Eastern culinary influences ranging from North East Asia to India and the Middle East.

Mr Hong is a contemporary rendition of the Chinese tea house concept incorporating culinary influences spanning South East Asia. Tea is the underlying theme infused in every aspect of the brand, from F&B recipes to interior design.

Act 5
Scene 1: There is no standing still...

PVR aims at expanding to 1,000 screens by 2018.

PVR Cinemas joined hands with Mexican family entertainment centres brand KidZania to launch a fifteen-screen superplex under a joint venture between real estate major Unitech and International Amusement Ltd, the biggest retail and leisure destination in the Delhi NCR region, spread across 147 acres in Noida.

PVR promises to be a force to reckon with in times to come in this space as well. While the country has a large urban population exceeding 300 million, PVR recognizes that the rural population is even larger and is working on creating products targeting this segment as well.

Scene 2: Shaping the growth of cine advertising in the country

Over the years, cinema watching has expanded its scope as a leisure activity. The movie watching experience has now evolved into a rounded entertainment activity, where the audience voluntarily surrenders to the environment, with higher receptivity to brand messaging as compared to any other medium.

Cinema offers an unrivalled advertising impact with low ad avoidance, helping form a deep connect between the advertising brand and audiences. Today, cinema advertising in India is largely known for the innovative methods that PVR has pioneered in the country. PVR's dominance in the cinema-advertising domain is so profound that its total advertising sales equal the combined sales of all competing players.

From ₹75 crore last year, cinema advertising has jumped to a whopping figure of ₹141 crore this year and is expected to touch ₹169 crore by the end of 2015. Rising at a 35–40 per cent year-on-year, cinema advertising is growing faster than online, radio or overall advertising, where annual growth is about 11 per cent.

	FY 2011–12	FY 2012–13	FY 2013–14	FY 2014–15
Turnover	₹62 crore	₹75 crore	₹142.5 crore	₹168.74
Screens	166	216	421	464
Cinemas	38	46	97	104

And...cut!!! Final word

PVR is listed as India's most trusted and attractive brand by The Brand Trust Report 2015 in the category entertainment and cinema display. The company commands a phenomenal 70 per cent of advertising revenue in the cinema space, and delivers 360-degree exposure and innovative opportunities to brands—both on-screen and off-screen.

Ajay Bijli said:

> Right from the beginning, if PVR Priya (the first screen opened) had not been a success, I would have been disappointed. Success in any initiative gives you the boost to go further, and do even better. I recently read a quote by Nelson Mandela which really touched me: 'Do not judge me by my successes. Judge me by how many times I fell down and got back up again.' I believe in this and that's what defines success for me.

Awards and recognitions

2015

PVR awarded India's most Trusted Cinema Display Brand in Brand Trust Report 2015.

PVR Ltd has been honoured with the following awards at The Fridays BW Businessworld Cinema Exhibition Awards & Conference:
» Fastest Growing Chain
» Best Chain, National
» Best Marketing Initiatives

2014

Ajay Bijli, awarded the Most Admired Multiplex Professional of the year, CMO Asia's Multiplex Excellence Awards.

Business Today India's Best 100 CEOs rankings—Ajay Bijli.

Images Most Admired Retailer of the Year: Entertainment.

Star Box Office Multiplex Chain of the Year.

2013

VC Circle Award for Media and Communication.

Ajay Bijli awarded the EY Entrepreneur of the Year Award for Business Transformation.

2012

Emerging India Award by CNBC.

2011

Business Icons Male Award India by *Entrepreneur India* magazine.

Industry Leadership Award at Indian Film Festival held in Los Angeles.

2009

EOY Videocon Youth Icon Award.

2007

Nominated among top Indians for Young Global Leaders by the World Economic Forum.

2005

Entrepreneur of the Year (Entertainment) by Indian Retail Forum.

2004
Business Leadership Award by Franchise India.
Newsmaker of the Year Award for 2003 (part of FICCI Frames).
Teacher's Achievement Award.

2003
Theatre World Newsmaker of the Year Award at FICCI Frames.

2003–2004
Retailer of the Year: Entertainment by Images Retail.

2002 and 2005
Finalist at Ernst & Young Entrepreneur of the Year.

PVR Journey so far....   PVR

Began with a single theatre, evolved to an integrated entertainment company and is now
INDIA's LARGEST MULTIPLEX OPERATOR

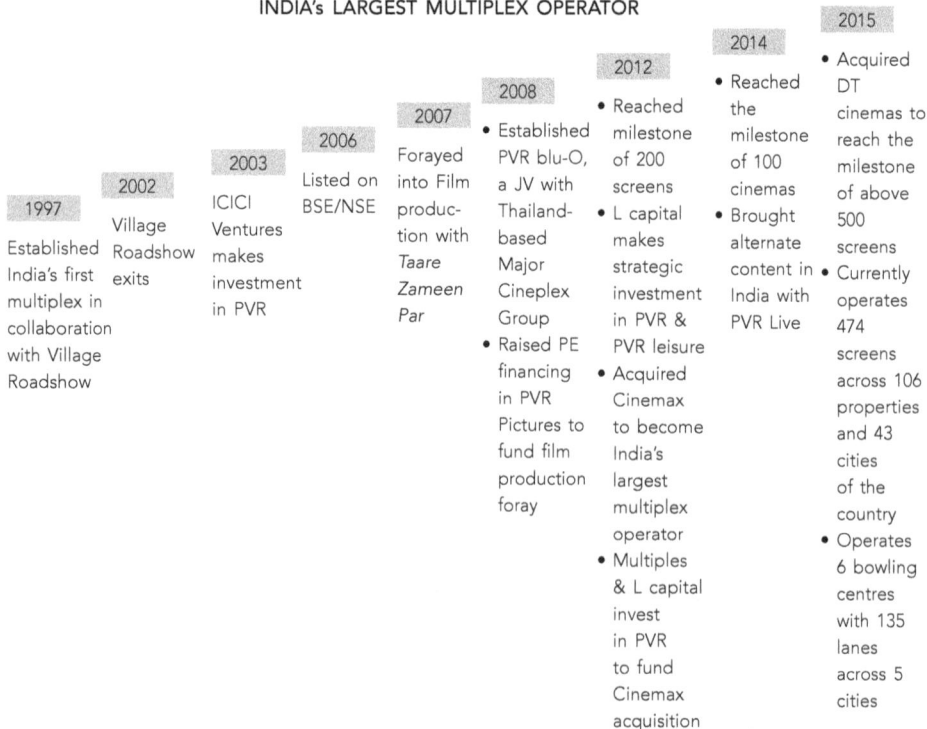

1997
Established India's first multiplex in collaboration with Village Roadshow

2002
Village Roadshow exits

2003
ICICI Ventures makes investment in PVR

2006
Listed on BSE/NSE

2007
Forayed into Film production with *Taare Zameen Par*

2008
- Established PVR blu-O, a JV with Thailand-based Major Cineplex Group
- Raised PE financing in PVR Pictures to fund film production foray

2012
- Reached milestone of 200 screens
- L capital makes strategic investment in PVR & PVR leisure
- Acquired Cinemax to become India's largest multiplex operator
- Multiples & L capital invest in PVR to fund Cinemax acquisition

2014
- Reached the milestone of 100 cinemas
- Brought alternate content in India with PVR Live

2015
- Acquired DT cinemas to reach the milestone of above 500 screens
- Currently operates 474 screens across 106 properties and 43 cities of the country
- Operates 6 bowling centres with 135 lanes across 5 cities

make *My* trip
Dil toh roaming hai

A JOURNEY OF COUNTLESS MILES AND BEYOND

*I see my path, but I don't know where it leads.
Not knowing where I am going is what inspires
me to travel.*
—Rosalia De Castro

It was with this belief that Deep Kalra, an alumnus of St Stephen's College, Delhi, and the Indian Institute of Management, Ahmedabad, conceptualized the business idea of MakeMyTrip in the year 2000. The entire online travel industry in India was pioneered by Deep with a single great idea—empowering the traveller. This is the story of MakeMyTrip, India's online travel leader.

The concept of holidaying together as a family has long been prevalent in India. But planning a family vacation, though fun, was not as convenient as it is today. Holidays were planned at least six months in advance, with a lot of deliberation and debate among family members. Families used to painstakingly collect brochures or keep cutouts of travelogues from newspapers and magazines to refer to for research. Recommendations from friends and relatives who had been to those destinations were an important source of information. The travel agent was the trusted expert and key guide before finalization. Booking the travel was the next big task with long hours in ticket queues. Value for money, however, an important criterion then, remains one even today.

A lot changed with the Internet boom in 2000. Business fundamentals reasserted themselves as users flocked to the web and the opportunity seemed boundless. Initial skepticism gave way to experimentation and mounting excitement as people began to believe in the power of the Internet.

Deep Kalra cashed in on this Internet boom with the insights gained as a result of his former role at GE capital. As the vice president, business development, Deep's mandate had been to develop and partner new distribution channels for GE Capital's consumer financial products, and he chose to focus on the Internet.

When he decided to venture out on his own, Deep first studied various verticals that could be well-suited to the Indian online market and his entrepreneurial instincts made him realize that the travel industry lent itself best to the power of online. A service-oriented industry with well-automated processes at the supplier end, the travel industry was also undergoing significant changes at consumer level—e-tickets were becoming all-pervasive and the success of IRCTC (Indian Railway Catering and Tourism Corporation), the online portal of Indian Railways, had demonstrated that consumers were warming up to the convenience offered by online ticketing. With the potential of offering never-before convenience and ease that would take away the pain of long queues and travel-planning blues, this industry was well-poised for driving behaviour shifts from physical channels to virtual ones. Moreover, there existed a vast gap in the service delivery standards for the average consumer who was dependent on the mercies of travel agents and other random support structures.

Deep envisioned MakeMyTrip as the defining portal for Indians travelling to, from and within India. Armed with rich insights, a lot of passion, a business plan and modest personal savings, Deep raised an initial round of funding from eVentures, an India-focused venture capital fund. Having worked in a large corporate, Deep ensured that MakeMyTrip had a professional team and hired his core from among seasoned professionals from the travel industry and managers who had worked with him in the past. This team worked tirelessly to develop a world-class travel portal to cater to resident Indians as well as non-resident Indians (NRI).

The first version of the site was launched in October 2000.

The first stumbling blocks in the journey

Upon launching the first version of the site in October 2000, MakeMyTrip received a favourable response from the NRI market in the US. In India, however, travellers were more inclined to research online but preferred to make the actual buying decision using traditional modes of payment. As a result, the team had to make the difficult call of stopping all marketing in India. In hindsight, this turned out to be one of the best decisions for the company. By focusing solely on the NRI market, MakeMyTrip managed to conserve precious marketing dollars while its competitors burnt their fingers in a premature online market.

> STRATEGIC SMART: Pulling off spends from the domestic market to focus on the NRI market.

The tightening of market spend (and other related expenses) turned out to be a timely move as it helped the company tide over one of the most difficult periods for the online travel industry. During the years 2001 and 2002, travel and tourism was ravaged by a series of storms—the aftermath of 9/11, the dot-com bust, the attack on Indian Parliament in December 2001 and the SARS epidemic. This took a toll on the travel industry as the demand for 'discretionary' travel and tourism plummeted. While it is difficult to isolate the impact of the events of 2001, they were a part of a chain of events that cost the industry three years of growth. However, the NRI market proved to be a highly inelastic and reliable market, mainly because the drivers for these trips were quite different. Providing NRIs the unmatched convenience of a 24×7 online travel portal and travel consultancy support, MakeMyTrip managed to survive these difficult years and soon became a well-known brand among NRIs in the US.

Around the same time, the company's investors, eVentures, withdrew all their investments in the country, including in MakeMyTrip, as a direct result of the dot-com meltdown. Saddled with a young business still in the red, the choices before Deep were to either wind up the company and go back to the corporate world or somehow muster further investment behind a potentially viable business. At this time, the cons of running the business seemed much larger than the pros. Internet penetration remained low, bandwidth was expensive and consumers were far from trusting online services. Deep Kalra, however, remined firm in his belief that his brainchild had immense potential to perform. Tempted though he was to sell the business at US$10 million at the time, Kalra finally decided against it.

> STRATEGIC SMART: Did not let a good idea float away: believed in the proposition of MakeMyTrip and stayed resilient despite the pressure of multiple adversities.

Perhaps as a testimony to Deep's conviction, came an opportunity. Ebookers, a UK-based online travel agency (OTA), came to India scouting for a development and support partner. MakeMyTrip was shortlisted as the India partner for Ebookers. However, this came at a price. Rajesh Magow, co-founder, chief financial officer and financial wizard of MakeMyTrip left the company to run the Ebookers venture full-time. (Rajesh and Deep had met through a head hunter in 2001 and had clicked immediately and as a result Rajesh had decided to join MakeMyTrip.)

Ebookers had a stake in the company, as well as some representatives from the management who may not have wanted to continue further with MakeMyTrip. In order to effect a complete management buy-out, Deep convinced other key members of the management team and some 'angel investors' (including individuals in eVentures who saw promise in the business) to invest in the company. Working on a bootstrap model for the next eighteen months, the company turned profitable in 2003. Strategic focus and persistence paid off as MakeMyTrip grew steadily over the next few years to emerge as the single-largest provider of travel services to NRIs in the US in the year.

Though Deep had temporarily lost the support of his long-time partner and confidante when Rajesh joined Ebookers, the cord was never cut and Rajesh rejoined MakeMyTrip in 2005. From 2001 to 2005, Rajesh oversaw a team of 1,500 employees, and migrated all processes from Ebookers to the India back-office. He also managed the transition of the business from Ebookers to Cendant (Cendant acquired Ebookers in 2005). For an entrepreneur, in every adversity lies an opportunity. Rajesh gained valuable experience in running the Ebookers business end to end which was to come in handy for MakeMyTrip in later years. His learnings from that stint (that helped him solve future business challenges for MakeMyTrip) included:

» Building operations from scratch—especially being a start-up—and subsequent scale-up.
» Domain experience—same model, multiple channels and processes of an Internet-based business model.
» Building a captive unit for Ebookers with transition of customer service operations, sales functions, technology back-end unit and financial services unit.
» Change management experience.

An idea whose time had come: The start of a memorable journey

While the NRI business continued to grow well, Deep never lost sight of his core vision of revolutionizing the way resident Indians bought travel. The changing industry and market environment in 2005 brought with it the dawn of a new era:

» The sudden emergence of new airlines (particularly low-cost carriers) along with fierce ensuing competition.
» Growing levels of the Internet and credit-card penetration in India.
» Growing propensity of the domestic consumer to buy online (as evident from the success of Indian Railways).

Deep was convinced that the time was finally ripe for the domestic travel market to go online. While the external environment was conducive, Deep was clear that a lot of marketing effort was needed to mould consumer buying behaviour. To meet the need for increased marketing investments, MakeMyTrip required external funding. The management, therefore, took the decision to raise private equity to fund its India launch. MakeMyTrip was fortunate to receive multiple offers and chose SAIF (Softbank Asia Infrastructure Fund) as investors.

MakeMyTrip.com was relaunched for the Indian market in 2005. With intensive work on the technology backbone, the site connected real time to all the airlines systems using direct connect and XML feeds. MakeMyTrip pioneered the concept of OTA (online travel agent) and guaranteed the lowest airfares and real-time bookings.

On the back of its unique proposition—a lowest airfare guarantee—the launch was an outright success. Soon after the launch, the site became the default place to research and buy air tickets, and even for other travel agents to find the best deals. Within the short span of a year, MakeMyTrip became India's largest OTA, issuing the highest number of domestic air tickets in the country, forever changing the way Indians bought travel services.

Under Deep's guidance, the company grew from strength to strength and soon became the top seller for virtually every airline in the country, ahead of established players in the segment—Thomas Cook, Cox & Kings and American Express.

The magic ingredients of success

Taking stock of MakeMyTrip's success unveils a holistic approach powered by the vision and spirit of each one of its employees, for whom no idea was too big and no problem too difficult.

» The success of the travel services provider can be attributed to the fact that it has been able to pre-empt trends and continually evolved its technology. It has set standards in service that competition had a tough time living up to.

» From the very beginning, the company deployed the best in technology to raise the bar as far as service standards were concerned. For instance, MakeMyTrip was fully powered by Amadeus, a state-of-the-art low-fare search tool that helps customers find the best match within their budget. Their payment gateways carried 'Verified by Visa' or 'Master Secure' protection layers for those who used credit and debit cards to make purchases.

» With untiring innovation and determination, MakeMyTrip proactively began to strengthen its product offering, adding a variety of online and offline products and services that clearly separated the wheat from the chaff as far as OTAs were concerned.

» While diversifying their product portfolio, they kept in mind the mental blocks that customers usually have. For instance, when holiday packages were being offered, they realized that, being a high-involvement product, it required a different strategy. Customers had a multitude of questions and concerns when it came to travelling overseas or on a long itinerary to multiple destinations in the country. While they were happy to do research online, the buying decision needed physical reassurance at least at this early stage of development of the market. *MakeMyTrip decided to address the holiday packages market by setting up its first retail store in 2007, the first to be launched by an OTA.* Initally these were just consumer touch points in cities like Mumbai, Bangalore, Kolkata and Ahmedabad to reach out to customers beyond the Delhi/NCR market. With such stores attracting customers, MakeMyTrip developed this concept into a hybrid business model of online and offline presence. This worked especially well in category B cities where customers wanted to come into a retail store and plan their holiday in the presence of a travel expert.

Hotels: The next destination

The next adjacent opportunity for growth for MakeMyTrip was the hotel business. While the opportunity was large and obvious, the challenges were even greater. The hotel business was a difficult market to capture since over 80 per cent of hotels in India comprised small, independent properties with abysmal levels of automation. Unlike the airline industry—which created the first global distribution system (GDS) in the 1960s largely to keep track of flight schedules, availability and prices, and SABRE (owned by American Airline) and Apollo (United), which began installing their proprietary internal reservations systems in travel agencies as early as the mid-1970s—hotels in India had no such system.

Challenge No. 1: One of the key challenges was creating a viable supply-chain that not only ensured availability of the inventory online but also a seamless purchase experience on the website.

MakeMyTrip endeavoured to overcome this by creating India's first extranet for hotels to load room inventories, either as a rolling stock with a cut-off date or on a real-time basis for sale on MakeMyTrip.com. So, the company took on the herculean task of bringing over 2,500 hotels in India online, irrespective of size and location. From stand-alone cottages in hill stations to shacks on beaches, all were now available to be booked real-time only on MakeMyTrip.

The cost for CMS (content management system) integration and automation was borne by MakeMyTrip. However, this also helped in forging deeper relationships and alliances with smaller, non-chain properties. As of 2015, MakeMyTrip offered access to the largest selection of hotel inventory in India (over 20,000) and nearly 200,000 properties worldwide.

Challenge No. 2: The next challenge was to ensure that once the bookings came in, they were honoured by the hotels and customers did not face any problems.

This was achieved by intense rigour put in by a young business development team that was placed in key commercial and leisure destinations across the country and supported by a central operations team that confirmed and reconfirmed bookings while obtaining future inventory. As MakeMyTrip established itself as the dominant travel brand in India, it got increasingly easier to sign up domestic chains and stand-alone hotels. However international chains, headquartered in faraway Europe and USA, had a much longer gestation period. By the year 2012, MakeMyTrip forged several direct connects with international bookings systems and offered thousands of hotels across the world with last-room availability. With MakeMyTrip's ability to fill rooms, the hotels on its lists experienced an increase in productivity that led to a virtuous cycle which ensured that getting new hotels on board was no longer a challenge.

Challenge No. 3: A fundamental challenge in customer-behaviour owing to the nature of the product still awaited MakeMyTrip. Purchasing hotels rooms in India was a fragmented affair—most people just showed up at the destination while many leaned heavily on contacts and friends and family to make bookings. This was unlike the established buying behaviour of customers purchasing air and rail tickets through travel agents.

To counter this trend, MakeMyTrip followed a two-pronged approach. It focused on creating awareness and building credibility around the promise of a hassle-free experience. The latter was strongly supplemented by building content, both proprietary and user-generated, which included photographs and customer reviews. In line with the psyche of the value-conscious consumer, MakeMyTrip offered a best-price guarantee with easy cancellation terms. Further innovations such as early-bird discounting, last-minute deals and launching a bundled flight+hotel-discounted product added even more value for the consumer.

Challenge No. 4: Seamless customer experience was the next big hurdle. Despite these mammoth efforts, MakeMyTrip's journey of selling hotels was just about beginning. There were plenty of hiccups along the way. For starters, customers who had used the airline ticketing services of MakeMyTrip booked hotels online only to find themselves in a place with a dirty swimming pool or with non-existent air conditioning. Besides, during the holiday season, small hotel owners refused to honour bookings. As a result, dissatisfied customers angrily renamed the portal 'RuinMyTrip'! The mistake the company had made was to assume that the hotel booking experience would be a standard experience like air travel, only to realize that on the ground experience for hotels was far more complicated.

Technology lay at the heart of the solution. MakeMyTrip realized that human effort alone could not ensure standardized experience across cities, hotels and customer types. It made amends by acquiring travel tech outfits and hotel aggregators and invested heavily in the backend. During second quarter of 2007, in order to cater to the evolving consumer preferences, a new version of the website was developed to empower the consumer and bring transparency into the process. The new site embraced elements of web 2.0 and allowed customers to post and read user reviews, check natural photos of accommodation and evaluate the hotel's unbiased ranking before taking a decision to book.

In addition, to strengthen its presence in the distribution of the low-budget accommodation inventory, the company made a strategic investment in 'My Guest House Accommodations Pvt. Ltd'. Soon enough, with the category maturing, MakeMyTrip's efforts started to pay off with hotel and packages contributing almost half of the company's revenues.

A dream debut in the stock market and some lessons along the way

By the year 2010, MakeMy Trip's revenues had grown tenfold to US$40 million since 2005. Customers had by then realized that MakeMyTrip was not just a 'call centre' or an outfit at the mercy of travel agents. The company was now on a growth trajectory and in need of funds to acquire strategic businesses and enhance its technology platforms. The company decided to unlock value and tap the markets to raise funds. However, it was faced with the choice of whether to go public in India or the USA. Finally, after much deliberation, it was decided that MakeMyTrip would list at the NASDAQ, because the US market had a better appreciation of Internet ventures.

Without any prior experience, the company took a mere six months to launch its initial public offering (IPO) under the stewardship of Rajesh Magow. *MakeMyTrip became the first Indian travel company to be listed overseas. It was valued at 5.4 times its next year's projected revenues and raised over US$1 billion in collections, with its shares soaring by 80 per cent after listing on the NASDAQ.*

STRATEGIC SMART: Listing on NASDAQ as against Indian stock exchanges, since US markets were more appreciative of Internet ventures.

Post its IPO success, the company went on an acquisition spree, making a total of four acquisitions between 2011 and 2012, each strengthening its foothold in various parts of the globe, beginning from Europe, South East Asia and the Middle East.

However, when Kingfisher Airlines stopped operations in 2012, it came as a bit of a jolt for the travel industry. Demand came down sharply as air travel costs soared. The woes of the industry were further compounded by a slowing economy in the aftermath of the global recession. As a result, MakeMyTrip ended the year 2012–13 with a loss of US$13 million. This taught it a valuable lesson that the time had come to diversify. A rigorous phase of transformation thus ensued with the hotels and packages component of the business receiving renewed focus. Once again, as consumer preferences changed and Indian travellers began looking for international packages, MakeMyTrip caught the pulse ahead of the curve and offered convenient and customized packages for international travel experience (Europe Packages). The rebalancing of the business in full earnest bore fruit and the non-air segment grew over 50 per cent in a single year. Additionally, the company's acquisitions in 2012, ITC Group and Hotel Travel Group, further strengthened its product offering and enhanced the competitive advantage in South East Asia , the key holiday market for Indian customers.

> STRATEGIC SMART: Looking beyond the bend and strengthening its international offering to diversify its portfolio and de-risk the business model

The road to success

Today, MakeMyTrip is much more than just a travel portal or a pioneering brand. It is one of India's largest online travel brands with the broadest selection of travel products and services. Collectively, MakeMyTrip covers virtually every aspect of travel from researching and planning to booking travel, from choosing the best mode of travel to ratings and reviews to making the most of your holiday. The portfolio serves a cross-section of

customers, spans local and international destinations and caters to both holiday and business travellers. The fact that it has relied heavily on innovation is what makes it an undisputed leader in online travel, a fact evinced by the trust placed in it by millions of happy customers. Some of the winning moves by MakeMyTrip have been:

» **Selling end-to-end holiday solutions:** Customers can search for a desired holiday, book a package of their choice and complete the entire purchase process on the portal. MakeMyTrip also offers instant assistance through a live chat service for any additional information required during booking. FPH (Flights Plus Hotels) was launched for an integrated user experience.

» **Influencing behaviours with lucrative offers on hotel bookings** 100 per cent money-back guarantee: The company offers customers a 100 per cent refund if the services offered at the hotel booked are not as outlined while booking. This intervention seemingly reversed the traditional business seasonality.
  Last-minute hotel discounts online and on mobile: This encourages online hotel booking and showcases benefits to the customer—best rate, widest range of hotels in the country and a hassle-free booking experience backed by the money-back guarantee.
  Pay at hotel service: This allows customers to confirm hotel bookings on the website for as little as ₹5, while the rest of the amount can be paid directly at the hotel.

» **A successful foray into bus services:** Volvo and deluxe buses had made inter-city travel by buses extremely convenient and popular, giving this service a fresh lease of life. As always, MakeMyTrip cashed in on this trend and launched bus services for travellers seeking good value and effort optimization. By the year 2013 the company offered lowest-price guarantee on bus tickets through 1300+ operators over 12,000+ routes across India.

» **Going places**
  Opening of new destinations like Phuket and Maldives to the Indian market: Over the years, MakeMyTrip has strengthened focus on identifying emerging opportunity areas in unexplored, uncharted territories and converted them into viable business ideas. It realized

that certain exotic destinations were being avoided by travelers as they were perceived to be expensive. Chartered flight-inclusive packages to Phuket and Maldives were created with the sole aim of rendering these destinations affordable and accessible. The competitive pricing of these packages set them apart from other packages to these destinations in the market and made them a huge success. From creating compelling itineraries, ensuring high service standards and positively influencing the commercials to make it a win-win proposition for the traveller, MakeMyTrip led the category with product innovations. On the back of these efforts, MakeMyTrip was rated as a top producer of attractive holiday packages to South East Asia destinations such as Mauritius, Thailand, Malaysia and Singapore.

Flexi Europe packages: MakeMyTrip also launched an exclusive travel option of Flexi Europe travel for both group tours and individual travellers. These packages offered customers the opportunity to see Europe without a pre-fixed itinerary. MakeMyTrip's Flexi Group Tours operate across twenty-two cities in Europe and offer city modules where a traveller can choose as many cities as he/she wishes to visit, with a minimum requirement of at least three cities. One of the finest innovations in holidays in Europe, Flexi Group Tour packages address key concerns of fixed itineraries, food preferences and assistance—i.e. aspects that form the bulk of concern areas for Indian travellers during an international tour.

Technology: The heart of MakeMyTrip

MakeMyTrip is leading the category with innovations in technology and user interface that have transformed the travel purchase process and information consumption related to travel.

» Innovation on mobile: With penetration of mobile Internet exploding, MakeMyTrip realized that the future of the travel industry lay in m-sales. With a clear strategy of tapping into this, the company used a two-pronged approach to target both ends of the market.

   MakeMyTrip invested in creating differentiators and value-adds for feature phones (used by price-sensitive customers) as well as smartphones (favoured by the tech-savvy traveller).

MakeMyTrip became the first Indian OTA to launch an iPhone app in July 2012 with features that gave 'real' value and benefit and were used uniquely around the mobile platform. Key drivers for this were delivering content around location-based services, minimizing the number of inputs, highlighting and offering selective but important information and local storage (on the device) of frequently used information (such as passenger/traveller details).

The MMT iPhone app was a huge success in the market and became the most downloaded app on the iTunes India store within a few days of launch. The iPhone App was also ranked as the Top free app on App Store (India) overall as well as in the travel category. The MMT Android app is rated 4.3 out of 5 in the Google Play store. *By 2014, MakeMyTrip iPhone and Android apps had received top billings and ratings, and had more than 5 million downloads.*

For feature-phone users, MakeMyTrip pioneered natural language processing (NLP) for SMS-based self-servicing and queries, enabling this technology innovation to solve natural-language ambiguities. NLP allowed the user to 'query' in an intuitive (natural) way as opposed to structuring the query in a standard template. To cater to the large segment of users without a data connection, MakeMyTrip built an assortment of value-added travel solutions that are available on SMS including India's first SMS-based bus-ticket booking service which enabled feature/entry-level phone users to harness the power of 'mobile'.

» RoutePlanner: This app enabled faster and easier trip-planning between any two destinations in India. RoutePlanner leveraged a highly scalable technology architecture that sifted through 1 billion possible routes and over 20 billion possible schedules in a matter of milliseconds, to give the best possible combinations to travel from one city to another. Post route selection, RoutePlanner displayed the best transport combinations down to the specific flight number, train name or bus operator with approximate fares and allowed the user to book the route, in a remarkably simple interface.

» Inspire: The tool helped users research and explore holiday destinations based on a variety of parameters such as interest areas, flight intersections and budget.

» Tripalong: In 2012, the company launched 'Tripalong', the world's first multi-airline social-seating app that allows users to share their itinerary within their social networks and plan 'intersections' (meetings) with their friends at airport-lounges and the city of travel and (if they are booked on the same flight) get seats together while checking-in.

Success, rightfully deserved

As of December 2014, MakeMyTrip's market-share was nearly 50 per cent of the online travel market in India (according to Phocuswright). In the third quarter of 2015, its hotels and packages transactions increased by nearly 47 per cent year-on-year and recorded 43.5 per cent growth in revenue less service costs, on a constant currency basis.

Awards and accolades

MakeMyTrip has received numerous accolades for providing best-in-class services to travellers. Over the last few years, the brand has been recognized by industry bodies and through various customer surveys as the best-in-class travel service provider.

Key wins

» Phocuswright Travel Innovation Summit Award 2013 for the innovative travel product—RoutePlanner.
» Lonely Planet Travel Best OTA Award for 2013.
» Top five Best Companies to Work For in India by the Great Place to Work® Institute 2010–2013.
» Lonely Planet Travel Best Travel Facilitator (Indian) Award 2012.
» Outlook Traveller Travel Best OTA Award 2012.
» Eyefortravel Award for the Best Mobile Strategy and Best Mobile Solution 2012.
» Safari India National Tourism Best Online Tour Company Award 2012.
» Franchise India Awards Retailer of the Year 2012.
» Times Travel Honours Best Domestic Tour Operator 2011.
» CNBC Travel Award 2009.
» Consumer Superbrands India-Superbrand 2009.

» Most-preferred Full-service Online Travel Agency in India in a user survey conducted by TravelBiz Monitor 2008.

» Galileo-Express Travel World Best OTA Award 2007.

MakeMyTrip has also won the Porter prize 2012 for Industry Architecture Shift and was recognized for 'outstanding performance in the industry' and 'redefining the industry structure by challenging the very basis of competition, creating new business models, challenging the status quo and exploiting change'.

The way ahead

Today, MakeMyTrip enjoys the reputation of being technology-forward and innovative and delighting customers with service and value-based offerings, moving from the proposition of 'customer satisfaction' to 'customer delight'. Another factor that has been a major contributor to the success story of MakeMyTrip has been its focus on suppliers. With more people planning and booking their travel themselves, India is at an edge of another boom in the online travel industry. This time it will be fuelled by hotels. In the coming years, MakeMyTrip will be focused on growing the share of the hotels and packages business in its overall revenue mix. Mobile apps will become an important point of sale for the company in the near future. MakeMyTrip will continue to use its core strength of technology to innovate with products and provide best-in-class service and be recognized for providing customer delight. The company aims to continue to be the primary consultant of the Indian customer for the entire basket of travel-related needs.

THE MIRCHI STORY
'It's Hot!'

T his is the story not just of a brand
called Mirchi, but of the rebirth of
a category called radio.

It's as much a business story as it is a
marketing and an advertising story.

The company behind brand Mirchi,
Entertainment Network (India) Limited,
ENIL in short, was born in 1999 into the
house of Bennett Coleman & Company Ltd
(BCCL), known as 'The Times Group'. The
Times Group had already been operating a
small radio 'business' from 1995 to 1999 when
it produced content for a few hours a day
to be aired on All India Radio (AIR). The
content was offered under the brand name
Times FM. In those early days, the company
focused on English content and targeted a
'yuppie' crowd. Many in India still remember
Times FM for its effervescent programming
and innovative packaging and marketing.
For the first time, drive-time audiences had
something entertaining to look forward to,
even as they stayed stuck in the pathetic traffic
in their cities. Bolstered by its early success,

and enthused by the vibrancy and vigour of the medium, the company decided to participate in the first round of auctions that took place in early 2000. In the meanwhile, the AIR slots had to be surrendered, and the Times FM business had to be shut down.

Spicing up the airwaves: The first wave of FM radio privatization

The year 2000 is perhaps best known for the dotcom bust that happened towards the end of the year. However, for radio broadcasters, it was the year in which FM radio privatization started. With privatization slowly spreading to all sectors after 1991, private FM finally had its 'eureka moment' in February 2000 when the government conducted auctions now known as 'Phase-1' auctions. Since auctions happened before the dotcom bust, and at a time when the stock markets were scaling new highs, the auctions attracted many groups from within the media and outside. Many of these surrendered their licences later, after winning, when their stock market-induced enthusiasm dropped. Since BCCL was a private limited company (and remains one), and since it had had excellent prior experience with radio, it decided to trudge on in what was clearly a very difficult policy regime.

The Phase-1 policy was based on the 'tender' form of auctions. The bidding was for the 'first year license fee'. The tender terms stated that starting from this in the first year, the licence fee would increase by 15 per cent every year. In hindsight, this 15 per cent annual hike was ridiculously high, but in those heady days, bidders went ahead nonetheless. Even the auction methodology was faulty, given the fact that winners could walk away with hardly any financial penalty being imposed, while leaving other, more serious players stranded at a much higher licensing figure. All of this, coupled with the effervescent stock market-fuelled froth, led to very high licence fees from the first year onwards.

In any case, at the end of the auctions, BCCL had twelve licences, including Mumbai, Delhi, Kolkata, Chennai, Ahmedabad, Pune, Hyderabad, Lucknow, Bhubaneshwar, Cuttack, Indore and Kanpur. The one big exception was Bangalore, where it didn't demonstrate the aggression that it later did in other cities. With a good network under its belt, it was ready to roll out its operations. BCCL was the only company to offer the 'four metros', even though Bangalore had already started replacing Chennai as the southern hub. It also had the strongest 'western' package including the four biggest cities (Bombay, Ahmedabad, Pune and Indore). The main competitors were Music Broadcast (Radio City) with four stations including the vaunted Bangalore, along with Mumbai, Delhi and Lucknow; Sun TV (Suryan FM) with stations in Chennai, Tirunelveli, Vizag and Trichy; the India Today group (then Red FM) with Delhi, Mumbai and Kolkata; the Zee group with eight stations (which it did not operationalize) and even the Reliance group (then still the combined entity) which did not operationalize its stations. Almost all stations played Hindi music, with the exception of Mid-Day group's Go FM, which offered English programming. There were also some passionate and committed individuals like Gautam Radia (Win FM in Mumbai and Delhi) in the fray. All in all, it was a motley mix of committed media professionals, rich corporates who wanted in on the media glitz and passionate individuals who could add chutzpah to the young medium.

Solving for early challenges

The biggest challenge was to get people to listen

People had grown up on a three-hours-a-day diet of TV. *India was perhaps the only country in the world where private FM came a good ten years after private TV.* In those ten years, private TV had made enormous strides with the launch of Zee TV in 1992 followed by Star TV that offered English programming. There were also a few notable news channels including New Delhi Television (NDTV) and Aaj Tak. The state broadcaster too experimented with Doordarshan (DD)2, run privately. This is also the period of time when cricket had already become dominant and sports channels like ESPN-Star Sports were in the thick of the action. In a scenario like this, getting people to even consider radio was a challenge.

So far, radio had suffered from a legacy of neglect from the times when AIR was the sole broadcaster. The medium best known for its youth quotient, innovative programming, irreverent stand on issues and non-stop spontaneity, was wanting on 'programming strategy'. Social objectives dictated content production, with every language segment getting a 'slot'.

Whether people wanted these programmes or not was not important.

However, this deficit of good entertainment for people 'on the move' turned out to be a blessing and ensured that FM radio in its private version picked up really fast. The earliest consumers were the youth, who found radio 'cool'. Radio jockeys became aspirational (this was before they started getting mocked for their jabbering). Suddenly, being seen with headphones stuck in the ears was the identity card for the 'arrived' segment. Around the same time, the iPod was launched globally, and music itself got a big lift.

The fact that Hindi music wasn't considered 'chic' was another barrier. The youth preferred to be caught humming English music and it was still considered passé to hear Hindi music. This was one reason why most radio jockeys spoke in English; some even pretended not to know Hindi at all! It's thanks to the work done by radio stations and jockeys after their launch that slowly but surely Hindi music became hip...giving a huge fillip to the Hindi music and film industries.

Post launch communication

Incidentally, because of the perception of Hindi music being uncool, Mirchi's programming at the time of its launch in Mumbai featured English music in the two drive-times (7–11 a.m.; 5–9 p.m.). The underlying logic was that the 'professional' crowd in Mumbai consumed English music. It was only after competition launched an entirely Hindi station and started closing in rapidly on Mirchi, that Mirchi decided to tone the English down and in a couple of months got to a 100 per cent Hindi music format.

The second and more significant business challenge was to get advertisers on board

Just like lay consumers, the marketing folk in the corporate sector had grown up on a diet of TV. Ditto the creative folk at ad agencies. No one wanted to make 'cheap' radio ads because they didn't find it 'sexy'. Radio work was delegated to the lowest person at the agency and client ends. There was also no research data available to make number-crunching media planners support the medium.

However, what everyone knew was that radio was a 'fun' medium, a medium that catered to the youth, and one that was largely irreverent, all important attributes for making a brand cool. The early experimenters used radio largely for these qualitative reasons, not for any serious media delivery. It was good to have a small radio campaign, even if it was only leftovers that were thrown at it. But starting from this small patronage, radio grew rapidly.

Mirchi played a very crucial role in these early days. When it launched in Indore, it got the station inaugurated by Bollywood actor Akshaye Khanna. It launched with a young, contemporary, and irreverent programming style, belting out the latest—and only the latest—Hindi hits. The jockeys were handpicked to give the brand a youthful feel. How these jockeys were recruited is a story in itself. Very soon, Mirchi had set the airwaves on fire.

Identifying the right talent for this nascent yet effervescent industry was the next hurdle

One of the jockeys was a front-desk manager at the Taj where the Mirchi team was staying. Two others were news anchors on a local cable news channel. One woman came to the Mirchi office and started singing. The programming head was hired in an interview conducted in a car the team was driving to the airport. The promo producer used to work in the church, mixing gospel music for the faithful. The station head came from a fast-moving consumer goods (FMCG) company, and was picked up partly because he loved music. In short, no one knew what to look for in a radio station employee. It's in that context that the station's success with its first hires needs is to be seen. Many of these employees were still there at the tenth anniversary celebrations of Mirchi in 2012.

Another tough one was the issue of music royalties

The relationship between music labels and radio broadcasters had never been smooth anywhere in the world, but issues were usually resolved with some give and take. In India, the music labels appeared to be there only to take. The ask for music royalties was exorbitant; to the extent that most broadcasters would have to pay 100–500 per cent of their revenues as royalties. Labels were organized as an influential and savvy association (Phonographic Performance Limited—PPL) which filed criminal cases even in cases of minor infringement. But most importantly, it was simply not willing to negotiate. The matter went to the courts; an interim rate order was passed in 2002. The order was onerous for radio broadcasters and it was supposed to be reviewed after two years. However, legal cases ensured that the matter stayed stuck in the courts, unresolved until August 2010. For this entire first decade, private radio suffered enormous financial damage. On the one hand were enormous licence fees payable to the Government of India as Phase-1; and on the other hand were even more humongous music royalties.

A bleeding industry

In just five years of operations, Mirchi ran up accumulated losses of ₹102 crore. Since debt was not easy to come by, this was entirely funded by the promoters through equity, and later through a private equity placement Mirchi was able to manage. Canadian pension fund CDPQ, Mirchi's private equity (PE) partners, not just provided funding but also introduced experts from around the world who helped shape Mirchi's professional management culture.

The fact that all broadcasters were bleeding was leveraged by Mirchi as an opportunity. Being one of the earliest to advertise itself, brand Mirchi became synonymous with radio. Cheap 'pen radios' from China were being sold for ₹50 a piece all around the country under the name of Mirchi. Various restaurants came up proudly flashing the Mirchi name and logo. Phillips radio even released ads in papers in cities where Mirchi was to launch, welcoming Mirchi even as it sold its wares. In a short span of time, Mirchi became the heart-throb of the nation.

Strategic smarts that went on to shape Mirchi's success

Naming it right!

The story behind choosing the brand name Mirchi itself is quite interesting. From the onset, the management team was clear that the brand name would be decided via a thorough, research-based, scientific process. All potential brand names—generated on the basis of brainstorming, vox-pops and global search—were subjected to extensive consumer research. And in every stage of research, Mirchi (the recommendation of Times Group's managing director [MD] Vineet Jain, the passionate visionary behind this success) would come LAST! Eventually, though grudgingly, research outcomes were overruled and the MD's gut prevailed. This, in hindsight, turned out to be an ace in the pack, as the name set the strategic direction for many things to follow. It was an instant hit with audiences…because 'when you've tasted Mirchi, everything else feels bland!'

The intuitive consumer promise

The birth of the brand's tagline, 'It's Hot', itself is another interesting story. A few senior people from the British Broadcasting Corporation (BBC) wanted to know the meaning of 'Mirchi'. The obvious answer 'chillies' led to one of them commenting 'Oh very hot!' That was it! A seemingly strategic decision was taken in the most casual of manners.

Borrowing best practices from the FMCG industry

So far, media companies were run in a rather haphazard manner. Typically, the content teams ran the show. They produced what they *thought* would work, and then hoped that it did. The marketing teams largely focused on buying other media to promote the content. This was changed entirely. It was decided to run Mirchi as an FMCG brand. It started by defining the brand's identity (youthful, energetic, vibrant, colourful, sunshine), the target audience (18-25-year-old male/female, aspiring for bigger things in life), the brand's personality (cool, confident, not trying to impress), the right packaging wrappers (vibrant colours, witty temperament) and the tone (liberal, progressive, irreverent).

Just like any FMCG brand would do, the revenue opportunity in each market was examined before finalizing the 'format' of the station and then came the content.

Mirchi was also one of the early companies to have started the whole culture of research in media. Mirchi started pre-launch usage and attitude (U&A) studies—lifestyle, entertainment, pastime (LEP)—which played a key role in shaping the content and programming strategy for each city.

Early programming that gave the brand the gloss

Starting off with a catchy jingle, innovative 'sparklers' (creative capsules), international-standards packaging, clever radio jockeys and a slick flow of widely researched songs, Mirchi quickly went on to break new ground.

Adding the glam quotient to spice up this erstwhile sarkari medium

One of the pioneering things Mirchi was able to accomplish, clearly using the clout of the Times Group, was to have every single station inaugurated by a film star. So Ahmedabad, which followed Indore, was inaugurated by Sonali Bendre; Mumbai by Aishwarya Rai; and Pune by Amisha Patel. The following year, Delhi was launched by Kareena Kapoor and Kolkata by Bipasha Basu. Much later, in 2006, John Abraham launched Bangalore, Vidya Balan, Jaipur and so on. The instant connect with Bollywood, the widespread media coverage, the glitzy launches...all went on to make a 'dead' medium come alive.

Establishing 98.3 as the frequency to remember

The Kismat Khol De (KKD) contest was a simple one. It tried to establish 98.3 as the frequency to remember. Anyone who had the numbers 9, 8 and 3 (in any order) in a whole series of items, taken one day at a time, was eligible for participation. For example, on one day, if your life insurance policy had these numbers, you could be one of the lucky winners. On another day, if your bus ticket had these numbers, it could get you some prizes. The participation in this contest was so extensive that it had to be stopped for a day just a day after it was launched, and restarted only after a much bigger call centre was put in place to handle the call traffic.

Funky contest communication

Adding spice to traditional marketing the Mirchi way...

Equipped with an evocative tagline, advertising and promotion campaigns made it cool to be caught listening to the 'humble' radio. The hoardings all around Mumbai, witty print ads, bizarre on-ground activations (people standing on the road in ice-buckets under Mumbai's May sun!) and of course consumer contests and film-star launches all added to the frenzy around Mirchi.

One of the early direct mailers to media agency heads was a big-sized TV box which many refused to accept, thinking Mirchi was trying to bribe them! Till they opened it, and saw a tiny TV set inside...the message blaring out loud that: 'TV has shrunk and radio is bigger than TV'. The idea was that radio's listenership (for Mirchi, it was some 30 odd lakh in Mumbai then) was comparable and comparing it with TV viewership of the No. 1 channel Star Plus (with a five minutes+filter), Mirchi numbers were actually bigger!

Mirchi activations: An idea ahead of its time

Mirchi was among the first media houses to launch 'non-traditional revenues' (NTR) that were basically advertiser-funded on-ground events that Mirchi supported with on-air campaigns. Commercially savvy as it was, Mirchi realized there were more clients willing to give it money for on-ground events than for radio advertising. The first event itself was a roaring success with more than 80,000 people thronging stalls of consumer products, food, etc. that were promoted on-air. In those early days, Mirchi even ferried potential advertisers to these fairs...to show them how radio worked.

The investors felt that such peripheral activities diluted the focus on core radio. However, the team convinced the investors that the strategic objective of these was to in fact strengthen the core radio proposition. This NTR initiative was later rebranded as 'Mirchi Activations'. This was much before Martin Sorrell said activations would be the next big thing in media. Mirchi Activations was born in 2002–3, and now contributes between 10 and 12 per cent of Mirchi revenues. While all radio stations today do activations in some form or the other, Mirchi has a dominant share of that business.

All these efforts paid off as early research indicated that people had taken to Mirchi like fish to water. Even though other stations had launched in Mumbai by then, Mirchi was consumed by some 80 per cent of listeners. Car research indicated that close to 75 per cent cars were tuned into radio and more than 50 per cent of those into Mirchi. Mirchi used these research reports (conducted by Indian Market Research Bureau) to educate media agencies that in turn appreciated this data.

The second wave of FM radio privatization

The next big opportunity for Mirchi came in 2006, when fresh auctions were conducted as part of 'Phase-2' reforms. The big change the government made was that it changed the licence fee structure from the fixed annual licence fee to a combination of a one-time entry fee (OTEF) and a small revenue-dependent annual licence fee. This one change made the radio industry not just viable but also lucrative. Post 2006, Mirchi never made reported any loss. (It had accumulated losses of ₹102 crore till 2006.)

The auction method was also changed. From Indian Premier League (IPL)-style 'ascending' auctions, the 'tendering' format (one-step bid) was adopted. This was a tricky style of auctioning. One had to estimate the potential of the market, the bidding strategy of the competitors, and also plan financial resources carefully because bidding went region-wise and was staggered over five weeks. The team was clear about the stations it wanted ('must haves') and those that were 'good to have'. It consciously 'over-bid' in Bangalore and Hyderabad, the must-haves, bid aggressively in other metros and state capitals and conservatively in the good-to-have ones. The success of the strategy was clear from the fact that Mirchi bagged all thirteen 'A+ and A' towns (20 lakh+ population towns). It also managed thirty-two of the next best towns with the only painful exceptions being Chandigarh and Kochi. Chandigarh's loss was not as painful (bidding ₹8 crore odd, when the lower of two successful bidders bid ₹10 crore). But the Mirchi team felt really bad about losing Kochi which it lost by a mere ₹18 lakh after bidding ₹9.12 crore (lowest of three successful bids was ₹9.3 crore).

Mirchi now had the best network and it has been the strength of this network that has powered the brand since 2006.

While the parent, BCCL, was well capable of funding Mirchi's growth, an initial public offering (IPO) was launched in 2006, with a vision to make Mirchi the gold standard in media. The listing was more to test the inherent strength of the business than to raise funds. The IPO was a huge success.

Just before the IPO, as part of a global strategy shift, CDPQ exited from all Asian markets including India with healthy returns.

By 2006, brand Mirchi had become a much-sought-after brand, even in markets where it didn't have any presence. So when it launched in these new towns, it found consumers eagerly awaiting the launch. Before the launch, there were even stories of people coming to Mumbai and Delhi and taking back recordings of shows! Now they had their own Mirchi to listen to. Not surprisingly, the brand was readily accepted. Years later, in 2014, Mirchi remained the No. 1 brand in 22–24 of the 32 cities it operated in (Indian Readership Survey & Radio Audience Measurement) and a close No. 2 in 8 more.

Mirchi continued to build on its successes year after year with new innovations and additions. By 2014, it was doing programming in ten languages (Hindi, Marathi, Gujarati, Konkani, Tamil, Telugu, Malayalam, Kannada, Bangla, Punjabi). It forayed into international markets with a presence in the UAE where it won the Best Radio Station Award twice in its first two years.

Keeping pace with the emergence of digital, nine online stations were created on radiomirchi.com and Mirchi became the No. 1 radio brand on all forms of social media, with 1.8 million fans on Facebook, 25,000 followers on Twitter and 7 million+ views on YouTube (as on March 2014).

For long spells, it has also been the No. 1 on the audio podcast business on itunes.

The sounds of success

Mirchi went on to win numerous awards including some truly remarkable Indian and international recognitions

» Pitch-IMRB award for 'media brand of the year' (2008), ahead of *The Times of India* and Star Plus.

» FICCI (Federation of Indian Chambers of Commerce and Industry) Frames 'radio business of the year' award, several years in a row.
» Golden Pegasus award for corporate social responsibility (CSR) initiatives with the visually impaired.
» Hundreds of RAPA (Radio and Television Advertising Practitioners' Association of India) and IRF (Indian Radio Forum) awards.
» International Radio Festival award.

But none of these awards was as satisfying for Mirchi as the ones from its listeners. By 2014, nearly 37 million listeners were tuning into Mirchi every week (IRS), 25 per cent more than its nearest competitor that had fifteen more stations. Mirchi became the No. 1 brand in the top eight markets aggregated (IRS), the No. 1 brand in north, west, central and east India and No. 2 brand in south India.

» As a ₹385 crore brand today, it is nearly 70 per cent bigger than its nearest competitor.
» With a healthy EBITDA (earnings before interest, taxation, depreciation and amortization) of ₹125 crore and PAT (profit after tax) of ₹83 crore, Mirchi had cash-on-books of ₹440 crore to which it added ₹118 crore in just FY2014.

There is still a lot of spice in the Mirchi story

The brand is truly ready for Phase-3 when even more towns will open up, and there will be a distinct possibility of acquiring a second and even third licence in some of the bigger towns. While growing its footprint nationally, Mirchi hopes to offer alternate music formats in the bigger cities. Then there is the global market opportunity of non-resident Indians and persons of Indian origin waiting for Mirchi to come to their shores. And there is the whole exciting world of online radio and music where it can morph from an FM broadcaster to a digital broadcaster. With exciting opportunities like extending Mirchi into various youth areas and creating IPs around the Mirchi brand (like Mirchi Music Awards and Mirchi Top 20), the brand promises to stay hot for a long time to come.

Mirchi's advertising campaigns:

Mirchi's innovative advertising strategies, particularly in the initial few years after launch, played a key role in the brand truly catching the attention of listeners. These campaigns defined the brand. The ad campaigns can be divided into the following categories:

A. Initial outdoor campaigns aimed at playing up the Mirchi name, visually dramatizing the 'fire'.

B. Building on the 'hot' theme to build curiosity around 'something hot is coming your way'. Using props like the simple chilli with an antenna or a toaster with an antenna. Tabasco/grenade and playboy ads. The campaign line was 'You like it hot. We play it that way'. 'Subsequent campaigns worked on 'Its hot' in more direct ways leveraging Bipasha Basu, Preity Zinta and Salman Khan.

C. Establishing Mirchi as *'aapka apna Bollywood radio station'*—another significant strategic initiative considering that all of its content came from Bollywood.
'Up close on Radio Mirchi' was launched to position Mirchi as the listeners' connect into Bollywood. Around this time, Mirchi was playing an average of 100 film-celebrity bytes/interviews every month. Competition was way behind.

D. The RJ Hunt, the first talent hunt on radio.

E. Eventually around 2007, as product parity started emerging between different radio brands, Mirchi decided to take the brand outside of the realm of the product and developed the *'Mirchi sunne waale always khush'* campaign. This was designed to play up the 'pep-up' promise of the brand.

There were many other brand campaigns run for the next few years. However, clearly the brand had been made in its early, formative years. It is that legacy that still holds Mirchi up.

One last word

The success of brand Mirchi is on account of many factors. But if there is one that stands out, it is the quality of its people—a bunch of aspirational go-getters, put together by A.P. Parigi, a maverick leader who came from the world of telecom. The earliest leaders were all brand aficionados, coming from diverse backgrounds. There was a banker-turned-jeweller, a paint-executive, an advertising guru, a techie with exceptional people skills, an entrepreneur born and raised in Gujju-land, and a money-making machine who was popularly called 'milkman' (he used to milk the clients in his earlier days!). Then there was the chief financial officer (CFO), who we often said could make an entertainment TV channel by merely pointing the camera at him, and an HR head who was so into emotional engagement with an often volatile bunch of youngsters that he often forgot to maintain even basic records. And behind all of these passionate leaders was Vineet Jain, the chairman and the visionary behind Radio Mirchi.

'REAL' SUCCESS

To accomplish great things, we must not only act,
but also dream; not only plan, but also believe.
—Anatole France

This is the story of a juice brand that emerged from the stable of a company manufacturing Ayurvedic products; it is the story of a brand that won the battle of public perception to emerge as the dominant player in the market.

The opportunity

In the mid-1990s, the freshly squeezed fruit juice market in India (home or local juice stalls) was more than 300 million litres annually. This literally translated into a whopping 150 crore glasses consumed annually or 40 odd lakh glasses daily. So fruit juice was not exactly an alien concept. What was alien, however, was the idea of packaged juices. It was a non-existent category. Amit Burman, vice chairman at Dabur India Ltd spotted this as an opportunity to take a strategic bet and create not just another product for Dabur, but

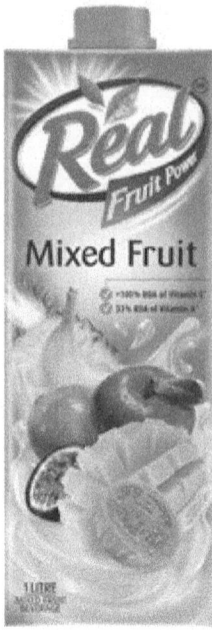

a whole new category for the country.

Dabur India had a history of thinking out of the box and developing innovative products emanating out of deep consumer understanding. In many cases, Dabur pre-empted demand and evoked new needs by introducing category-creating products like Chawanprash, Gulabari, Vatika and Hajmola. This visionary thinking has been key to Dabur's success as a leading Indian FMCG (fast-moving consumer goods) company. In this case, too, Amit Burman observed the sharp contrast between the easy availability of packaged juices overseas and their unavailability in India. This was what, in the summer of 1996, led to the birth of Real—India's first completely natural, healthy, packaged fruit juice with no added preservatives that was soon to dominate the Indian juice market.

Solving for multiple challenges: Brand equity, product fitment, branding, product, packaging, positioning

Thinking back, it wasn't an easy step for Dabur India, an Ayurvedic company with almost no equity in foods, to embark on a bold and ambitious journey and launch what would later become the dominant brand of juices in the Indian market.

Many fundamental questions had to be addressed. Was the Indian consumer ready for packaged juices? Was the concept a mere imitation of the West? What would be the acceptance of this product from a company known for Ayurvedic products? And most importantly would consumers be ready to pay for what is traditionally associated with homemade or freshly made?

The answers lay in going back to the basics of Dabur's core business philosophy of comprehensively understanding consumer needs and designing innovative solutions.

The whole concept of fruit juices revolved around freshness. Also, juice stalls facilitated out-of-home consumption, providing variety and convenience. To convince consumers that packaged juices were as good if not better than fresh juice was a mammoth task. The tangible proof of possible freshness lay in adopting the new tetrapack packaging technology instead of the traditional glass bottles that Indian consumers were used to for beverages. Early adoption of advanced packaging technology contributed to a premium image which tends to get decoded in the minds of consumers as better quality.

The fact that Indians have a sweeter palate and also that mothers and fresh juice stalls add sugar to freshly squeezed juice to enhance its taste appeal was a key input by the research and consumer insight team to the new product development team at the Dabur Research Foundation. Merely aping the texture (which was more fibrous), taste (which was less sweet) and flavours (which were western fruit variants) of the West would have been premature for the Indian market. In a market where sweet lime and orange were the most juiced fruits, orange seemed to be the more appropriate variant from a profitability point of view. Hence, the first flavour to be created and launched was orange with the right balance of tangy and sweet to suit Indian taste buds.

Consumers' acceptance of a non-medicinal non-Ayurvedic juice from Dabur was another big question. The solution was actually quite simple. By not highlighting the company name alongside the Real brand name, as was conventional Dabur practice, two objectives were served. The authenticity of the product was highlighted while the very different traditional product portfolio of the parent company didn't act as an obstacle to acceptance.

It was a brave sacrifice and bold strategy within the organization to create a whole new brand, create and develop a new category not just within the organization but for the country itself and launch it in a relatively new-format packaging.

The launch pack was dark blue with strong branding and such that the fruit stood out. However, in making the pack premium, the need to convince the consumer of the authenticity and taste, somehow seems to have got diluted. This was a learning from the first phase of launch that was quickly corrected along with other tweaks post the first year of launch.

However, the most important achievement of Real was highlighting the taste dimension in a category traditionally driven by health, without compromising on the wholesomeness factor.

Business problems	Solution design
• As fresh as home-made juice	• Packaging innovation 'tetrapack' that helped preserve freshness
• Taste as important as health	• Choice of orange flavour as the launch variant with the right texture and balance of tangy and sweet
• Dabur's overt perception as an Ayurvedic company a barrier	• An authentic brand name like 'Real' not pre-fixed with 'Dabur'

A comprehensive overhaul

The first year of launch did not turn out to be very encouraging. While many of the strategic decisions paid off, critical concerns related to distribution and supply-chain management emerged as barriers in market acceptance. Added to this was the wrong choice of packaging design and missing links in communication. A demotivated team, including the sales crew, nearly forced a defeat. The bottom line was that the packs were not being picked off the shelf.

A sales meet in Mussoorie proved to be the turning point. An open mind and sheer grit and determination helped identify, course-correct and chart the course forward by the team led by Krishnakumar Chutani, the marketing head. A patient ear to the woes, complaints and issues highlighted and helped translate these into tangible actionables.

To bring back faith and confidence and re-energize the team, some fundamental components required re-engineering:

» Supply chain: Some of the packs were getting puffed due to delay in the supply chain. The then existing supply chain was not fully equipped to handle food products with specific storage needs and short shelf lives. This was one of key concerns that was addressed on war footing, and Real is reaping the benefits even today.
The internal systems were improved to ensure that quality was maintained till it reached the consumer by strengthening distribution and better packaging.

Real developed a food-sensitive warehouse management training programme at all levels of the channel to ensure that the freshest product reached the market.

» Design and aesthetics: The first pack, though premium looking, lacked food appeal. In India, dark blue is conventionally seen as a negative colour and not very appetizing—clearly disassociated from foods. Real redesigned to enhance food and fruit appeal by using bright and attractive colours that enhanced retail shelf impact.

» Packaging enhancement: Dabur Foods was also the first company to introduce cap-on packs which gave consumers the flexibility of re-use. This, in addition to the tetrapack spin cap, cold-fill technology and spill-proof double seal cap packaging, helped in keeping the juice fresher for longer and also making it easier to pour.

» Revamped product portfolio: Launching preferred popular variants like orange and mango to start with, proved an effective fruit variant strategy. The stringent action standards in consumer product testing ensured the acceptance of the product by consumers and thereby the success of the brand.

» Communication: Consumer research had already tabled the lack of belief in packaged foods and fresh juice. This issue was addressed in communication by highlighting no added preservatives and no added colour.

Having addressed each issue systematically, the brand tasted its first success in the year 2000. The changing consumer, impacted by urban India's rapid globalization, was actively embracing the concept of 'Time is money'. The 2–minute noodle generation wanted everything fast and was willing to pay the premium for the convenience.

Real was an idea whose time had come.

Segmentation plays a pivotal role in market expansion

Today, Real commands a more than 50 per cent market share in the packaged juices and nectars market (AC Nielsen). This growth was made possible on the strength of innovative segmentation to tap into diversified consumer needs.

Real was able to successfully segment the market early, thus effectively creating a differentiated niche even in the no added sugar juice category with its sub-brand, Real Activ, in the year 2000.

Real Fruit Power: Focusing on children while promising health with happiness

Real's proposition is that fruits can be fun, colourful, juicy, delicious and exciting. Its ongoing endeavour is to bring fruit goodness and health to the home, without compromising on the happy. To cater to different needs, occasions and taste buds, the Real Fruit Power range today has fourteen exciting variants. The range includes exotic Indian mango, international favourites pomegranate and cranberry, and classic orange and pineapple among others. Real Fruit Power has no added preservatives, delivering on the promise of real fruit power.

Real Activ: Appealing to a health-conscious young India

The Real Activ brand was created keeping in mind the needs of health-conscious young executives for whom fitness is a way of life. The product comprised unsweetened juices that had 0 per cent added sugar, no added colour or preservatives and that were naturally rich in antioxidant nutrients. The Real Activ range expanded to three categories of juices—100 per cent (single fruit) juice, Fruit–Veggie, a combination of fruit and vegetable juices and Fibre+ with added fibre.

Fruit–Veggie: Dabur's most successful innovation

The new Fruit–Veggie juice category was created by Dabur Foods in 2006. Globally, the fruit+vegetable combo juice market was a fast-growing niche that appealed to health-conscious adults who wanted their juice to 'deliver more'. Interestingly, this was not an entirely alien concept to the Indian consumer who was accustomed to drinking mixed fruit and vegetable juices from the neighbourhood juice stall but did not have this choice when it came to hygienically packaged juice.

Real's strategy to launch this category was an outcome of an innovative product development plan that combined product ideation and extensive consumer feedback. The company's research showed that consumers were looking at an orange+ option, i.e., a way of making the all-time favourite orange juice more nutritious and healthy. Several options were considered and the orange-carrot combination was chosen for various reasons: it made the healthiest combination; the two flavours blended well with each other creating a more flavourful juice; and there was a high degree of comfort with the combination as carrot juice was also traditionally consumed in India and its health benefits were well known.

Real Activ was the first and remains the only juice that offers a combination of fruits and vegetables. The innovations in the 'health' space continued with the launch of Real Activ Fibre+—the first fibre drink—and Real Activ Yoghurt—the first yoghurt drink—both of which directly benefited gut health in addition to weight management.

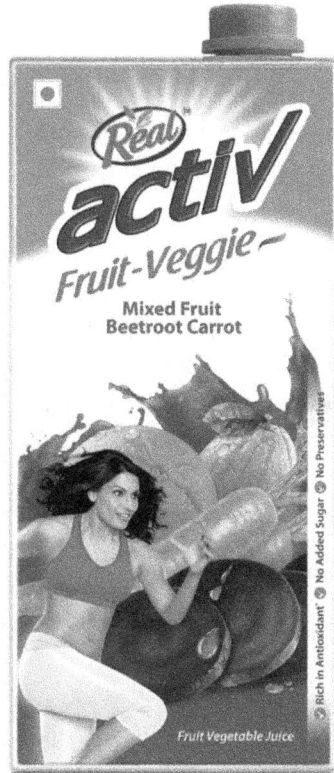

Real SupaFruits: Promising supra health and enhanced nutrition

Superfruits are a special category of fruits which are exceptionally nutrient dense and rich in antioxidants. These are among the most exotic and premium fruits that are difficult to obtain throughout the year. Superfruits and their juices enjoy great popularity the world over. These superfruits and their juices are a perfect blend of exotic fruit appeal and exceptional fruit nutrition. Hence they are not only great tasting but also provide extra nourishment that boosts well-being.

Dabur continued its innovation stint with the launch of Real SupaFruits, another first for India. Real SupaFruits combined two super-fruits (Goji berry and Plum) in each pack to deliver the promise of more nutrition per millilitre.

Real Fruit Shakes: Becoming every mother's best friend

With the launch of Real Fruit Shakes, Dabur forayed into the packaged milk fruit shake market. The objective was not only to extend brand Real to give consumers more choices but also make the experience of having milk more enjoyable and nutritious for kids.

Real has grown from strength to strength and will continue to create a disruption in the market with innovations and speed to market with the numerous variant launches and sub-brands.

The role of communication

Communication strategy relied heavily on launching and communicating new variants. The launch of popular variants to start with, before moving on to more exotic variants, was an important and effective part of communication. It helped create familiarity and acceptance for the packaged juice category among Indian consumers without compromising on nutrition and taste as fruits are almost always associated with freshness and seasonality.

Once familiar with the concept of packaged juices and the more niche 'no added sugar' Real Activ variant, the market and the consumer were now ready to experiment with newer variants, some of which were exotic fruits not juiced at home like apricot, plum and cranberry. It is this nimble-footedness and ability to deliver a variety of products and variants under each category that will continue to fuel growth.

In a short span of time, the communication traversed from 'Fruit in a pack' to 'Eight times more fruit (nutrition)', 'As good as fruit' and 'Drinking a fruit'. Krishnakumar Chutani, the marketing head, followed the simple philosophy of 'brutal simplicity leading to engaged creativity', that became the cornerstone of all communication.

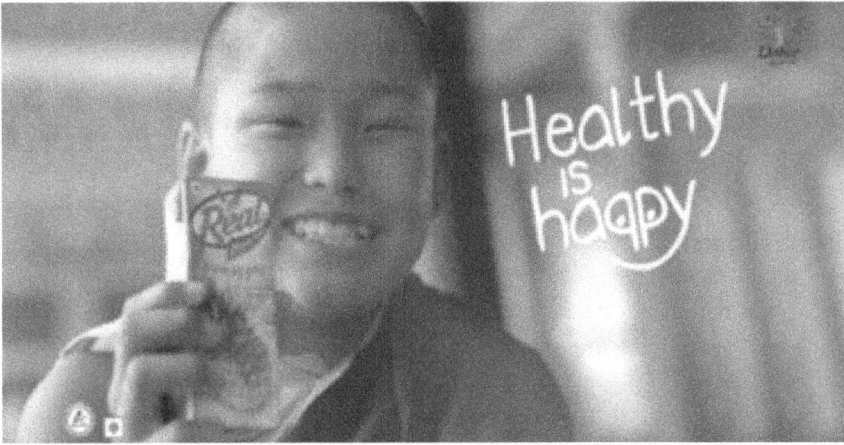

Rooted in the insight that 'kids make faces at healthy foods', Real Fruit Power took on a compelling platform of fruit nutrition for fussy eaters (i.e. kids). This was different from the competition's aggressive communication on owning a particular occasion or time of day, like breakfast. The brand endeavoured to involve mothers through real stories to help them overcome the barrier of children finding fruit boring. This was brought alive through fruit stories, recipes, fun facts and innovative digital initiatives to drive home the proposition of Happy=Healthy.

High-impact, below-the-line engagement—'Real taste challenge'—supported the campaigns by establishing the authenticity and freshness of real fruit in a pack. In fact, in 2013, in some Durga Puja pandals, Real packs were distributed as prasad in lieu of the conventional fruit prasad. This is a sign of the high respect the brand has earned.

The brand philosophy of 'A Happy Child is a Healthy Child' captured in the latest communication is a guiding and driving force for the brand.

In a world where milk food drinks (MFDs), amongst other brands, focus on the physical or mental dimension of health, here is a brand that goes beyond. As often heard from paediatricians—if a child is happy then it's a sure sign of health.

In line with its intent of targeting a health-conscious young India, the communication for 'Real Activ' focused on the positioning of weight management. The earlier campaign was based on the powerful insight of 'fitting into purani (old) jeans' as the benchmark for successful weight loss. The recent campaign captures the rising health trends, inspiring the urban masses to lead a more active and energetic lifestyle. Celebrity endorsement by Sonali Bendre for Real Fruit Power juice and fitness icon Bipasha Basu for Real Activ also contributed significantly by giving communication the desired fillip.

Real leadership

Real has been a category creator and has driven the growth of the packaged fruit juice market in India. *The brand witnessed its fastest growth in the past five years, from a ₹250 crore brand to a ₹700 crore brand. Real and its sub-brands served a whopping 15 crore juice helpings in 2013. It is said that the number of packs sold, if laid side by side, would far exceed India's coastline of 7,516 km.*

Real was a pioneer in every sense of the word

- First to launch packaged juices with Real Fruit Power.
- First to launch over sixteen variants.
- First to launch functional juices with Real Activ in eleven flavours, in the year 2000.
- First to launch summer coolers, in 2006.
- First to launch soya-based beverages, in 2007.
- First to launch Indian ethnic drinks, in 2011.
- First to introduce the concept of 'super fruits' through the SupaFruit launch in 2013.
- First to launch milk-based juices with fruit nutrition.

Accolades and recognitions

» Real was voted the Most Trusted fruit juice brand by consumers for the eighth year in a row in the Reader's Digest Trusted Brand Gold Award in the Food and Beverages (Juice) category.

» Real was ranked amongst the Top 100 Most Exciting Brands in India (Milward Brown).

A stable team spanning marketing, sales, operations, supply chain and even vendors, motivated and inspired by Sunil Duggal, the current chief executive officer, and led by Krishnakumar Chutani, has been the core of Real's success. It's a team that dreamt of, believed in and eventually built and nurtured the business to be the most successful fruit juice brand in India.

Challenger

THE JOURNEY OF A BILLION CUPS

Thou shall not:
- » *have advertising*
- » *have a marketing team*
- » *recruit extra manpower*
- » *blend tea*

decreed Darbari Seth, long-serving chairman of Tata Tea.

Steve Jobs, while addressing the graduating class of 2005 at Stanford University, said, 'You cannot connect the dots looking forward; you can only connect them looking backwards.'

Back in 1983, when Tata Tea acquired Finlay, little did Darbari Seth know that, thirty-two years later, his people would be narrating the story of the brand/company he had helped build, and that they would be doing so by connecting the dots looking backwards.

But, unlike what Jobs said, these dots are not mere acts of coincidence. They are simple yet meaningful actions taken time and again in the face of adversity; they are decisions that went on to become trends; they are a series of stories woven together that form part of the DNA of a legendary brand.

It all started when Tata Finlay was set up as a joint venture (JV) between Tata Sons and the UK-based tea plantation company, James Finlay and Company in 1962. In 1983, Tata Tea was born after James Finlay sold his shareholding to Tata, heralding the start of a new journey.

Tata Tea: A brand that was not meant to be

In the early 1980s, Tata Tea's primary business—growing and manufacturing tea in the lush green plantations of Assam and Munnar—was flourishing. The company leadership at that time was debating the need to add value to the plantation business and also protect it from the uncertainties of a commodity business. Thus was born the idea of launching the Tata Tea brand. The key motivation behind the thought was to add to the plantation business rather than create a 'branded business', in line with the intriguing tenets laid down by Darbari Seth. In other words, the motivation behind founding the Tata Tea brand was to maximize value for the plantations and not to create a brand.

Competitive environment in the 1980s: Nothing Indian about it

Branded Tea: In the early 1980s, tea was a commodity tightly controlled by a handful of companies.

Ironically, in the early years, i.e., the first three decades of the century, the Indian tea trade was predominantly controlled by foreign entities. As one website put it: 'There was nothing Indian about Indian packed tea.' The names were all foreign—English names based on colours—Red Label, Violet Label, Green Label.

Of these, Red Label had the most significant share and was sold in carton packs.

At that time, with over 70 per cent market share, loose tea dominated the market. Of the remaining 30 per cent, one player, Hindustan Unilever, controlled the majority share (70 per cent).

An insight into supply chain management led to the creation of Tata Tea's unique brand promise

To create a dent in the marketplace, the team was clear that it needed to do something different. It became imperative that the company develop a 'competitive advantage'—something that was 'unique' and of real value to the end consumer.

A close scrutiny of the tea business at that time (and to a large extent, holding true today as well) revealed that tea was sent from the plantations to the auctions. Companies or agents bought this tea and then blended or mixed it as per a standard that in their understanding would deliver a certain taste and profile of tea or simply a recipe (at least for the branded players). They then packed and dispatched the tea to the respective markets for sale. This process took a whopping eight months or so from production to consumption. Now tea, like other food products, deteriorates when it comes in contact with moisture and air and hence loses its natural properties over time.

Hence the customer was drinking stale tea, at least eight months old, and no efforts were being made by any player to preserve the product in any manner.

It is important to note that the companies that owned brands rarely, if ever, grew the teas they marketed, and this was even more so for the loose tea players.

And so Tata Tea discovered its unique competitive advantage. *Why not pack the tea at the gardens it owned and then sell it 'garden fresh' to the consumer?* It was an unmet need of the consumer and a clear differentiator in the market place.

For the first time in the country, tea was packed on the estates where it was grown.

And was born, Tata Tea's brand promise—*garden fresh tea*. The pack itself, of course, was green.

A packaging innovation, the use of polypacks over cartons, which were the industry norm, helped enhance this brand promise. Polypacks, which are laminates of polyester and polythene have very high barrier properties to keep both air and moisture out.

Product innovation

In line with Darbari Seth's fourth tenet, a conscious decision was taken not to blend this tea. Unlike regular blended teas in the market which were sieved and had uniform grains, Tata Tea was made of a combination of big and small grains. The small grains gave the tea strength or 'kadakpan', while the bigger grains gave it 'khushboo' or aroma. Mystically, what Seth didn't know then was that years later, this very tenet would form the core brand proposition for brand Tata Tea Premium—promise of a mix of badi and choti patti (leaf) which gave a balance of strength and aroma in every cup of tea.

| 1985 | 2001 | 2002 | 2004 | 2010 |

Current

Evolution of the visual identity of Tata Tea and the introduction of Tata Tea Premium

Another of Darbari's tenets said that the company would bear no extra cost behind marketing—which meant no investment behind manpower, excessive trade spends or even advertising. It was simple: the brand had to prove itself to command investment.

Sweet-spot pricing

Thanks to state-of-the-art machinery from Japan and a handful of workers at the gardens, tea was now packed into branded Tata Tea packets which were then transported along with Tata Salt and distributed further through a third party distributor.

Because of the lean cost structure and removal of supply chain layers such as auctioning and blending, *packets of Tata Tea were available to the end consumer at prices that were marginally above those of the 'loose' teas they were purchasing and significantly lower than those of packet tea players.* The brand had already found a way of addressing the clear gap in the customer requirement of 'freshness'.

It was only a matter of time before the consumer bought into this brand. After all, any consumer, anywhere in the world, would prefer fresh food products at a reasonable price. There was a surge in demand and Tata Tea became a significant player, soon eating into the share of Unilever as well as of the loose teas.

By now, the brand had become so significant that the retailer community expressed its desire for the brand to advertise. The local (kirana) trade in India is built on wafer-thin margins where traders make money on volume. Hence, when the local trade accepts you, it means that you are their asset. And this community was telling the brand that it needed to advertise for it (the retailer community) to take pride in selling more of it.

The inadvertent brand journey along the 4 Ps, for a brand that was not meant to be

Packaging at source to retain freshness; polypacks instead of cartons to keep air and moisture out.

Product: Non-blended tea that retained its strength and aroma.

Proposition: Garden fresh tea.

Price: Strategically positioned between loose tea and branded teas.

The brand was thus ready to command investment and the fifth P, 'Promotion', was a natural outcome.

By 1987, having proved itself in the market, Tata Tea had by now earned its right to spend on advertising. That is when advertising and creative agency, Ogilvy & Mather, went on to create the first Tata Tea TV advertisement. The film featured Amjad Khan as the protagonist educating a young lady about how Tata Tea was freshly packed at source with freshness sealed into every packet. This was followed in a few years by a piece of communication which became one of most iconic ad films of the decade. This film featured Anu Agarwal in a 'tea' rendition of the superhit Bollywood song, '*Jumma Chumma de de*', where a group of men with tea cups in their hands demanded a cup of 'taazgi' or freshness and Anu Agarwal promised that with a packet of Tata Tea.

At a time when Unilever was positioned on strong emotional credentials of being a family drink cuing bonding and togetherness, Tata Tea went on to create a new segment for tea—one that desired freshness. This 'unique' feature became so fundamental to the brand that even today it comprises its core equity.

High quality tea, low trade spends, competitive pricing and a differentiated and unique proposition of freshness resulted in Tata Tea's ascent to fame. Having changed the dynamics of the tea market in India, Tata Tea's flagship brand, Tata Tea Premium, saw phenomenal growth from 1986 until 1999.

Running out of breath

But by its very nature, an advantage only remains competitive so long as it is unique. Tata Tea soon saw competition catch up and erode its erstwhile competitive advantage.

The tea trade is one with low entry barriers, so local businessman could buy good quality tea from the auctions, pack it in pouches and begin to sell—all at highly competitive prices. The crash in commodity prices made it even more lucrative for new players to enter. By now, most packs in the market were green and promised freshness. The polypack packaging was no longer a differentiator either.

Trade and consumer promotions started eroding market share

By the end of the 1990s the market saw a mushrooming of 'local' brands, each operating in its respective geography. Typically, local players operated in a specific area and they quickly understood that tea in India is sold at the recommendation of the retailer. Hence, incentivizing the retailer (who also happened to be in his close network) to sell was a sure shot path to success. This was also the time that the stainless steel industry was going through a boom—making stainless steel items (with high perceived value) very reasonable to procure. These made for attractive free items, luring the consumer into their franchise.

In a sense, history repeated itself with local players doing to Tata Tea what Tata Tea had done to the industry a decade earlier. This was not good news for the brand—for the first time since inception, the brand shrank by 4 per cent in 1999. After a decade or so of phenomenal growth, Tata Tea clearly needed to stop and rejuvenate itself.

The business environment was challenging, no doubt. And yet again it was time for change.

In former managing director and chief executive officer (MD and CEO), Harish Bhat's book, *Tata Log*, he mentions: 'A pioneer has to find the way around challenges that appear insurmountable because he is attempting to scale a peak that has never been done before.'

And a breath of fresh air

Along with the dawn of the new millennium, came a ray of hope.

In 2000, under the leadership of R. Krishna Kumar, Tata Tea became one of the first Indian companies to acquire a company overseas, a company that was much bigger than itself. This was in line with Krishna Kumar's belief that 'if you want to be a strong player, you can't not be a global player'.

Tata Tea acquired Tetley, a heritage British brand with a presence around the world—and with that, it found its place on the world map.

Tetley, the market leader in the UK and Canada among others, had a distinguished history of innovations to its credit, including the original teabag and the drawstring bag. Tata Tea, with this acquisition could leverage Tetley's expertise in marketing and innovation, in its quest to become a global player. While the mood in the economy was good, brand Tata Tea continued to shrink and the brand ended FY 2001 at 11 per cent market share. *It was clear that the garden fresh story and the original pack which had stayed the same since inception had run their course.*

Up until 2001, Tata Tea operated with only one brand and that was 'Tata Tea Premium', tasked with addressing all segments of the market. But that was an approach not suited for the Indian tea market.

Tea in some ways mirrors the multifaceted culture of India—with differences in grain sizes, tea colour, taste, method of preparing tea and so on. But with diversity also comes complexity, and to paint a canvas as wide as the Indian market, one colour just wasn't enough.

In the words of Sushant Dash, vice president marketing, India:

The biggest challenge the brand faced was that it needed to compete at both ends of the spectrum with the likes of Red Label at the upper end and Taaza and local brands at the economy end. Hence, it was important to move from a single brand offering to a portfolio of offerings that catered to various price points and value segments in the market.

Portfolio brand strategy

And so began the journey of building a portfolio, one brand at a time.

Unique consumer insights from across the country coupled with tea expertise led to the creation of several brands in the three-four years that followed. This was a crucial period in the expansion of the brand.

Geographical segmentation

Tea preferences across the country weren't uniform. In Bihar, for example, bolder-grain teas were consumed and considered superior. But knowledge of tea dictated that bolder-grain teas were in fact inferior teas and least preferred in the hierarchy because they took longer to release colour and taste. Unlike other markets, housewives here would first add water and sugar—a process by which the sugar would get caramelized giving a unique flavour to the tea. This flavour compensated for the lack of delivery of the bolder grains. This realization allowed for an offering that could cater to a consumer need at a lower cost. And thus was launched Tata Tea Danapur Leaf—a yellow-coloured pack which promised the goodness of bold grains.

In some parts of the country like Maharashtra and Orissa, consumers had a preference for 'dust' tea—dust tea was fine tea and consumers of dust liked their tea thick and strong. To address this need, Tata Tea Premium Dust was launched in a red pack, the colour red connoted strength and was differentiated from the original green pack. Today Tata Tea Premium Dust defines the tea market in Orissa and enjoys dominant market share—the only other presence in the market is local players, who, of course, come in red packs.

As the variants of Tata Tea Premium grew, so did the footprint of the brand.

Affluence-based segmentation

Premium

But it was not enough to grow in different markets. It was also important to grow across different consumer segments—by now Tata Tea Premium operated in the 'popular'/mid segment of the market while lacking a presence in the upper and lower segments.

Extensive research was undertaken to understand in detail the tea consumption habits amongst the higher socio-economic classification (SEC), urban audience. And research said that these consumers desired something that was very fundamental to tea—aroma. Aroma was the signifier of a superior cup of tea. At that time, it was a habit amongst some consumers to buy CTC tea (CTC stands for crush, tear and curl: a method of processing black tea) and mix it with orthodox tea or long-leaf tea (Unlike CTC tea, orthodox leaves are manufactured through a more gentle process, thereby allowing them to retain more aroma and flavour). CTC offered a strong full cup and the orthodox added a unique flavour or aroma. And that, right there, was an opportunity for consumer delight.

This led to the birth of one of the few successful innovations in the tea category—Tata Tea Gold. The brand was differentiated by the presence of orthodox long leaves (15 per cent), and enjoyed a unique packaging which allowed for the pack to stand on the shelf and a clutter-breaking name.

The Tata Tea Gold launch was a huge success. The brand was stocked out within two months of launch. It became a 2 per cent share brand within two years of launch, and, a decade later, it is now the face of the Tata Tea portfolio in the eastern parts of the country.

In 2013, brands like Taj Mahal, Taaza and a host of locals have launched long-leaf variants with 15 per cent long leaf—ten years too late.

Economy

At the same time, Tata Tea also owned 'Agni', a brand that the company had launched in 1998 to address the economy segment. Agni stood for strength and came in a red pack with the brand name written in Hindi. It was launched with a lot of fanfare and had Sridevi as its brand ambassador. It grew rapidly but declined just as fast. As soon as investments behind advertising were stopped, the brand became undifferentiated from the plethora of local brands. Neither trade nor consumers saw any reason to buy into the brand. By 2004, Agni was struggling to find a foothold and Tata Tea was debating if it should withdraw the brand.

Strategic revival of the Agni brand by leveraging the equity of 'Tata'

A strong presence in the large economy segment of the market was important for Tata Tea as it provided an opportunity for bringing a large number of consumers of loose and local teas into the Tata Tea franchise. And so instead of closing down a brand that was struggling to survive, fresh life was infused into it. Agni was transitioned under the Tata Tea mother brand in 2005. It was rebranded Tata Tea Agni. Another smart business tactic deployed to make the brand aspirational for the economy segment was to transition the nomenclature from Hindi to English while retaining its bright red colour. The Tata Tea name gave Agni the required differentiation from the local brands. Importantly, it gave trade a reason to stock Agni. That was a turning point for the brand with it breaking all previous sales records in the post transition period. Today, Tata Tea Agni is the only successful national branded player in the economy segment.

Tata Tea started with a single brand offering and became a portfolio of brands, each addressing a distinct segment of the market with a relevant consumer proposition. It was now a portfolio in the true sense and it flourished.

From volume leadership to thought leadership

By 2007, the company had seen great success in tea and was now a global player. Along with volume and turnover, even ambition became larger.

However, tea was perceived as a beverage for 'older people'—youth didn't seem to engage with tea and so the immediate task was to appeal to this segment which had been excluded from all marketing plans so far.

In the legendary words of the then MD and CEO Percy Singanporia, 'With the limited growth potential of a single beverage brand play, it was evident earlier that growth utilizing the same business model in adjacent beverage space was an accelerator. Other than that the decision to look at youth oriented and fast growth new age beverages was the next definitive milestone.' In line with Percy's vision, youth couldn't be left out of the Tata Tea story anymore.

It is these very constraints that pushed the team to, for the first time, stop applying the lens of tea to the world and instead broaden its perspective and look at everything afresh—from a perspective that transcended gender, income, age, habit and any kind of segmentation that conventional marketing wisdom dictated. And thus was born one of the most iconic campaigns in the history of Indian advertising—'*Jaago Re*'.

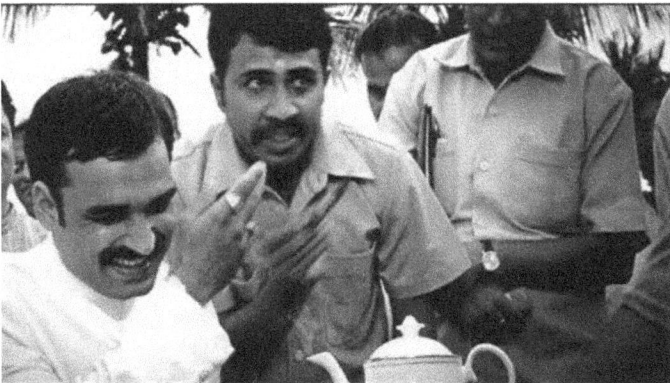

Jaago Re *campaign*

Conceived by creative agency Lowe Lintas & partners, it was an idea that was exciting and challenging. The possibilities were infinite.

Tea, with a penetration of more than 90 per cent, is consumed by millions of Indians several times a day. In that sense tea is a leveller; everybody drinks it, for the same reason—to wake up.

Jaago Re was conceived with the objective of making Tata Tea the agent of social change, broadening the role of tea from a beverage that facilitated physical awakening to one that also brought about mental and social awakening. That allowed for it to bring under its fold not only the older age group that currently consumed tea but also youth, who, in some senses, represented the restless generation 'X'. Youth who wanted social and societal change were also the consumers of tomorrow. *Jaago Re* managed to generate appeal across segments because of the cheeky manner in which it pointed the finger inwards on key social issues.

In his address to Tata Tea employees, ex MD and CEO Harish Bhat said: 'When Tata Tea embarked on the journey of Jaago Re, we took a big leap of faith. We wanted to make a humble cup of tea an enabler of social change by "awakening" people to be the change that they wanted to see.'

Jaago Re touched upon issues like corruption, bribery and voting well before they became topical.

In a nutshell, with *Jaago Re* Tata Tea broke all the rules. In a category which is considered old and boring, Tata Tea created advertising that was tongue-in-cheek and edgy. In a category that was associated only with physical awakening, Tata Tea introduced a new dimension—one of *social* awakening. When people were blaming each other, Tata Tea pointed the finger inwards. But it was not enough only to voice all this. The brand had to walk the talk which has always been core to the Tata value system. And with that thought, in 2009, ahead of the Indian general elections, *Jaago Re* facilitated over six lakh voter registrations through Jaagore.com. This at a time when social media was still at a nascent stage and had yet not become a buzzword in the Indian context like it is today.

At each stage where the brand faced a challenge—market entry, difficult commodity environment, stagnation in business—it reinvented itself and changed the rules of the game altogether. This reinvention happened at various stages through different levers—marketing mix, disruptive packaging, new product innovation based on consumer insight, and communication.

Business results followed when in 2007–8, Tata Tea as a company overtook Hindustan Unilever in volume market share. This was a historic moment for the company. In 2011–12, Tata Global Beverages overtook Hindustan Unilever to become the No. 1 tea company in the country.

And there has been no looking back, with every campaign, *Jaago Re* and the Tata Tea equity have only become stronger and all brands continue to be leaders in their own right—surging forward towards profitable growth.

2014: Racing ahead

On 21 March 2014, ahead of the 2014 general elections, Tata Global Beverages and the Tata group unveiled a first of its kind women's manifesto, aggregating issues raised by more than a million women from across India. Who would have thought that a tea brand could pull this off?

The times are indeed changing but Tata Tea is geared up more than ever to embrace that change. And looking back, the dots paint a reassuring picture—that being a challenger is in the very DNA of Tata Tea. For the company, the only constant is change!

Post Note: Tata Tea does have a marketing team now and has recruited some of the brightest minds in marketing. What has not changed is its desire to challenge and do things differently

WHAT INDIA'S BEST MARKETERS DO DIFFERENTLY

This is the story of a brand born against the backdrop of a young India brimming with confidence, eager for success and riches. It is story of a brand that has created a new segment in a hotly contested space by playing the game differently. In an orbit-shifting strategy, Sprite redefined and systematically displaced competition to emerge as category leader.

1998 could have been any other year. But in hindsight, it was one of the most momentous years in independent India's history.

This was the year when, demanding change, India elected Atal Bihari Vajpayee as prime minister, who then went on to become the first non-Congress prime minister to complete a five-year term. Announcing its rise as an emerging global power, India conducted its second nuclear test, standing up to the world.

This was the year when new icons were born, symbolizing the youth's admiration for confidence, success and riches. Sachin

Tendulkar was anointed a youth icon for years to come when he single-handedly beat Australia with back-to-back hundreds in Sharjah. The stupendous success of the candyfloss college romance *Kuch Kuch Hota Hai* transformed Shahrukh Khan into 'King' Khan—teen matinee idol and media darling.

This was the year when the 'Cola wars' were at their peak with the two cola competitors locked in intense battle for the rapidly growing sparkling-beverages market. By signing on two of the biggest celebrities—Sachin Tendulkar and Shahrukh Khan—Pepsi became the numero uno youth brand with the launch of its iconic *'Yeh Dil Maange More'* campaign.

This was also the year when Sprite—a clear lime sparkling-beverage brand from the global Coca Cola portfolio—was launched in Goa in December.

David takes on Goliath

Post economic liberalization in 1991, the sparkling-beverages category was abuzz with the return of Coca Cola India in 1993 and its takeover of the Parle brands. This was close on the heels of PepsiCo setting up operations in India in 1989. With these two global giants in the fray, sparkling beverage was no longer just about a sip of refreshment, it was an entry into a world of wide-eyed dreams, Americana and glamour. And India entered into this world with much gusto, leading to explosive growth in the 1990s. The market was dominated by the faster-growing colas—Pepsi, Coca Cola and Thums Up—which accounted for almost two-thirds of the total pie. The flavoured-beverages segment—comprising lime drinks like 7UP and Limca and orange drinks like Fanta and Mirinda—formed the balance of the pie and grew slower than the category.

As is the case even today, the youth were the most attractive demographic segment for this category, by virtue of sheer size and consumption potential. While every brand talked to youth, the colas held the greatest appeal—thanks to high-energy communication, celebrity endorsements, heavy investments across media and distribution.

Since Sprite was a lime sparkling beverage, the natural instinct was to pit it against the rival lime brand. But the company realized that it would always remain a niche brand if it did so. If it wanted to become a large brand, it would have to win the hearts of the youth—the most lucrative segment of the market. In other words, it would need to take on the colas and more specifically the rival cola brand—head on.

> As we will realize later in the journey, this decision was pivotal. This strategic bet of positioning Sprite against it's competitor changed the cola game forever. Proof that if the purpose is set right, the path follows.

Rome wasn't built in a day

Cola Cola Ltd knew that coming up with a few good campaigns would not be enough to dislodge competition. It needed to create a powerful brand identity for Sprite that would serve as the launching pad for all their marketing efforts in the future.

The colas were talking to the youth as well and had carved out unique spaces for themselves. Coca Cola stood for 'innocent' fun, encouraging the youth to enjoy the simple pleasures of life. Thums Up addressed the 'hero', asking the youth to bring out the daredevil in them. The rival cola brand urged the youth to have a great time by living in the moment. Thus there was a need to identify a distinct persona for Sprite—one that resonated more with the youth than that of the dominant cola brands.

Coca Cola Ltd conducted exhaustive ethnographic studies with college-going youth across major cities in the country, to enter into the minds of twenty-year olds in India. The studies observed how they lived, how they talked, what they loved and what they feared.

Universally, across regions and economic strata, the youth expressed an inherent desire to be their true selves. They wanted to explore life further, but were restricted in some way or the other. They wanted to carve their own path but were under pressure to conform to societal norms. Coca Cola Ltd realized that every youth brand across categories was telling the youth what they ought to be, but not to be what they actually were!

The company leveraged this powerful insight to create the brand essence for Sprite. Sprite as a brand would simply ask the youth to trust their own instincts and make their own choices. It would be an 'explorer' brand, encouraging the youth to discover themselves and the world. It would never preach or tell the youth what to do, but merely act as a mirror to who they really were.

Hyperbole punctured: 1998–2001

The opening up of the Indian economy saw a host of global brands entering India. As the disposable income of consumers grew, so did their aspirations. Feeding into this frenzy, brands across categories, from candy to soaps and cars, created fantasy worlds with tall claims and glamorous advertising—literally taking the consumer for a ride.

Sprite knew that it was up against formidable brands and that it had to change the rules of the game in order to win against the glitz of the cola brands. It needed to create a dent in the sparkling category and stand out with a differentiated proposition. It was in this context that Sprite chose to play a challenger brand, not just against colas but against everything they stood for—thus was born the anti-cola.

The first communication campaign revealed the secret of Lisa Ray's beautiful skin—bathing in a tub full of Sprite! Taking a dig at the way celebrities endorsed brands, Sprite asked youth not to trust everything they saw. The iconic campaign: *'Sprite bujhaye only pyaas, baaki all bakwaas'*—which is recalled by consumers even today—helped establish Sprite as a brand meant to puncture the hyperbole and be seen as a 'no-nonsense' alternative for the youth. Little did the brand realize how central this proposition was to be for all its future campaigns.

Studies had shown that while teens were inherently aware the world of hype was fake, many of them suffering from a lack of confidence, often became pretentious themselves and relied more on style rather than substance to impress their peers. In the years that followed, Sprite continued to take on the world of pretence, hype, over-exaggeration and false promise. At the same time, it slowly but steadily pushed its footprint across the southern and eastern states.

The results were phenomenal. Within the first year of launch, the spontaneous and total awareness levels crossed those of all the other flavoured brands and were only below the colas. Sprite saw a staggering 44 per cent growth in volumes till 2002, overtaking the competition's sparkling drinks in the process. Sprite had arrived in style—creating a new presence in the market place with a distinctive, confident, unpretentious and straightforward point of view.

The coming together of brand persona and functional attributes: 2003–2007

While a distinctive personality was defined for Sprite, it was still to be linked with an equally strong functional differentiator. Unlike the black opaque colas or other flavoured drinks, Sprite was clear, transparent and had a crisp, refreshing taste. 'Clear' also fit in naturally with the Sprite persona—honest, straight talking, unpretentious. But the brand realized that 'clear' had a far deeper meaning attached to it.

With greater exposure to media and information, teens in India were inundated with choice like never before. Every day they were confronted with new situations where they were inclined to follow outdated, tried and tested methods, and failed to achieve the desired results. How does one get youth to think differently, to be smarter?

Clarity of thought not only cuts through thirst but also liberates you and allows you to have a clear-cut perspective. Sprite demonstrated its clarity of thinking and wit by presenting a modern twist to the age-old way of doing things from popular fables in India—coming up with smart, unpretentious solutions for any task at hand. Simply put— *'Clear hai!'*

Armed with a cut-through refreshing product formulation and perception as a healthier option, Sprite was strategically set up to recruit consumers from the largest beverage opportunity—tap water. This was followed by the largest distribution drive focused on affordable glass bottles targeting rural India. On top of this, Sprite leveraged the telecom buzz to create its first national promotion to popularize PET bottles in urban markets. '*Sprite kholega to bolega*' was a first-of-its-kind digital innovation on a mega scale—a whopping 5.3 million participants chose Sprite to top up their talk time, setting it up as a cool brand of the future while expanding PET distribution. By 2005, Sprite, growing at 11 per cent while the category declined by 16 per cent, had become the second largest brand in the Coca Cola India portfolio.

In 2006, Sprite signed on a celebrity—Sania Mirza, the first mainstream female sport star in India. How could Sprite, which had always been against celebrities and tall claims, sign on one itself? 'Heresy, hypocrisy!', shouted everyone. Of course, that was before they saw how Sprite used the 'celebrity' in their communication campaign. Taking a dig at advertising that literally worships the very ground celebrities walk on, Sprite got Sania to reveal the secret behind her success—Sprite, what else! This was again, of course, tongue-in-cheek, before Sania bust such pretences by revealing that she only drank Sprite to quench her thirst—nothing more, nothing less.

This came at a time when the competition, first realizing the threat posed by Sprite, pumped even more money into glitzy, celebrity-laden campaigns and promotions. The gloves were off and it was time for war. In line with its fundamental proposition of being an honest, straight-talking brand, Sprite decided to take the competition head on by openly mocking it for its outrageously pompous and glamorous communication.

Sprite was becoming the talk of

the town! It had now built a formidable presence, almost doubling its national footprint, and with a 34 per cent growth in this period, it had become the No. 3 player in the sparkling category.

Becoming a youth icon: 2008–13

By now consumers already saw Sprite as a youth brand built on cut-through refreshment credentials and high levels of likeability. It was time to change gears and take things to the next level—becoming the youth icon by displacing its rival cola brand competitor from pole position.

Exhaustive ethnographic studies had shown that teens were a much more 'confident-in-my-skin' generation and were exploring and crafting their own identity—without the aid of any crutches. They believed in 'walk the talk' and not just 'talk the talk', i.e., straight talking rather than putting up an 'act' to achieve their goals. There was an undercurrent of annoyance if they were branded empty followers of a made up image.

Taking a cue from this insight, Sprite's campaign built a clear contrast between the guy who succumbed to a convoluted way of doing things, and the Sprite protagonist who was always his true self and got straight to the point. The iconic articulation was: '*Seedhi baat, no bakwaas*'—using youth lingo that connected famously with the target audience.

As the nation's No. 1 passion, cricket, succumbed to Indian Premier League (IPL) fever, Sprite brought its credo to life with none other than the likes of King Khan and team KKR. In line with its geographical expansion, a massive on-ground consumer engagement was created in 2009—Sprite Gully Cricket epitomized street cricket. The competition which went nationwide in 2010 reached 110 cities and satellite towns and registered 45,000 teams. Each game was watched by thousands as the local heroes were egged on with free samples of Sprite.

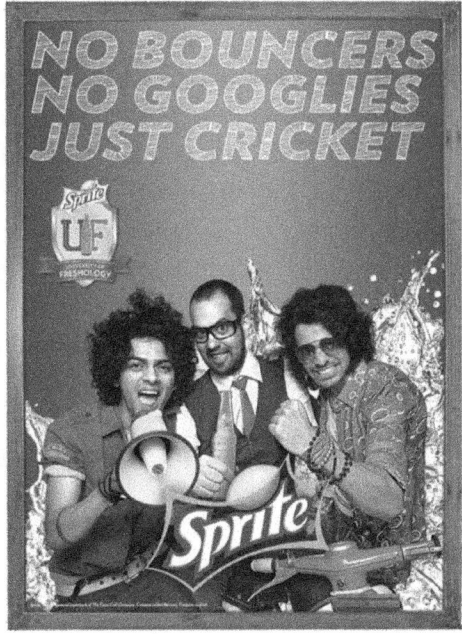

By 2009, creating 60 per cent brand recall across rural markets to match its expanding rural distribution, Sprite had finally ousted its nearest rival and emerged as the No. 2 drink in the sparkling-beverages market in India.

Having finally knocked the competition off its perch across all parameters, Sprite had achieved the objectives set at the time of launch. It had gone from being the hunter to being the hunted, with the competition pooling all its brands against Sprite to regain its lost position. So where does Sprite go from here?

Clearly, Sprite had to start looking beyond its biggest competitor so far and set its vision higher. It would need to continue embodying the youth ideal by capturing insights from their life better than anyone else. Rather than pit itself against the category, Sprite is now benchmarking its efforts against iconic youth brands like Axe and MTV. Thus the new vision for Sprite is to become an iconic brand for the youth—one that leaves an impression on their lives beyond the product.

Teens communicated that they aspired to be masters in life management. Everyday existence required constant negotiation with their environment— gone were the days of confrontations and rebelliousness. This generation knew that it had to be street smart and not just intelligent.

This was a perfect evolution for Sprite—here was a brand that embodied smart thinking to navigate the 'heat of the moment' moments. It started to create a brand personality in harmony with the aspirations of the nation's youth. Simultaneously, in rural India, Sprite undertook the largest sampling programme to continue recruiting new consumers. Gamification of the consumer engagement was designed to play up the 'water-plus' credentials of Sprite, leaving behind an unequivocal cut-through refreshment experience. Focusing the sampling programme to rural villages, combined with expanding the distribution network, ensured that Sprite became the most widely distributed brand in the country.

On the back of this two-pronged approach, by the end of 2013, Sprite finally became India's numero uno sparking-beverages brand—both in terms of hearts as well as revenues.

The consumer: the brand ambassador

In a category that focused primarily on emotional imagery, Sprite outperformed its rivals without piggybacking on a celebrity or heavy investments in brand building. The brand was able to outmanoeuvre and outwit competition by leveraging cultural and societal insights from the teenager's life, reflecting who he truly was rather than preaching to him.

While Sprite's communication has evolved over time, its brand essence, personality and tonality have stayed consistent. Rather than using a celebrity, the Sprite ambassador has always been the teenager himself—confident, smart and spontaneous.

'And miles to go before I sleep...'

The landscape in 2015 is completely unlike the one in 1998 when Sprite was launched. Sachin Tendulkar has retired, Shahrukh Khan is more Khan than king, the competition is no longer the king of cool with AAP leading a social activist wave across the country. In the midst of all this, Sprite has grown from a scrappy new entrant to the leader of the sparkling-beverages market, on its way to becoming an iconic brand for the youth of tomorrow.

Consumer Needs

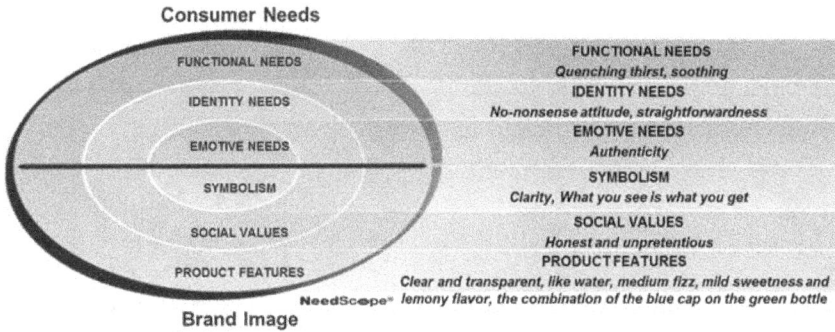

Brand Image

Sprite's journey

Period	Insight	Role of Brand	Milestone
1998	An inherent desire to be their true selves, trust their own instincts and make their own choices	There'll be a mirror to who the youth really were	Launch of Sprite
1998–2001	Expose the ad claims, false pretences and hyperbole in the category that teens inherently knew were fake	Encouraged teens stand against conventional societal norms. *'Sprite bujhaye only pyaas, baaki all bakwaas'*	In 2002, Sprite's growth rates were two and a half times that of the category, reaching a market share of 4 per cent overtaking its rivals Starting Leverage brand in the process
2004	Teens inundated with information overload and confused with the plethora of choices and diverse opinions	Liberated the youth to cut through the maze and have a clear perspective. *'Clear hai!'*	In 2005, Sprite, growing at 11 per cent while the category declined by 16 per cent, was the second largest brand in the Coca Cola India portfolio.
2008–13	An undercurrent of annoyance among teens if they were projected as phony or fake	Appealing to straight-talking no nonsense youth. *'Seedhi baat, no bakwaas'*	In 2008, Sprite beat its major competitor in volumes, emerging as the No. 2 drink in the sparkling beverages market in India. By the end of 2013, Sprite finally became India's numero uno sparkling beverages brand in market share, preference, brand love, consumer intent and deepest consumption, an unprecedented achievement.

HOW A CHALLENGER BRAND BECAME THE MOST TRUSTED PRIVATE SECTOR BANK BRAND

AXIS BANK

Tracing back to the year 1980, 91 per cent of the banking sector was under government control. Although private sector banks and foreign banks coexisted with the nationalized banks, their activities were limited through entry restrictions and strict branch-licensing policies.

In 1993, the Reserve Bank of India (RBI) issued banking licenses to ten players including UTI Bank, HDFC Bank and ICICI Bank. These new players, along with the entrenched foreign banks, ushered in a new era in Indian banking through their investments in technology, processes and customer service.

Legacy

Operating under the borrowed name of UTI (Unit Trust of India) at the time of its formation, Axis Bank capitalized on the UTI lineage. Over the years, there was a need for the brand to stand on its own and thus came the change in its brand identity. In 2007, UTI Bank was rechristened Axis Bank.

However, by that time, its competitors had already acquired an edge in brand recognition and recall, leaving Axis Bank to play catch up.

In 2009, under a new management, everything within the Bank was introspected under a new lens. There was pressing need to move on to a more consumer-centric approach and to review existing processes. The task at hand was clear—to create a differentiated 'Axis' brand, not just in banking, but in the entire banking and financial services category.

To establish its 'differentiated' position in the mind of the consumer, Axis could not just replicate what its competitors were doing. It had to challenge convention and do things differently.

The journey of reinvention begins with understanding the consumer

Various industry-level researches reflected that 54 per cent of the Indian demographic was under twenty-five years of age. Times were changing. So were consumer choices. It was a time of rapid transformation in lifestyles, preferences, opinions and choices.

This brought about a sea change in terms of consumer expectations of brands, which had to be in sync with the evolving consumer value system. The once clearly defined dividing line between the metros (big cities) and smaller towns had been blurring. This was evident in the penetration of global brands into these smaller markets across industries and in an overall spike in service delivery to these consumers. The consumers of India had suddenly taken charge, and brands across industries had sat up to take notice. However, one industry, until recently not much affected by this change, and still operating within set parameters, was banking.

Problem: An undifferentiated brand with no clear proposition

With consumers becoming increasingly discerning and the market reacting to the volatility of these changes, the Axis Bank team scrutinized the market and came across a peculiar problem.

While business was growing for the bank, the brand (Axis Bank) did not have spontaneous recall across geographies and neither was it considered relevant by the younger audience. With no clear positioning, it was confused with various other brands.

There was clearly need for a new brand image that would connect with and make itself relevant to the new and emerging India, including its aspirational youth.

Identifying opportunity

As one would imagine, trust was the biggest factor in the banking financial services category and it was firmly held by the biggest Indian bank—State Bank of India (SBI)—owing to sheer size and sovereign lineage. Indian consumers had three clear categories of banks to choose from—public sector banks, Indian private banks and multinational banks. The team had to find a way of leveraging the legacy of the UTI brand, at the same time transforming its image from dated to contemporary and from ordinary to distinctive. A brand with global standards had to be built. Mere plastering over the surface wasn't going to be enough for reinventing the brand. Through extensive research, a few insights were uncovered. To begin with, the new generation of consumers had its own set of values and beliefs fuelled by boundless opportunities. By the age of thirty-two, these new-age consumers were consuming all financial products at least once, and their past experience would shape future purchases. Hence, it only made sense to shift focus to this younger consumer segment.[1] Digging deeper, it became apparent that the new generation was forward looking and aspirational while remaining grounded and aware of its responsibilities. It needed a partner, not a banker. This insight helped shape the new imagery of Axis Bank, and thus began the journey of partnering this new, emerging consumer.

---

[1]AC Nielsen, Usage and Attitude Study 2011.

The way the brand needed to gain mind share, and eventually business, from this set of consumers, was by truly imbibing and embodying their value system; by becoming a brand they could relate to—a young and progressive bank for the new-age Indian.

This manifested itself in a brand essence defined as '*Progress without Pause*'. It was rooted strongly in the philosophy that the modern Indian believes that life is a series of milestones that every individual wants to cross. *Every success is a milestone in the journey called life.*

'Progress without Pause' came to form the DNA of Axis Bank. The positioning reshaped the bank's strategy and it was activated at every single consumer touch point. And thus began the quest to become a more relevant, preferred, and differentiated contender among the more established private sector players. The challenge now was to transform this brand essence into each and every aspect of the brand that a consumer came in contact with.

The journey to this transformation in terms of the seven Ps of service marketing is related here.

Innovative 'products' designed to address specific consumer needs

Banking used to be a commoditized industry, with little innovation and customization in the products offered to customers. And there was nothing to deter competitors from quickly copying what little innovation there was. Consumers made choice of bank based on proximity to their home/ office or recommendations by friends and family.

With new-age consumers customizing everything from ringtones to cars, there was clearly need to create differentiated products that would be relevant to them.

A more youth-centric tone of communication was not enough; designing unconventional products that appealed to the young, progressive consumer was imperative for drawing in this segment. So while most other banks were taking the route of slashing prices or increasing the rate of interest, Axis Bank identified and created product propositions to address specific consumer needs.

For instance:

» The Ladies First Card designed especially for homemakers, with features that helped manage, spend and track household expenses better. This product was based on the insight that homemakers usually got a fixed household budget from their husbands, mostly in cash. They managed the house with this money and stored the balance they saved within the home—in the kitchen or in their cupboards. Managing cash was a hassle, since they had to keep a detailed tab of what was spent where. Keeping the cash safe was another problem. The Ladies First Card addressed all these issues.

» The Happy Ending Home Loan, where customers had their last twelve equated monthly instalments (EMI) waived off, simply by being punctual in paying their EMIs. The insight here was that while most salaried customers were regular in repaying, there was no benefit in being regular. It changed that convention by rewarding these customers.

» A range of credit cards aptly titled 'MY Cards', which allowed customers to customize their cards according to their spend pattern. So, the 'MY Wings' card got travel enthusiasts extra discounts and cashback on all their air, rail and bus spends, while the 'MY Zone' card was designed for entertainment lovers, giving them discounts on movie tickets and extra reward points on shopping and dining on weekends. For those who wanted to customize everything on their card, there was the 'MY Choice' card. Here, they could choose the categories they mostly spent on, and get a 5 per cent cashback on those.

» The YOUTH Account: Axis Bank realized the potential of the 222 million-strong youth market and sought to launch a savings account product to tap into this consumer segment. Initially, the product was aimed at migrant college/university students who were living away from home, possibly for the first time in their lives. Living alone made it essential for them to manage their own finances to some degree. They weren't financially independent because they still received money from their parents, but having their own bank account now became necessary. Axis Bank decided to adopt this as the core around which the YOUTH Account would be created. It decided to empower individual youngsters. The YOUTH Account would allow them to customize their debit cards and mobile apps, and they could even draw money from their parents' linked bank accounts with just a few clicks. All of this without ever having to step into a bank.

» Taking the offerings to the digital and social space: To appeal to the younger and contemporary target group, it was imperative for Axis Bank to take a leadership position in the digital and social media space. This came in the form of a dedicated focus by the brand on new and innovative digital products like a mobile banking application with features like bill pay, funds transfer, customized offerings which were state of the art when it came to the industry standards. In 2015, the bank also came up with a first-of-its-kind multi-social payment application called PING PAY. The application allowed users to make or receive payments across multiple social media platforms without knowing any bank account details of the other person. PING PAY challenged the existing ways of money transfer by excluding traditional requirements and platforms.

In addition, the Bank launched its most premium personal banking service, Burgundy, in FY2015. Designed especially for the busy, affluent high-net-worth (HNI) customer, Burgundy offers end-to-end personalized banking, wealth management solutions and business solutions to meet investment needs of HNI individuals. Burgundy also serves corporate advisory needs of families in business. It brings solutions offered by various business groups (both retail and corporate) within the bank and different group entities on to one integrated platform.

The brand has since continued to improvise and innovate in this medium not only with its product and service offerings but also by creating a substantial footprint in the social media space. As on 31 March 2015, it had over 3 million likes on Facebook, over 75,000 followers across its handles on Twitter, over 75,000 followers on LinkedIn and over 43 million views on its YouTube channel. It also launched a blog by the name of www.itsallaboutmoney.com. On this blog, it hosted content around everything to do with banking and finance to engage with its audience groups.

Axis Bank had not only paved the way for innovative products, but also an innovative approach to banking. And the results showed in the new-age consumer taking to these innovations instantly.

'Pricing' it right for the Maximizer Mindset

For young and progressive Indian consumers, time is of the essence, and they seek simplicity in everything they do. Axis Bank applied this insight to reprice its products. With extensive research, the bank discovered it was almost impossible for the average customer to understand the complex maze of charges and keep track of their average quarterly balances (AQB). It decided to go through a massive restructuring to move away from the conventional AQB charges model, to an average monthly balance (AMB) charges model.

Axis Bank also discovered that consumers could not be bothered with maintaining monthly balances on their credit cards. Thus, in an industry first, it introduced annual fees on products like the YOUTH Account and Ladies First Card.

Not only that, Axis Bank was one of the first banks to waive off pre-payment charges on its home loans.

The bank did not stop there—it introduced eDGE, its first pan-service loyalty rewards programme. Unlike the loyalty programmes of competitor banks which rewarded customers on card spends, eDGE was designed to reward customers for every relationship they had with the bank—savings account, cards, loans and electronic channel transactions.

The new pricing strategy resonated with the 'maximizer' in this young and progressive consumer set, and the impact reflected on the business as well as the brand.

Boosting financial inclusion through a unique 'placement' model

Axis Bank challenged convention to deliver financial services at affordable cost to all sections of society. The bank was aware that with only 50 per cent penetration of its banking products and services, there was huge potential for expansion. The result was a unique business correspondent (BC) model.

Under this initiative, Axis Bank partnered with two leading telecom operators to leverage their massive networks, to reach out to various parts of the country and service the unbanked populace. India has more than 500 million mobile phone subscribers, compared to just 240 million individuals with bank accounts. This served as the perfect distribution platform for reaching out to the masses and taking banking services to all corners of the country. The mobile companies partnering with the bank also stood to gain by providing this value-added service to their customers.

Rural agricultural lending is another key focus area within retail banking. It allowed the bank to serve the multiple needs of the farmer— both as a producer and as a consumer. In order to provide a strategic focus, the bank has adopted an area-centric approach in agriculture-intensive areas with the presence of decentralized area offices following a hub and spoke model.

The model was simple—customers would access designated retail outlets for cash-in, cash-out and transfer of funds. Other banking functions such as balance enquiry, mini-statement and change of mPIN, would all be supported by the mobile platform. This provided a highly accessible, convenient, secure and cost-effective solution to customers who had thus far remained financially excluded.

Axis Bank in partnership with Suvidhaa Infoserve, recently announced the launch of the Axis Bank–Suvidhaa Prepaid Card, a first-of-its-kind initiative in the banking industry, which leverages the e-KYC platform for instant on-boarding, cash deposit and withdrawal for the customer. The card is built on three components—the large reach of the BC network; instant eKYC, based on Aadhaar; and the ability of prepaid cards to be usable everywhere (interoperability). These come together to create a unique solution for the migrant population, which had hitherto found it difficult to access basic banking services for savings or money transfer.

The bank's efforts continued with the BC model going even beyond telecom partners. The model ensured that visiting a branch was no longer a necessity.

These inventive business models enabled the bank to reach out to all parts of the country and make banking accessible for different sections of society, thereby fostering the growth of not only the bank's business, but the nation's as well.

From a typical office-style branch to a modern retail-style 'Physical' presence

The Bank initiated an effort to ease the customer's journey in the branches, for which research played an important role in getting an in-depth understanding of the customer. Customers were closely observed and interviewed, and role plays were conducted to get a deeper insight into branch functioning with reference to customer expectations and behaviour. The idea here was to provide an immersive retail experience for customers.

The exterior zone of branches was redesigned with the purpose of creating awareness and engagement, using visual language. The new branch fascia and pole signage made it easier for people to locate the branch on a busy thoroughfare. Interiors were redesigned with designated zones—self-service, retail and transaction. The key principle was to anticipate each and every aspect of the customer journey, communicating relevant information and making the banking process smooth for the customer.

The self-service zone was fashioned to allow customers to perform their most basic transactions, such as cash withdrawal, cash deposit, cheque deposit and request for cheque book, on their own. This area was made accessible to customers 24X7.

The retail zone had a dedicated area to showcase retail products from the bank, along with a sales lounge and a premium lounge to serve high-net-worth customers.

The transaction zone, which included teller counters, was placed at the extreme end in the new branch layout, similar to checkout counters in a mall.

The idea was to move branches from being '*transaction-heavy*' spaces towards '*financial advisory*' spaces. This would help attract the new and emerging tech-savvy generation, which was seeking alternate channels for simplifying its financial transactions.

In today's scenario, Axis Bank is the first private sector bank to introduce recycler ATMs that enable customers to deposit as well as withdraw cash from the same machine. The recycler ATMs reduce the frequency of loading cash in the machine as well as the cost of idle cash, as they allow cash-recycling operations by dispensing deposited cash for future withdrawal transactions, thereby improving the efficiency of the bank's cash operations. The bank has deployed around 300 recyclers and plans to scale up the same in the coming months. The same approach was extended as the brand expanded its network through the year.

On the other hand, the bank's digital initiatives have continued to make significant progress and remain integral to providing a superior customer service proposition. As a part of the same, the bank also launched a free Wi-Fi service, available to all Axis Bank customers across key branches, during FY2015. The bank also embarked on its journey of providing multi-format branches to serve its varied set of customer segments in different geographies.

» **Flagship branches**: The bank has re-launched twenty-five strategic, high-footfall branches as 24X7 flagship branches that have been designed to provide its customers with an immersive retail banking experience. The innovative design-led approach for these branches has been arrived at after extensive ethnographic research.

» **Express branches**: In a move to facilitate digitization of banking services, the bank recently launched 24X7 'express branches' offering services such as cash withdrawals, instant cash deposits, cheque deposits, instant account opening, Internet banking, instant issuance of gift and foreign currency cards, online buying of insurance and advisory services. These express branches will be conveniently located either in malls or office complexes or business parks.

'Omni-channel approach to connect to consumers

The creation of alternate channels was necessary in a context where consumers were transacting in nuanced ways through different mediums. The new Indian was always on the move, with no time to visit branches on weekdays. Since banking seemed like a chore to them, they did not want to spend their weekends at a branch. Options that allowed them to bank from the comfort of their home and office were therefore the need of the hour.

As the number of ways to connect with customers increases and self-service channels become the primary way of banking, a simple multi-channel strategy fails to suffice anymore. Instead, an omni-channel approach, characterized by consistent processes, consistent data and seamless integration across various channels provides the bank a competitive advantage. Technology has enabled customer accessibility to all products across all channels through seamless multi-channel integration. The bank has been simultaneously focusing on 'digitization' of its backend processes and empowerment of its customers with mobile-led, simple, anytime anywhere 'digital' banking.

Axis Bank decided to take this to the next level with a secure, user-friendly Internet banking platform and cutting-edge mobile application, both built with features that made banking-on-the-go simpler and more convenient. The new mobile app pushed customization to a new level, by letting customers personalize everything from account details to menu options, navigation style, and even adding photos of beneficiaries from Facebook or the phone album or by clicking a new picture. It truly was the new way to bank.

The bank did not stop here. To help customers save time, it launched instant account opening at its branches, online opening of savings accounts, and even online application for home loans, car loans and credit cards.

With more and more customers voicing their feedback and grievances on social media, the bank decided to move beyond conventional customer service channels such as its call centre. It started responding to customer queries and complaints on social media. Every complaint, request and question received through these platforms was addressed swiftly, ensuring that every customer was satisfied and happy.

Our 'People', our brand ambassadors

Experience is the key promise that the service industry makes to consumers. While consumers build preference on touch and feel when it comes to buying tangibles, they have only their experiences to rely on when it comes to intangible products. How consumers perceive the brand is a factor of their experience of service from the bank's employees.

Axis Bank realized that to build a young and progressive brand, it needed to deliver the new, revamped brand through its 40,000+ employees. Crafting and communicating a new brand promise alone was *not* good enough. The brand promise had to be delivered to the customer on the ground. With this vision in mind, the bank launched its customer service credo, aptly termed 'PROGRESS'. The driving idea behind it was to move away from the the conventional, staid banker image and adopt 'insightful banking' in everyday practice instead. The ultimate goal was to be seen as a partner in the progress of its customers.

The customer service credo of the bank, PROGRESS stood for:

- P—Proactive in approach, do not wait for the customer to complain
- R—Right for the customer, never mis-sell
- O—Own the solution, never pass the buck
- G—Go deeper, sense the real need
- R—Remove the jargon in your conversation
- E—Error free, try and get it right in the first instance
- S—Simplify processes and products
- S—serve enthusiastically

The new credo became the cornerstone of customer service at Axis Bank.

360-degree brand promotion

Then came the time to take all these to the market under a unified brand proposition that resonated with the consumers. The key point that emerged from all the consumer research was that the new set of Indian consumers believed deeply in the philosophy of success being a never-ending journey. It was no longer about having accomplished a goal but about setting newer and newer goals and achieving each of them progressively. Every success was momentary and just another milestone in the journey of life. There was a need to embrace an idea so large and evolving and articulate it in a manner which encompassed its true nature of progress, continuity and evolution.

The brand essence of 'Progress without Pause' manifested itself beautifully in the new brand positioning:

> **Axis Bank**. *Badhti ka naam zindagi...* **Or Axis Bank**. Progress On...

The positioning speaks about a life that everyone wishes for and works towards. It symbolizes that Axis Bank will be there to help you move forward at every milestone and every stepping stone in the journey of your life—through first job jitters and marriage vows, through buying a first car or home, through family responsibilities and joys, Axis Bank will be there all the way, to celebrate this journey called life. The new positioning took the brand a step forward by articulating the role a bank should play in the lives of people. The promise was that of a partnership with them on their path to progress.

The *Badhti ka naam zindagi* campaign was split into three phases:

Phase 1 (February–December 2012) was the story of an individual, with life being compared to a film without intervals.

After narrating the story of an individual's progress in Phase 1, it was important to pay attention to the diverse and multicultural population of India.

Phase 2 was about 'collective progress' with the insight: 'In the journey of life, we never progress alone'. The 'circle of progress', as it was aptly termed, was successfully converted into the campaign thought, '*Zindagi ke highway pe koi akela nahin badhta*' (No one progresses alone on the highway of life).

Much like the new brand philosophy, the rebranding efforts reflected a continuous journey. The efforts to extend the brand essence and make the brand presence stronger did not abate. The circle of progress idea led to a platform that could be amplified digitally. Progresstogether.in was created as a way of connecting people online. Users could log in with their e-mail IDs or their Facebook accounts to be part of the ProgressTogether network, where they could acknowledge those who had played a part in their progress.

The microsite was promoted extensively on the digital platform, besides TV and out-of-home (OOH) media. Challenging the staid bank-like image, the brand made the idea come alive with interactive, game-like videos that communicated the product proposition. This not only made the communication interactive but also fun, thus increasing receptivity. Four product videos were created and hosted on the microsite.

Continuous exposure was ensured on other impactful platforms that complemented the bank's idea of progress, like one of India's highest-grossing television shows, *Kaun Banega Crorepati,* and the bold talk show, *Satyamev Jayate.* The Axis Bank team took this as an opportunity to take PROGRESS to another level.

The success of these campaigns set the tone for Axis Bank's communication, and it has been possible only because the dialogue with the customers has been meaningful. The idea was not to stop here, but rather to create an all-round banking experience—where every interaction that Axis Bank had with its customers, resonated its core philosophy.

With dedicated focus on the brand positioning over two phases of the campaign, Axis Bank had achieved what was one amongst its many brand objectives. The brand had gained significantly on spontaneous salience and stood strong amidst its competitors, ICICI Bank and HDFC Bank, in terms of recall and recognition.

The next task for the brand was to improve its preference and consideration amongst them (largely the younger audiences). It was clear that now was the time to change gears and take its communication to a new level and this is exactly what the third phase of the *Badhti ka Naam Zindagi* campaign was designed towards.

To improve consideration amongst its consumers, the brand understood that it had to give them a tangible reason to subscribe to the brand and start using its products and services. Thus the communication had to be woven around stories of these products more strongly but under the aegis of the brand idea. It was important that each of the products and services the bank offered was seen as enabling the progress of its customers, thus extending the idea to everything that the brand had to offer.

Phase 3 was about the many meanings of progress. Furthermore, it was found necessary to offer products and services that were distinct from similar ones of competitors. To amplify its youth image, it was felt that using a known face that had pan-India appeal, was modern and yet rooted, young and not normally associated with a heavy category like banking, was important. Leading Bollywood actress Deepika Padukone was signed on as the brand ambassador for Axis Bank. The choice of Deepika Padukone as brand ambassador was a strategic move that would not only help improve consideration but also amplify the image of the bank without alienating any of the multitude of segments that it catered to.

The creative idea was to portray stories of what progress meant to someone who was in the journey of progress herself. The communication brought out those aspects of her life. The campaign tapped into the human side of Deepika, portraying instances from her life where she used and endorsed Axis bank products depicting different facets of progress.

Badhti ka naam zindagi...

AXIS BANK

#myideaofprogress

Since the campaign idea was all-encompassing in nature, people were invited to participate and contribute their ideas of progress. A microsite—www.myideaofprogress.com—was created for people to post their ideas and thoughts on what progress meant to them. It was not just a crowdsourcing activity but a contest where people could create their progress diaries and stand a chance of winning a grand prize.

Mutlimedia strategy for a multidimensional campaign

While TV was used to play up endearing stories from Deepika's life to promote the products, other media like print, outdoor and below the line (BTL) were used to promote specific features of the products.

Last but not the least, the new generation of Indian consumers, while being very focused on its own progress journey, was equally sensitive to its responsibility towards broad-based and sustainable development. The brands which it related to were all brands that echoed this belief in the way they did business.

Corporate Social Responsibility

In 2006, Axis Bank set up Axis Bank Foundation (ABF) as the corporate social responsibility (CSR) arm of the bank

ABF is working ceaselessly towards creating one million sustainable livelihoods by the year 2017. Today, it partners over forty NGOs in delivering programmes in the areas of sustainable livelihood, education and health.

For its efforts, the Foundation was conferred an Outstanding Corporate Foundation award at Forbes India, Philanthropy Awards, 2014.

A consolidated and synergistic effort resulted in what the team had set out to do—boost a brand that was seen as a midget amongst its peer competition group. Within a span of just four years, the brand was far more recalled and preferred, and commanded a unique and differentiated positioning in the minds of consumers.

Spontaneous awareness: Now the most spontaneously recalled private sector bank

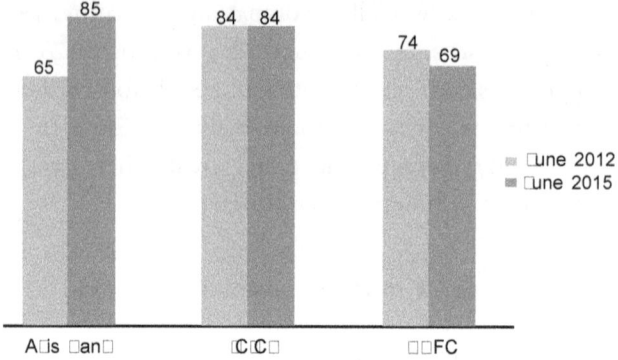

Source: AC Nielsen Brand Track.

Brand consideration: Now the second most considered amongst private sector banks

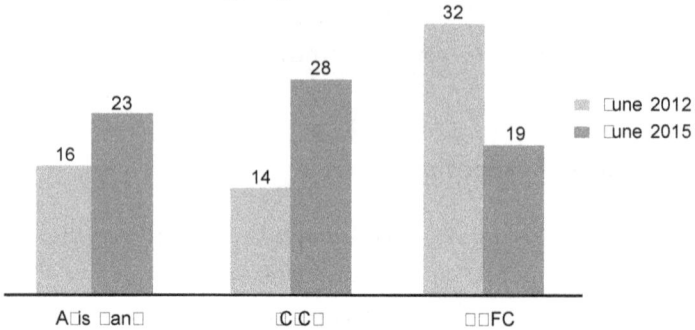

Source: AC Nielsen Brand Track.

Improving imagery perceptions over the years

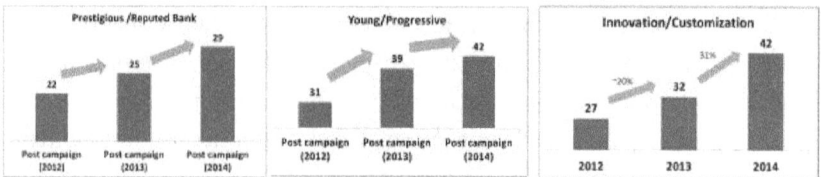

Source: AC Neilsen Brand Track.

Consistently attracting a younger audience set

Savings A/C acquisition	Mar. 2012 (%)	Mar. 2013 (%)	Aug. 2014 (%)	Credicard acquisition	Mar. 2012 (%)	Mar. 2013 (%)	Aug. 2014 (%)
Below 18	3	4↑	4↑	Below 18	–	–	–
18–35	63	65↑	66↑	18–35	5	8↑	9↑
36–55	28	25↓	24↓	36–55	78	74↓	73↓
55+	6	6	6	55+	17	13↓	13

Source: Internal data.

Axis Bank's success can be attributed to many factors, but none as significant as its steady focus on customer-centricity and innovation.

Within a span of just four years, Axis Bank has moved up from being the third most trusted private sector bank, to *the* most trusted. It has been voted the Most Trusted Private Sector Bank Brand in the country, two times in a row, in Brand Equity's Most Trusted Brand Surveys (December 2013 and October 2014).

Brand Equity Most Trusted Brands			
Rank amongst private sector banks			
	2011	2012	2013	2014
Axis Bank	3	2	1	1
ICICI Bank	1	1	2	2
HDFC Bank	2	3	3	3

Source: Brand Equity, *The Economic Times*, 28 September 2011, 7 November 2012, 18 December 2013, 22 October 2014.

The brand's journey has just started and there are many milestones to come. And just like its journey so far, the many initiatives under way at Axis are a work in progress.

THE CHEETAH-INSPIRED XUV500

Prowls the Global Automotive Arena

Creating a new segment: Advantage Mahindra

While international sports–utility vehicles (SUV) were already available in India at the time the XUV500 was conceptualized, they were highly priced and selling in small volumes. There was no brand that offered a premium 'global SUV' meeting international standards at an affordable price point. Mahindra saw this opportunity and took on the challenge of creating a world-class yet affordable SUV for the value-conscious Indian. The market opportunity lay between Mahindra's own Scorpio and Toyota's Fortuner in the ₹10–20 lakh price bracket. XUV500 was conceptualized to take brand Mahindra to the next level not just in India but also keeping in mind the global consumer.

Challenging norms

The design and development of a car is all about managing the future, because it takes around four-five years for a major new product to come to life from the concept-development stage. The design and marketing team at Mahindra gathered needs of not only current consumers, but also looked for indications on how these needs would change and evolve by the time the product was ready for launch.

The team that conceptualized XUV500 reached out to consumers across five continents in countries like Italy, South Africa, USA, Australia and in Latin America to conduct a 100-day study and collect the voice of consumers (VOC). This VOC was then clustered into common themes and also translated into technical and product requirements through a process called quality function deployment (QFD). These consumer insights coupled with emerging consumer trends, futuristic technologies, international and domestic benchmarks and styling preferences were assimilated by the marketing, product planning and R&D teams to define the product concept for the 'global SUV'. The outcome was an adrenalin-powered expression—'Feeling the Power'—that eventually went on to win the hearts of the consumers.

'Feeling the Power' became the 'driving emotion' behind every sphere of design decision during product development. 'Power' had many connotations among consumers. To some it meant sheer physical power of the SUV while to others it was manifested in the aggressive styling, muscular looks and macho stance of the vehicle. Even the high seating position was conceptualized to give a commanding view of the road while driving, which is an interpretation of 'power'. Some consumers equated 'power' with the status and respect they can inspire when they are seen driving or when they arrive at their destination in their powerful vehicle.

During this journey of creation there were numerous such challenges and turning points where significant decisions were taken. There were many firsts and trade-offs and each had inherent risks associated with it. At one stage, the management team was torn between two equally powerful designs based on two distinct inspirations from 'Feeling the Power'. One of the designs was more in line with the existing SUV design themes in the Mahindra portfolio, while the other was more evolved and futuristic, something that Mahindra had not attempted in the past.

Mahindra eventually took the road less travelled and decided to go ahead with the more futuristic concept which was inspired by the fastest animal on land—the cheetah. *The cheetah was the epitome of 'Feeling the Power' in every sense—speed, agility, stance, aggression, muscle.* Thereafter, many design elements took inspiration from the cheetah to bring alive the concept of 'Feeling the Power' from the pouncing cheetah-inspired bodylines and stance to the muscular wheel arches, the cheetah jaw-like front grill and even the door handles which represented the paws of a cheetah.

The glimpse of the clay model that rendered the design in its full physical form was enough to give confidence to everyone in the team that this was the winning concept that would enable Mahindra to make its presence felt not just in India but in the global automotive arena. And thus was born 'Advantage Mahindra'.

A monocoque body, inspired by the cheetah's agility, was adopted for the SUV to create a differentiated and unique styling coupled with superior ride and handling experience. *Mahindra was the first Indian manufacturer to indigenously develop a monocoque body for an SUV.*

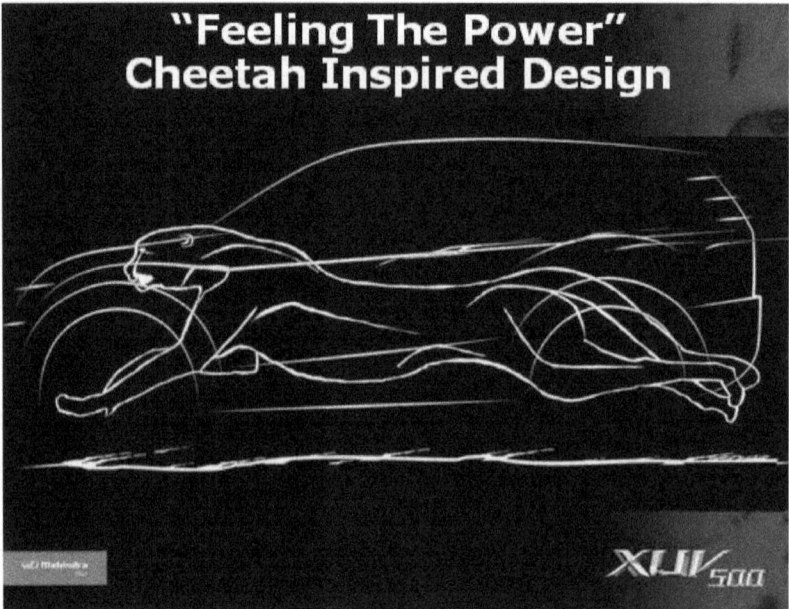

"Feeling The Power"
Cheetah Inspired Design

XUV500

Three projects rolled into one

The enormity and complexity of the project was a major challenge. The global SUV project was actually three projects rolled into one:

» Setting up of the high-tech R&D facility, Mahindra Research Valley (MRV) at Chennai.
» Simultaneous product development project for the XUV500.
» Construction of a world-class manufacturing facility for the XUV500 at Chakan, Pune.

The most crucial thing was that all three projects were interlinked and had to be completed so as to feed into each other's dependencies.

The technological risks were high due to many firsts which were included to make the product world-class. Mahindra wanted to give consumers high-end technologies like electronic stability program (ESP), touch-screen infotainment system with GPS, hill hold and hill descent and six airbags.

The company partnered with world-class vendors who had the expertise and capability to deliver these cutting-edge technologies to consumers at the right time and at a price that was significantly below those of international brands.

A multi-pronged approach to creating a category

Mahindra already had successful brands in its portfolio, but wanted to develop a new category-creating brand to take the Mahindra brand to the next level of aspiration. It took on the challenge of creating a category higher than its iconic Scorpio, of a world-class SUV priced above ₹10 lakh.

Tapping a new consumer segment

Mahindra and Mahindra (M&M) decided to reach out to urban, sophisticated consumers who either did not consider SUVs or only considered premium international sedans. M&M created a distinct brand identity for XUV500 while retaining the Mahindra DNA of making tough and rugged vehicles.

Premium brand nomenclature

M&M decided to adopt an alpha-numeric nomenclature to signify a premium and exclusive brand. This also helped M&M ensure minimal cannibalization among portfolio brands.

» The 'global SUV' was christened XUV500, chosen from among thousands of potential options (pronounced as '5 double O', where the 'double O' stood for the 'oomph' factor of the vehicle).

A deal-clinching price point

The XUV500 was launched at a jaw-dropping price of ₹10.8 lakh (ex-showroom Delhi). Auto experts were amazed and consumers delighted with this price point that offered a 'never before' package of head-turning style and hi-tech features at a price significantly lower than its international counterparts. It was way below the expectations of industry experts and consumers who were anticipating a price of more than ₹15 lakh—given the design and features. Such an attractive price point became possible because of the ingenuity of Mahindra engineers coupled with the 'Mahindra Rise' philosophy of accepting no limits to make things happen. This challenger spirit galvanizes the Mahindra engineers to constantly push the envelope and raise the bar as they strive to deliver better value to their customers. The result was that the team was able to pack in features like electronic stability program, static bending headlamps, tyre pressure monitoring system, state-of-the-art infotainment system with touch screen and apps in the XUV500 which many brands even above the ₹25 lakh price point were not offering.

Unique clutter-breaking positioning

The positioning strategy was based around the consumer insight that experiences are the new wealth in today's world. Having created a state-of-the-art product with breakthrough pricing, the challenge was to let the consumer connect it with his everyday life. The XUV500 was positioned as an SUV that *helps create memorable stories in your life and keeps you asking for more.* The sign-off line for the brand: 'May your life be full of stories', captured this aptly. The brand used the cheetah as the communication inspiration to help it stand out from the clutter and connect XUV500 with a powerful, agile and aggressive persona.

A sneak-a-peak launch strategy to create curiosity

Work on the market-entry approach began one and a half years before the launch. The team took on the challenge of making the XUV500 the 'most anticipated, most sought after brand' with the audacious task of creating a one-year booking pipeline even before the launch. The consumer was engaged at every aspect of the launch—be it the date, the design, the logo or the price—before the vehicle was unveiled in its full glory. M&M crafted an innovative digital media strategy to create a buzz for the brand before and during the launch of the XUV500. The digital medium allowed consumers to share and have conversations around the brand. This helped increase consumer involvement to create exponential launch impact and buzz.

» Building on the curiosity and interest surrounding the XUV500 launch among enthusiasts online and in social media, M&M decided to reveal the XUV500 bit by bit.
» Anand Mahindra himself announced a contest on Twitter, calling for the participants to guess the launch date. And the winner was invited to the launch of the XUV500.

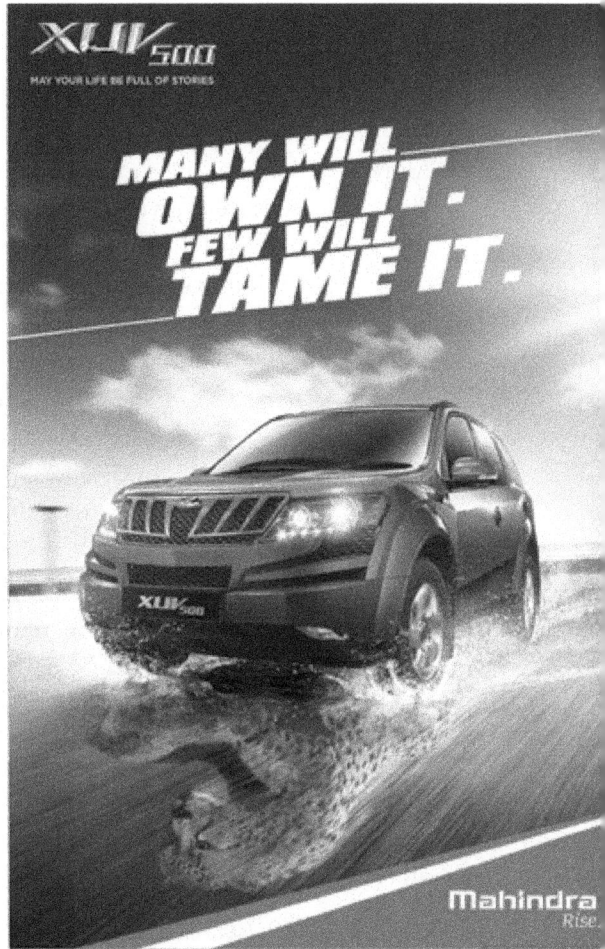

» Consumers were then invited to the first-of-its-kind website to uncover and launch the brand name logo themselves and also share it with their friends. An audio clip with the pronunciation of the brand name was also seeded into the website.

» A pre-launch micro site showed a webcam feed of a covered XUV500 that consumers were given the opportunity of seeing from different angles. More than 4.5 lakh likes were required to reveal parts of the covered XUV500 from different angles.

» Just a few days before the launch an exciting 'guess the price' and win an XUV500 contest was announced. An unprecedented 1 lakh consumers started visiting the website daily.

» On the XUV500 launch date M&M gave all fans and enthusiasts the opportunity to watch the live webcast of the media launch online and the momentum resulted in online viewership of more than 1.5 lakh consumers. This was the highest live webcast viewership for any auto launch at the time.

» The buzz generated pre-launch resulted in more than 40,000 test-drive requests and more than 5 lakh website visits.

Once the launch was over, the micro site morphed into an advanced interactive video animation where people could unveil the XUV500 themselves in a very interactive way. And finally, the much-anticipated details, images and videos of the product were released on the product website on the day of launch.

High-end sales and service experience

To create a fitting high-end experience at dealerships, M&M deployed specialized manpower recruited from outside the auto industry from categories like hospitality and retail. These personnel were trained on technical and soft-selling skills and enabled with technology aids like tablets and kiosks for the first time in the auto industry.

Purple Club: XUV500 customers are guaranteed an extraordinary ownership experience filled with personalized services and exceptional privileges through the Purple Club. In an industry-first initiative, XUV500 owners were assigned their very own personal relationship manager who was their main point of contact. Some unique benefits to owners include privileged access to in-house and lifestyle events such as the 'Mahindra Great Escape', invitations to popular auto-related events, holidays to exotic locations by Club Mahindra, golf and photography workshops and a host of service-related benefits like a car spa, monsoon wash, etc. Purple Club has redefined the way consumers look at the vehicle ownership experience. Till 2015, four 'Torque Day' events had been conducted since launch at Budh International Circuit and Madras Motor Race Track, where the Purple Club owners had a once-in-a-lifetime experience of driving their own XUV500s on a race track.

A successful debut

» XUV500 was completely sold out for sixteen months from its launch in September 2011—with four months of production booked within eight days of launch.

» The XUV500 achieved the 50,000 sales milestone faster than any other premium SUV it its segment.

» In line with the objective, XUV500 successfully managed to create an altogether new niche between the Scorpio and high end SUVs (HSUVs) and lead the HSUV segment with a 56 per cent market share in 2012–13.

» The sales of all premium sedans put together (like Altis, Cruze, Civic and Elantra) in the similar price range dropped by 29 per cent from 4118 (October 2010 to September 2011) to 2934 (October 2011 to September 2012) after the XUV500 launch, as can be seen from Figure 1.

» The exceptional success of the XUV500 can be gauged from the fact that it was the only Indian SUV above ₹10 lakh ex-showroom price, to cross the 1 lakh sales mark within just thirty-four months of its launch. XUV500 has more than 2.1 million fans on Facebook and more than 10.9 million video views on the XUV500 YouTube channel till December 2014, which is a testimony to its popularity amongst customers.

Taken volume away from Premium sedans

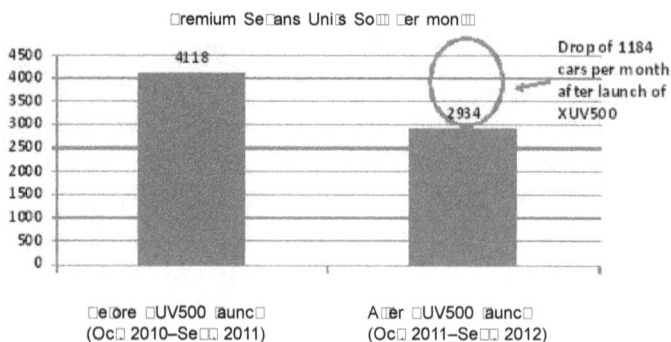

Premium Sedans Units Sold per month

- 4118 (Before XUV500 launch, Oct 2010–Sep 2011)
- 2934 (After XUV500 launch, Oct 2011–Sep 2012)

Drop of 1184 cars per month after launch of XUV500

Before XUV500 launch (Oct 2010–Sep 2011)

After XUV500 launch (Oct 2011–Sep 2012)

Figure 1

HSUV industry share before and after launch

Apr–Aug 2011
Market Size 12,949
XUV500 Share 0%

Sept 11–Mar 12
Market Size 33,848
XUV500 Share 41%

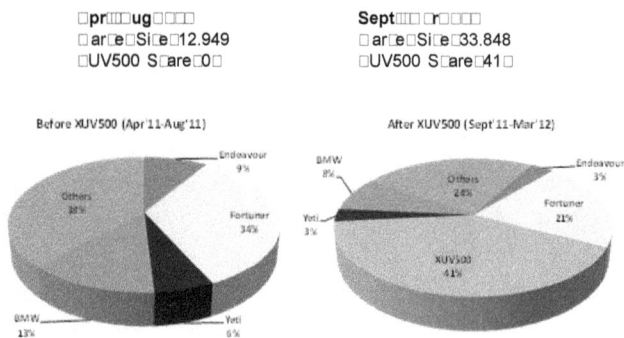

Before XUV500 (Apr'11-Aug'11)
- Endeavour 9%
- Fortuner 34%
- Yeti 6%
- BMW 13%
- Others 38%

After XUV500 (Sept'11-Mar'12)
- BMW 8%
- Others 24%
- Yeti 3%
- Fortuner 21%
- Endeavour 3%
- XUV500 41%

Figure 2

*HSUV: High–end sports utility vehicle

Recognitions

» The XUV500 received tremendous response from customers and reviewers alike and was the most awarded car in its year of launch in 2011–12. It received over twenty-five awards from auto experts and numerous other recognitions.

» It was also rated the most reputed auto brand in the Reputation Benchmark Study conducted by Bluebytes with a 74 per cent lead over the second most reputed car brand.

» True success is determined by how customers react to or rate the product. The XUV500 topped in customer satisfaction in the SUV segment, in the TNS Automotive India study 2012.

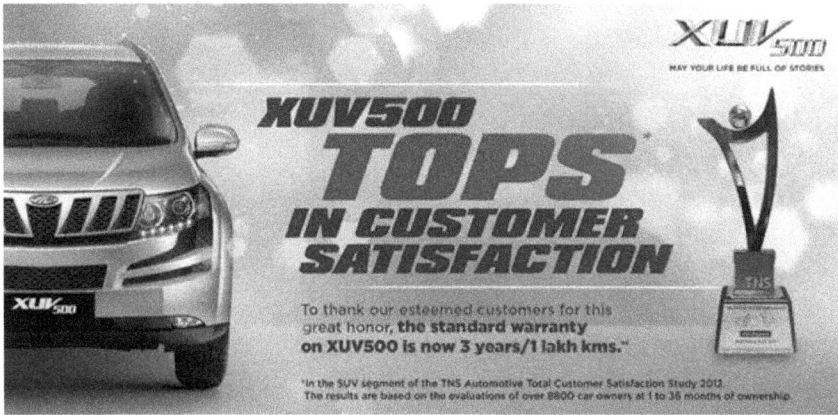

New stories to sustain the momentum

» M&M continued to engage consumers with more stories of the XUV500 playing an enabling role in fulfilling the brand promise: 'May your life be full of stories.'

> A television commercial based on the incredible experiences of three young friends who embark on a journey to find a cheetah became very popular. The advertisement exhorts the young at heart to seek out memorable experiences for themselves. The XUV500 was seamlessly integrated to showcase its on-road and off-road capabilities. The surprise element of two cheetahs emerging, and one of them jumping on the bonnet of the car towards the end of the film, leaves the viewers thinking of those incredible experiences that make for life's memorable stories and thus ties in with the positioning of the brand. A two-minute uncut version first premiered on YouTube and has garnered a phenomenal 3.4 million views on YouTube. An award-winning dual navigation website was also launched where consumers could read and share memorable stories of their road trips and journeys.

» To keep feeding the buzz around the brand with more interesting content, a unique 'XUV500 Memorable Stories Short Film Festival' contest was launched in 2012 among short film makers to create films around the theme of 'memorable stories'. This received tremendous response with twenty-two short films featuring XUV500 in different themes. These were launched on the XUV500 YouTube channel and XUV500 Facebook fan page.

The story of creation of the XUV500

The team worked with Discovery Channel to create a 'Making of the XUV500' programme on their 'Inside Out' show. This film is the story of the XUV500 from its inception till launch. It takes you through the journey of the XUV500's design evolution and also provides you glimpses of its birthplace, Chakan, where a state-of-the-art manufacturing facility has been put up.

Association with rallies to reinforce the rugged off/on road capabilities of XUV500:

» XUV500 became the exclusive vehicle partner for the ASEAN India Car Rally 2012. This three-week-long rally saw twenty-eight XUV500s travel through eight ASEAN countries over 8,000 km.

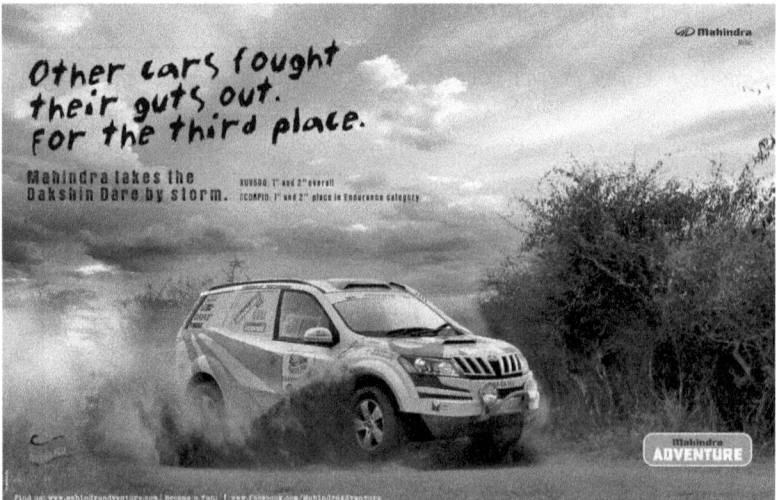

» XUV500 showcased its performance capabilities by winning several rallies like Dakshin Dare, Indian National Rally Championship (INRC-2013), Desert Storm and Indian Rally Championship (IRC-2014).

The road ahead

Having received phenomenal response in India, and also in Australia, South Africa and Italy, the XUV500 is poised to make its mark in other international markets.

More experiences will be created by building value for consumers through upgrades, refreshes, limited editions and new variants of the XUV500 to provide luxury at an affordable price. An entry-level variant W4 was launched below the ₹11 lakh price point to make the XUV500 more accessible to compact SUV and sedan buyers.

The Purple Club programme will continue to create unique experiences for XUV500 owners through exciting lifestyle-enhancing privileges and exclusive service privileges, as well as special events like adventure drives and Torque Days at the Buddh International Circuit.

The new-age XUV500 has been launched recently, which will further enhance the finesse and driving experience while retaining the DNA of the cheetah-inspired XUV500. It is packed with a host of new cutting-edge technology features like an electric sunroof, first-in-class logo projection lamps on ORVMs, six-way power-adjustable driver's seat, push button start, passive keyless entry, 18-cm (7-inch) touchscreen infotainment system with GPS to name a few.

Advantage mahindra delivered

Crossing the milestone of 1 lakh sales in India, faster than any other premium SUV above the ₹10 lakh ex-showroom price, is a testimony to the phenomenon of the XUV500 and the overwhelming response from consumers.

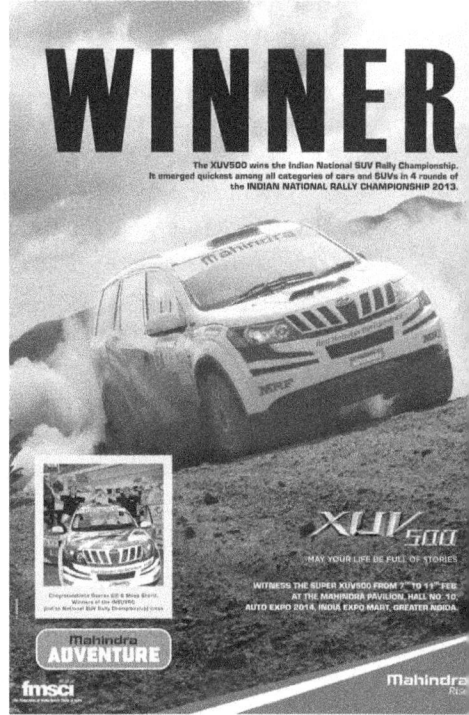

What was different about the XUV500 success story?

1. A clear vision and an audacious goal with a rallying war cry to enthuse the team *(creating a one-year booking pipeline)*.
2. Built anticipation prior to launch with great intrigue value *(teasing with titbits of information before launch)*.
3. Created disruption. Did the unexpected.
   a. What's in a name? you might say. Most Indian-manufactured automobiles tend to have alphabetical names. Mahindra did the unthinkable with an alpha-numeric name for the XUV500 that lends a lot of exclusivity to the product.
   b. Digital and social media were used as effective buzz-generating, cost-effective, lead medium in a launch. Proving that launches need not necessarily lead by traditional media like TV and press.
   c. Why does an auto salesman need to be the only one who can sell an automobile? Mahindra hired from outside the auto industry to get people who could sell to a more evolved, high-end target audience.
   d. A salesman is a salesman is a salesman. Mahindra created 'experience executives'!
   e. Designer clothing to dress an automobile salesman? Ritu Beri designed the uniforms worn by the XUV500 experience executives.
   f. Whoever heard of using digital technology and tablets to detail product information in the auto industry? Mahindra did it successfully.
   g. Leveraged loyalty programmes otherwise restricted to airlines, retail, hotels, etc. Mahindra did the unthinkable and created the Purple Club with an exclusive relationship manager, both firsts in the auto industry!
   h. Stunned customers, critics and competition by offering a hell of a lot more value in the product at a wow price than can ever be imagined. Static-bending headlamps, six airbags, ESP, hill-hold and hill-descent control, 6-inch touchscreen infotainment system with GPS, voice commands, lounge lighting…all in the XUV500 at significantly lower price than the price of global auto brands in India.
4. Provided the consumer with a world-class surround experience. Dealerships were upgraded with carpeted and leathered customer lounges.

5. Viralized consumer opinions about their product in the early stages of the launch itself via social media.
6. Made consumers a part of their launch such that they feel they are launching the product.

AN 'ITEM NUMBER IN THE MOUTH' THAT KEEPS FAMILY FUN TIMES ROLLING

The story of Kurkure is one of a brand that created a completely new segment in the salty snacks category, created value in consumer life and did it all with a sense of humour. And along the way it challenged many beliefs.

How much value can a small crooked piece of a salty something that crunches and melts away in your mouth in no time at all, create? Turns out, plenty—the value of navigating between tradition and modernity, the value of aspiration, and last but not the least, the value of embracing imperfections and loving with a laugh. The belief that families that snack together and laugh together, stay together, will continue to be the bedrock of the Kurkure campaign strategy.

Truth, quirkily told

When it comes to describing the success of the fifteen-year-old brand Kurkure, the

₹1000-crore-plus snack brand of PepsiCo India, old timers often talk of providence. Over the years, Kurkure has come to be identified as a quintessential family brand and has brought joy to many families, consistently highlighting thought-provoking contemporary points of view on the Indian family and its myriad interactions.

'Tedha fun' has been at the forefront of product and marketing innovation and the brand has constantly reinvented itself to remain relevant to the Indian ethos and culture. India's most loved snack brand, since its launch, has been engaging Indian families with its inimitable taste and highly addictive, full-bodied offerings. Right from the beginning, Kurkure has been steering between tradition and modernity: made with familiar kitchen ingredients but in shape and format and flavour delivery, a 'twist on tradition'. As we will discover, this would go on to become a cornerstone of brand Kurkure. *Be it in product, format, flavour or shape, in brand communication and the characters it portrays, Kurkure has followed the 'twist on tradition' formula.*

Mood, twists and turns

Kurkure was launched in 1999 and has since then transformed the way Indians snack. At its core, Kurkure questioned the existing norm that salty snacks were divided into two large segments, traditional and potato chips. Kurkure introduced a new sub-segment within namkeens, creating a new palate experience for consumers. Armed with its unique product proposition: 'Familiar taste in an innovative format', the brand broke category codes and transformed the landscape of snacking in India, both sensorial and visual. It introduced a sub-segment that was not palm food, but finger food—so if namkeen was eaten in a bowl, Kurkure was eaten out of a bag. *Kurkure bridged traditional Indian snacks—namkeens—and the modern potato chips. It also substantially modernized the codes of namkeens while still appealing to the spicy Indian palate.*

Brandishing a strangely addictive, intense chatpata taste, Kurkure was launched as Lehar Kurkure, a sub-brand under the umbrella of Lehar (which was positioned at that time as an irresistible snack). It used traditional Indian 'kitchen ingredients' like rice, lentils, corn and Indian masala seasoning; and the story goes that it took 220 trials to make Kurkure. Consumer testing had people loving the crunchiness and saying it was very 'kurkura' (crunchy)—and from there came the name.

When it was launched in Chandigarh, the sales team literally 'painted the town orange' with all three-wheelers carrying the packs being painted in that colour. One of the fastest market placements, Kurkure had near 100 per cent coverage in ten days, something that was repeated in many other markets soon after. A significant retail merchandizing innovation that marked the initial years was the 'rack', which gave consumers a modern trade experience in traditional trade, today an accepted and ubiquitous sight. The small packs hanging in 'ladis' (hangers) outside shops rather like shampoo sachets, was another innovation that became a category norm.

With its zesty, multi-sensorial taste that was energizing and mood transforming, and as a consumer once put it, an 'item number in the mouth', it was launched with the tagline: '*Kya karen, control nahin hota*' to drive home the addictive taste of the product. Focusing on the value of mood transformation, Kurkure tapped into a variety of flavour buckets, giving its consumers a range of experiences, sometimes coming from regional palates, sometimes emerging as fusion flavours with a hint of the west but always Indian at heart.

The 'Great Indian Family' brand

While in the initial years, Kurkure leveraged the product's irresistible and unusual taste to establish itself and create the category, in 2003 it shifted its fun positioning to encompass the entire family. With this, it also stepped out of the shadow of Lehar, as a brand in its own right.

The brand created a context for itself by appropriating the territory hitherto occupied by namkeens enjoyed as moments of family togetherness over a cup of tea. Kurkure took the battle into namkeens' own backyard by developing its contemporary perspective on Indian family dynamics.

In a country so rooted in family values, few brands came across as truly 'family brands'. Kurkure talked to snack-loving, spice-loving, variety-loving, conversation-loving Indian families. Kurkure rooted itself in the family social context and became a commentator on the changing Indian family, always bringing its own insightful observations on quirky truths of the great Indian family.

Kurkure professed that families that snacked together and laughed together, stayed together. In a country where family love was historically deep-rooted in duty and responsibility, obedience and sacrifice and codes of conduct; where Bollywood idealized family love, lump-in-the-throat melodrama, replaying mythology themes of duty, sacrifice, protect and save; where advertising revelled in portraying the perfect mother, the perfect son, the perfect wife; where TV serials paraded the dark side of family life, kitchen politics, conflict, jealousy, manipulation, power, marital violence, and money fights; with its strangely addictive, intense chatapata taste, Kurkure assumed the role of a catalyst. It portrayed a family that was happily, unabashedly idiosyncratic and playfully imperfect, always accepting that 'we are like this only' and that 'in our family it happens like this only'. It loosened stiff, formal relationship hierarchies in Indian families and let in fresh masti-filled air!

Introducing a 'Kahani mein twist'

When other players started trickling in, sensing the opportunity, Kurkure had to reassert its uniqueness and elevate itself above the mass of copycats. It did a re-jig of the product (extra spicy) and linked the product's transformational experience to the 'twist' in any regular and staid situation. The 'twist on tradition'-centred promotion continued till 2004 even as the brand then signed on the bubbly actress, Juhi Chawla in 2004 in an attempt to target housewives who were the 'gatekeeper' audience for the brand.

Kurkure wanted to do something special with Juhi and decided to leverage her cheerful personality, her amazing sense of comic timing, her non-glam doll image and the fact that she was a mother and housewife too. Since housewives were generally hooked on TV serials, Kurkure decided to target them by making a spoof on *Kyunki Saas Bhi Kabhi Bahu Thi*, a popular TV soap at that time. The campaign continued with many a spoof, be it of Bollywood classics or television soaps that helped tell product stories of '*Kahaani mein twist*' (A twist in the story).

If masti (fun) and Kurkure were synonymous with each other, so were masti and Juhi; and what could be better than having all three (Juhi, Kurkure and masti) packaged together. Spontaneous, fun-loving and witty, Juhi helped shape Kurkure as a great family brand with a sense of humour.

'Masti' continued with new consumption occasions

Having appropriated 'masti', the next strategic growth bet for Kurkure was to increase penetration by appropriating new 'regular' consumption occasions and expanding its portfolio with innovative offerings.

'The Kurkure family' was a powerful platform to plug-in the brand firmly into 'family teatime moments' as well as the brand's innovation roadmap. Starting with 2005, Kurkure strategically targeted evening teatime, at the time the largest occasion for snacking—consuming macro snacks, i.e. biscuits and namkeens—as the consumption occasion. It reached out to the homemaker who desired 'evening tea' as the moment for changing gears and to other members who looked forward to evening tea as a moment of relaxation and a joyful collective family huddle. When every member tended to relax in his own individual style, Kurkure stepped in not just as a snack but as a bonding factor that brought the family back

into the same living room, creatively rendering '*Chaitime masti bole to Kurkure!*'. The timing could not have been better with the large family as a unit beginning to disintegrate into nuclear set-ups. The brand evoked the nostalgia of the quintessential large Indian family set-up.

Kurkure aimed to breach the traditional stronghold of Indian snacking: teatime, the biggest gap between meals. Beyond just positioning and advertising, product sensorial work was done to pair Kurkure with tea. Extensive in-home promotions with tea brands were launched nationwide. To further enhance its share of teatimes, Kurkure launched two sub-brands 'Kurkure Solid Masti', as new-age substantial snack options for that 'evening peckishness' and 'Kurkure Masti Squares', as an aid to the homemaker who desired versatility in teatime snacks. Both sub-brands, however, did not find much traction with consumers.

Kurkure kept raising its standards in terms of variants, flavours, formats, occasions and communication to deter copycats that posed a serious threat. Multiple promotions, many of them first of their kind for this category, were conceived that encouraged families to spend time together, with gratifications ranging from holidays to a tea party in the sky. Disruptive large-scale consumer engagement programmes like 'Kurkure Mast Family Jackpot', 'Kurkure Jupp for the Cup' (during the ICC World Cup 2007) and 'Kurkure Chaitime Achievers' were launched to drive consumption.

'Kurkure Chaitime Achievers' (family face on the pack communication) was not just engagement, but consumer-generated participation, another first from the ever-innovative Kurkure. Families were invited to share interesting, ingenious chaitime recipes using Kurkure. The winning recipe made out of Kurkure was the 'family's passport to fame', with the winning families having their photograph featured on one million Kurkure packs. This was the first-ever consumer-generated participation in the history of advertising in India; and with over 100,000 responses, it lead to a surge in business.

To leverage yet another consumption occasion, Kurkure came up with '*Zyada meetha ho gaya? Muh Kurkure karo*' for Diwali, which was traditionally a sweets-centred feasting time. This was again in line with the brand DNA: a twist on tradition. *Kurkure boldly pitched a salty snack as part of the festive repertoire by beautifully blending two unrelated insights—the fatigue with excessive sweets at Diwali time and the changing equation between mother-in-law and daughter-in-law.* Kurkure took on the controlling and disciplining mother-in-law whose household was liberated with fun when Kurkure appeared on the scene as an opportune gift from the new daughter-in-law's maternal home just when the mother-in-law was tired of excessive sweets. In keeping with this, highly decorative gift packs were introduced. Kurkure went on to expand its 'festival' strategy by introducing a whole range of chilli flavours, the premise being 'when you get a strong dose of it, your real self comes out and you start taking liberties and breaking the shackles of formality'.

'*Tedha hai par mera hai*': Flavours transcending tastes, geographies and cultures

In its bid to drive habits and enhance its share of teatime, Kurkure started facing a host of challenges primarily due to aggressive competition from many local and one large national player entering the market with products in the same space.

Kurkure launched its 'X-treme' edition of flavours to connect with the youth, which in turn reinforced its positioning as 'always doing the unexpected'. Unearthing yet another insight into the great Indian family, Kurkure launched its iconic tag-line '*Tedha hai par mera hai*' in 2008.

'*Tedha hai par mera hai*' became a part of everyday conversations and advertising folklore. Some of the novel initiatives during this period included new, unusual ingredients; introduction of regional variants; fl avours inspired by master chef sessions around chutneys/pickles; and creating rituals—Kurkure bhel via on-premise bhel carts at PVR. Constantly giving consumers new taste experiences, over the years, Kurkure has created many limited edition flavours that included extreme flavours like Risky Chilli, tangy flavours like Electric Nimbu; regional flavours like Punjabi Kadhai Masala, Mumbai Chatpata Usal, Bengali Jhaal and South Spice Mix; the judwa pack which was loaded with two collet packs that looked alike but tasted different: the irresistible zing of Tirchhi Mirchi (crazy chilli) and tangy zest of Chulbuli Ambi (raw mango) in one pack; the chilli range: Chilli Achari, Chilli Garlic, Chilli Mustard, Chilli Saucy; and indo-international flavours: Punjabi Pizza, Andhra Bangkok Curry and Rajasthani Manchurian.

Many of these flavours were co-created with chefs who specialized in regional cuisines, or those who loved experimenting with fusion food. While some of them remained limited edition flavours, others became a part of the regular Kurkure portfolio as they acquired a huge consumer fan base—Naughty Tomato for example is one of the most popular flavours in the south.

Kurkure also introduced the puffed range, again stealing the show with new shapes. Puff corn has been one of the most successful launches for Kurkure in the puffed segment—it grew share by playing to the category code of 'play' by creating fun play rituals with the product. This puffed portfolio of Kurkure has seen many innovations since, with new shapes and differentiated textures and flavours.

To take on the money-for-value players, Kurkure launched ₹2 and ₹3 packs and created the 'houseful pack' at the ₹5 price point, a name that implied quantity and all the masti of a Bollywood movie.

Through this phase, the brand's communication always tapped into timeless as well as emerging trends in consumer behaviour, and remained a brand with a point of view—be it the changing mother-in-law–daughter-in-law relationship, motherhood, the disintegrating family, the modern housewife, mixed marriages, mother-son relationships, husbands expressing, or not expressing, their love for their wives, the returning NRI—but always connecting back to the product basics, the pack price proposition, the extra quantity or the promotion offer.

Consolidating its leadership with new promotions, packs and price points

Kurkure revamped its communications strategy in late 2012, scaling up its *'Tedha hai par mera hai'* proposition, creating a first-of-its-kind 'Kurkure screen family'. With a very modern 'remix bahu' at its centre, India's Most Crooked Family is a joint family, bubbling with conversation and energy, disagreements and conflicts, negotiating between the individual and the collective, balancing tradition and modernity, and always looking for ways to resolve everything with warmth and laughter, abundance and abandon. And this quirky family told every new story, be it new taste, new pack size, or new price point.

To help drive sales in the large pack segment, the family gathered in the living room and tapped into the insight of 'the making of the guest list'—that, in an Indian family, there is no such thing as a 'small family party'! The large pack helped Kurkure become a planned purchase in an otherwise impulse category. Kurkure thus managed to get on to the kitchen shelf where the housewife stored it and then served it with pride.

The ₹5 pack, a salient and recognized price point, was amplified through the campaign '*5 rupaye mein khaane waali cheez khao*' and addressed the conversion and upgradation opportunity, taking on lookalikes and unbranded competition/local brands and low-quality snacks. While consumers do look out for an affordable treat, research showed that they do not necessarily give too much thought to their choice of snacking options available at ₹5. This indifference and lack of discretion by consumers formed the basic premise of the campaign that asked consumers for a reappraisal of current choices, even if it was only about spending ₹5, that could make both their purchase and consumption experience more worthwhile.

The launch of the new ₹15 price point was another category disruptor. Enabling greater sharing between two or three individuals, Kurkure wanted to add some spice in those moments of sharing. Family life is supposed to be all about sharing, but there are some things that just can't be shared. The campaign played on the unwillingness of a mother-in-law to share her most prized possession, her son, with her daughter-in-law. The mast share pack showed that it could even get them to share the man in the middle, so to say.

A classic 'challenger' brand success

In its bid to become an iconic family brand, over the years Kurkure used a varied mix of penetration conversion and upgradation strategies, to increase consumption and frequency, i.e. share of tea tray and kitchen shelf, portfolio strategies by experimenting with flavours, taste and format, new price point strategies and packaging strategies for special occasions.

On consumption occasions, Kurkure dared suggest that it could replace the 'traditional' namkeen at teatime with its more mood transformational bold taste and later, even, that Kurkure snacks could be gifted on festive occasions in place of sweets.

In retail, Kurkure challenged the belief that packs had to sit on shelves, instead creating the 'ladi' with snack packs hanging like sachets, now a ubiquitous sight.

In pack sizes, Kurkure turned the practice of calling a ₹5 (23 g) chota (small) pack, 'houseful' instead.

In engagement, Kurkure was the first to challenge the thinking that snacks are an end in themselves, and tapped into the insight that housewives like to create their own signature dishes—creating the first-of-its-kind invitation to send recipes with Kurkure as an ingredient, with the promise of 'consumer on pack'.

In communication, Kurkure challenged the traditional notion that a housewife-centric brand cannot be humorous, and not just humorous, but over-the-top funny.

In the deeper promise that it offered in the space of family bonding, Kurkure challenged the traditional notion that family togetherness comes from every member of the family being perfect and functioning within their role boundaries. Kurkure was the first brand that dared portray a housewife who proudly and happily admitted her family was full of imperfections.

So how much value can a small crooked piece of a salty something that crunches and melts away in your mouth in no time at all, create? Turns out, *Kahaani abhi baaki hai...*

Kurkure: The journey to sustained leadership

Leadership retention for Kurkure has been no cakewalk. It has faced many challenges along the way.

Challenge of product novelty: Consistently declining product uniqueness with the Kurkure stick (referred to as collet in the industry) becoming a category generic and proliferation of a lot of 'copycats' from a host of local players.

Challenge of growing competition: The total number of branded players in the salty snacking category more than doubled in a matter of three years (2009 to 2011).*

Challenge of new and emerging formats: Taking the cue on shapes and attempting to excite the consumer, feeding from the collet category and further expanding consumer repertoire.

Challenge of commanding a premium: Increasing pressure on commanding a premium when competition is offering less than acceptable quality but with more grammage per bag (more bites per pack).

Today, Kurkure is a megabrand with a portfolio that straddles four distinct snack formats:

- **Core Collet range** with several flavour offerings—Masala Munch, Hyderabadi Hungama, Green Chutney Rajasthani Style, Chilli Chatka, Naughty Tomato
- **New and Emerging range** under Kurkure Solid Masti Twisteez
- **Puffed Snack range** that has six variants—Monster Paws, PuffCorn, ZigZag, Monster Smileys, CornCups and Crunchy Rings
- **Innovative Namkeens range** with the launch of Papad O Nutz in two flavours—Jeera Hing and Chilli Masala—this year

*Source: Nielsen

THE WIND BENEATH THE WINGS
Honda's dream run in India

In the derby of global mobility, Honda Motor Company, Japan, is a certified thoroughbred with the rich legacy of being the undisputed leader when it comes to two-wheelers. This is the journey of a brand that challenged convention and rewrote destiny. Since 1948, Honda Wings has symbolized Honda's two-wheeler business worldwide and has been synonymous with quality, innovation and technology. Most importantly, Honda has earned the trust of over 300 million two-wheeler customers worldwide. That 60 per cent of the contribution comes from Asia shows the importance of this market and brings India to the forefront. However, the trust that Honda enjoys today has not been handed to it on a silver platter. Rather than promotions claiming a No. 1 world ranking in two-wheeler manufacturing, a claim that would not be false, in every country Honda operates in, it has, instead, studied the needs, wants and aspirations of the people. Only after careful scrutiny and analysis has Honda made the best use of technology and expertise to come up with country-specific innovations. This is what has enabled it to carve a special place for itself in the hearts of its customers worldwide. This is the unique story of Honda's journey in India.

Testing the track (1999)

When Honda decided, in 1991, to make its mark as a two-wheeler manufacturer in India, things were none too easy for it. India posed a peculiar problem. Not only was there tough competition from local players, Honda also found itself grappling with daunting geographical diversity and the fast-evolving attitudes of Indian consumers. Further, while technology and R&D were innate strengths of Honda, understanding which technology would be applicable to India was a challenge. It contemplated bringing in technology that would reduce emissions, but this would escalate the cost, as most of the parts would have to be imported. On a daily basis, the Honda team found itself asking whether its Indian customers would be willing to pay a premium for a better and greener riding experience? But, as it turned out, that was *not* the only issue facing Honda officials...

Since 1984, Honda had been in a joint venture with the Munjal family-led Hero Cycles—India's largest bicycle company at that time. In the 1980s the Hero Group was also diversifying its product lines and emerging as a strong player in the auto component industry. When Hero decided to join hands with the Honda Group in the early half of the 1980s, it was in a position to call the shots and had therefore imposed certain restrictions on Honda by way of business and product parameters. So the the biggest question before Honda was whether or not to embark upon a a solo journey in India at this juncture. These challenges, notwithstanding, Honda Motor Company, Japan (HMC) took up the daunting task of replicating its resounding global success head on, and set up a wholly owned two-wheeler sales and production subsidiary in India—Honda Motorcycle and Scooter India (HMSI) Pvt. Ltd—in 1999. At the same time it walked the tight rope of maintaining confidentiality and trust with the Hero Group, in a joint venture that operated amicably for close to thirty years and became one of the longest in Indian automotive history.

Honda's vision for India was built on what has been the core philosophy of the group the world over. This philosophy is encapsulated in their communication tagline, 'The Power of Dreams', that has been driving the group since 1948. Keeping the 'Power of Dreams' at the core of their vision for India HMSI put together a 'dream team', every associate of which would be encouraged to pursue their dream and produce revolutionary ideas to spread the joy of riding to millions across India. This young, go-getter, interdisciplinary core team was handpicked to structure a robust and resilient business model for HMSI. Plans were being implemented full steam from HMSI's makeshift office at Nehru Place, Delhi, while the first factory was under construction at Manesar district Gurgaon, Haryana.

Saddling the horse: 2000–2001

The core team knew only too well that it would have only one chance of proving its worth with the very first Honda product in India. Zeroing in on which segment to focus on was a huge challenge in itself. Till the late 1980s, the scooter was the traditional vehicle of choice for middle class Indians, but with economic liberalization at the turn of the decade, there was a sea change in the demands of the two-wheeler customers. In the 1990s, customer preferences had shifted from the economical and convenient scooters to the more stylish, young, fuel-efficient, four-stroke motorcycles powered by advanced Japanese technology. While motorcycles were becoming extremely popular, scooters were perceived to have an 'aged' profile and were on the brink of extinction. Assuming that scooters were losing flavour with the Indian consumer, Bajaj, the No. 1 two-wheeler manufacturer then, focused all its energies on manufacturing motorcycles that were flying off the shelves. *But the existing partnership for Hero Honda clearly stipulated that the new Honda Company—HMSI—could not launch any motorcycle in the first three years of its Indian operations.* This put well over 80 per cent of the Indian two-wheeler market out of bounds for Honda. The remaining niche market, comprising automatic scooters (ATSCs) like Kinetic DX and Bajaj Saffire, was not a volume driver, being limited to urban households, and contributed less than 10 per cent of the Indian two-wheeler industry.

Adversity vs opportunity

In this scenario, HMSI decided to turn the scooter industry's existential crisis into an opportunity, much to the shock of industry watchers. The core team at HMSI decided that Honda's first product for India would be an ATSC. Industry experts declared this a 'strategic suicide' and started writing obituaries for the brand even before it took its first independent step!

Far from being fazed by the criticism, the dream team worked with new-found fervour to bring back excitement into the ATSC category and came out with the Honda Activa as its maiden launch. Here was a 'scooter' in a new avatar that was trendy, stylish and unisex in appeal. Far from the geared scooters that were cumbersome, heavy and archaic, the Activa came with all the features of a motorcycle. This included superior four-stroke technology, V-matic (gearless) transmission, durable all metal body, convenient lift-up independent cover (CLIC) mechanism and Honda's patented puncture-resistant tuff-up tube (that minimized sudden punctures by 70 per cent) ensured convenience like never before.

With Activa, therefore, Honda achieved all that it desired in its maiden launch. On the one hand it completely changed the perception of a scooter in the mind of the consumer and on the other it reopened a 'dead' segment, thus throwing the competition out of gear!

Honda Activa-i

The product completed to perfection, Honda set about putting the last piece of the strategy in place, that is to register presence and tap customers in the first phase. Taking cognizance of the fact that it was near-impossible to instantly create a pan-India presence, the Honda team shortlisted top potential markets for ATSCs in India. This included obvious key growth drivers of urban consumption, led by cities like Bangalore (India's largest market for ATSCs).

Innovative distribution strategy

The next step was to invite applicants for Honda Exclusive Authorized Dealerships (HEADs). In India, Honda wanted to be the pioneer in providing world-leading standards under one roof which was more than the trio of sales, service and spares.

Globally recognized for its transparency of approach, the same blueprint and profit and loss (P&L) projection was shared with prospective dealers who would sign up as exclusive dealers of products from the Honda stable. Honda had taken into account every exigency to prepare a three-year survival plan, and provided proof in no uncertain terms of how sustainable and wise a business decision it was to invest in brand Honda.

Itself a young brand in India, Honda chose young blood over experience when it came to its HEADs. A majority of the sixty-two HEADs chosen in Phase I were entrepreneurs in their thirties. This dedicated and enthusiastic team of founder dealers laid the path for future Honda success in India.

Results of this momentous first step: 2001

By the year 2001, everything had started falling in place. In May 2001, mass production of Activa commenced in Honda's production facility at the industrial model township (IMT) of Manesar, Haryana. With the grand entry of Activa, Honda successfully reactivated the dying Indian ATSC market, and the rest, as they say, is history.

With the success of Activa giving Honda a solid foundation, the brand soon trailblazed its way to record sales. In 2001 itself, Honda sold over 55,000 units from its limited network. The next fiscal (2002–3) saw Honda striving to meet unanticipated demand as sales climaxed at the peak annual production capacity level of 1.5 lakh units. More than a decade later, the legacy and pace continue unabated. Honda Activa holds the distinction of being the numero uno among automatic scooters in the world. It has over 10 million happy customers in India. *So phenomenal has been its success that 'Activa' is now the generic name used for all automatic scooters!*

Mastering the stride: 2001–2004

Honda expanded its ATSC portfolio step by step in order to meet the evolving needs of its Indian customers. Initial customer surveys indicated that Gen Y loved the convenience of a scooter, but dreamt of a ride that also amplified its style quotient. In other words, it wanted something that was not a family scooter, but an individual style statement in motion.

» To realize this dream of Indian youth, Honda innovated with the 102cc Dio, which created a new sub-segment within ATSCs and was India's first unisex moto-scooter.
» This was followed by Eterno—the geared surprise from Honda in mid-2003, targeted at hard working professionals.

The new product pipeline was fortified by a steady addition of network outlets. Every new city was finalized keeping in mind the future product line. Ensuring dealer viability was paramount. From sixty touch-points in FY 2001-2, the network grew to 252 outlets by FY 2003–4.

Undisputed Leader

In just three years, Honda's ATSC sales skyrocketed by 515 per cent to 3.41 lakh units in FY 2003–4. From a new fringe player that had its hands tied at the time of its entry into India, HMSI was now the undisputed leader with a 52 per cent market share in the ATSC market.

Trotting ahead: 2004–2011

As per its agreement with Hero, Honda could not enter the motorcycle segment for the first three years of its independent operations. However, as it entered into its fourth year of operations, HMSI was free to eye the largest share of the two-wheeler pie: motorcycles.

From a brand standpoint, it made sense that the first model be a premium performance motorcycle as the Honda network's reach was predominantly in Tier-I cities. Further, the first motorcycle had to personify Honda's R&D innovations and superior technology. Gradually, as the network would grow to include Tier II and Tier III cities, the product portfolio would grow to address the masses. Thus, the top-down approach was adopted, keeping the demands of the consumer in mind.

It was with this background that HMSI launched its first motorcycle—the 150cc CB Unicorn. This was India's first motorcycle with a state-of-the-art mono suspension (Honda's original technology from the world of international racing) and an enviable list of other novel features. Unicorn was the only motorcycle in India with Honda's patented puncture-resistant tuff-up tube (that minimized sudden punctures by 70 per cent) and had best in class pick-up (clocked 0–60 in just five seconds) and incredible mileage (60 km to a litre) coupled with an international design guaranteed to bring out the 'Wing Rider' in every customer. Globally, Honda's two-wheeler operations are symbolically representated by wings while the car operations are represented by the letter H. Wing Rider was the tag line for the CB Unicorn.

With CB Unicorn getting a thumping response from customers, Honda rapidly grew to reach the one million happy customers milestone in January 2005.

2004: Honda's first motorcycle

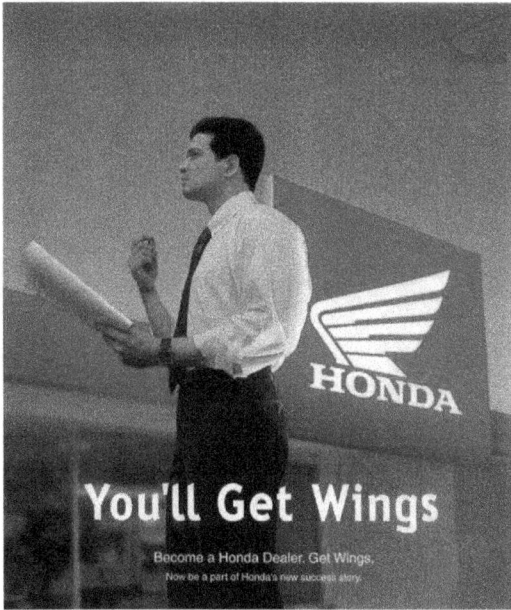

You'll Get Wings

Become a Honda Dealer. Get Wings.
Now be a part of Honda's new success story.

0–60 in just five seconds

From 2006 to 2010, Honda's operations picked up pace, and the motorcycle line-up stretched from 150cc to 125cc. In 2006 came the 125cc CB Shine. In the nine years since, CB Shine sales have jumped from 10,000 units to more than 70,000 every month. Customer satisfaction has ensured that despite severe competition, CB Shine continues to rule as India's largest selling 125cc motorcycle.

This was followed by the introduction of a sporty, fun bike in the 125cc CBF Stunner in 2008. With its expanding product portfolio, HMSI's network had now started penetrating deeper beyond urban India, into the heartland of Bharat.

However, the global economic meltdown, lay just around the corner and by October 2008, the Indian two-wheeler industry was in the throes of a contraction. The sole exception to this was Honda, the only two-wheeler company to witness no drop in sales even for a single month.

In contrast to the overall decline of 7.92 per cent in the two-wheeler industry in FY 2007–8, HMSI sales had jumped up 27 per cent. While the motorcycle industry, which contributed over 70 per cent to total two-

CB Stunner

wheeler sales, witnessed a colossal de-growth of 11.9 per cent, Honda's motorcycle sales grew at a phenomenal 65 per cent. In just two years, by FY 2009 end, HMSI had gained a substantial 5 per cent market share by making the most of the opportunity that lay in adversity.

Engaging with society at large

As the fastest-growing two-wheeler company in India, Honda left no stone unturned to catch the pulse of the nation and convey the message that the well-being of its customers was at the core of its philosophy. Working towards this goal, Honda introduced a separate 'safety riding' vertical to its organization. Honda's skilled safety instructors started engaging with all age groups, starting from children as young as five years old to adults. Riding trainers were introduced at HEADs across India to aid new riders to experience over hundred possible risks on the road in a virtual safe mode. From regular safety trainings at schools, colleges, corporate offices and public sector units to mega camps in Tier II cities, the importance of responsible riding and safety of self and others on the road was driven home.

Observing the increasing trend of female riders, Honda also became the first in the two-wheeler segment to extend its two-wheeler riding programme to women, enabling them to experience the freedom of riding. The unique Dream Riding initiative is the next step wherein women can learn to ride in just four hours. All they have to do is to drop an e-mail and Honda's safety instructors will get back to them. Already, this empowering initiative is seeing an overwhelming response from eighteen-year-old college students to forty-eight-year-old professionals and housewives.

A new era begins

From 2000 to 2010, India had become the world's second-largest motorcycle market after China. Sensing the opportunity that lay in the increasing diversity of the Indian motorcycle market and its potential to grow business both inside and outside India, both JV partners (Honda Motor Company, Japan, and Hero) expressed a desire to mutually end their twenty-six-year-old partnership in December 2010.

With this new development, HMSI was all set to unleash its mega plans of expanding Honda's footprint in the Indian two-wheeler market on its own, this time without any restrictions.

Picking up pace: 2012–2014

HMSI's new innings as the only Indian Honda two-wheeler company had now begun.

This translated into 'simplicity, concentration, speed and communication' on all fronts—product, production capacity, R&D, penetration, manpower, investment and expansion of supplier base.

The challenge now, as the core team saw it, was 'to provide good products to our customers with speed, affordability and low CO_2 emissions'. The plan was to develop India as the centre of Honda's global two-wheeler operations, build it as an export hub, and increase its contribution to Honda's overall two-wheeler sales from 13 per cent in 2010 to 30 per cent eventually. Honda's then global chief, Mr Takanobu Ito, president and chief executive officer (CEO) Honda Motor Company, Japan, reaffirmed that Honda would go all out to leverage its vast resources and expertise for emerging as the leader in India. Towards this end, Honda launched its new India-specific, three-pronged corporate direction in May 2012.

Following a *three Cs strategy*, Honda would *communicate, connect and create* for India. Simple as this sounds, behind it lay years of experience in building trust and continuous innovation.

There was vast opportunity in taking the spirit of the Honda global brand slogan 'The Power of Dreams' and communicating it to a country of a billion in a way that showed that Honda was here not just to share a dream, but to power it into reality. That is how the Indian brand slogan '*Sach kar denge sapne*' was conceived.

At the heart of it was a simple but powerful insight that revealed what drives today's India. As a nation, Indians are in a rush to turn their dreams into glorious reality. Across geography and demographics, they are impatient to participate in the march to progress, and all they need is a two-wheeler to get them there faster. This dovetailed perfectly with Honda's own mission, across the world, and here in India.

To establish an emotional connect with the Indian masses, Honda roped in Bollywood superstar Akshay Kumar as its brand ambassador. Kumar, as the marquee ad for HMSI conveyed, had seen this journey from dreams to reality up close, succeeding as he did in Bollywood without a godfather, coming in from the unknown. He embodied that journey, knew its ups and downs, but also knew that once it got a little boost, nothing could come in its way. Aspiration and perspiration for turning dreams into reality were matched perfectly in Kumar, making him a credible spokesperson for Honda.

Bollywood superstar Akshay Kumar as brand ambassador

Most importantly, Honda was proceeding full throttle to create new benchmarks of success in the two-wheeler industry. This entailed challenging and ambitious network expansion, product innovation, aggressive investment for production expansion and more.

On the product side, Honda was finally free to enter the 100–110cc motorcycle segment which commands a nearly 42 per cent share in India's two-wheeler market. In this highly competitive mass motorcycle segment, Honda introduced Dream Yuga, its first 110cc mass motorcycle, in May 2012. The Dream series has originated at the hands of Honda Motor Company's founder Soichiro Honda, and is a perfect embodiment of the Power of Dreams, created as it was with the dream of providing mobility for all. With its accessible style and value offerings, Dream Yuga sales crossed 1 lakh units in just four months of its launch.

Creating capacity

By the end of 2011, Honda's first factory at Manesar was already running at its full annual production capacity of 1.6 million units. To serve its waiting customers better, the HMSI announced its second plant at Tapukara industrial area of Rajasthan, and it started operations in July 2011 with an initial annual production capacity of 0.6 million units. Still, with waiting time going up to a year on some products, demand for Honda's products far exceeded supply.

Taking a dynamic leap to accommodate present and the future demand, Honda announced plans to double the capacity of its Tapukara plant, and build a third two-wheeler plant in Narsapura area of Karnataka even while construction of Phase-I at Tapukara was being completed. The second plant started production in FY 2011 and expanded to its full capacity of 12 lakh units annually by FY 2012. Following this, the third plant started operations in May 2013 and expanded to its full capacity of 18 lakh units annually by FY 2014 end. It is noteworthy that in just three years, Honda has blazed new trails by almost trebling its annual production capacity from 16 lakh units in FY 2010–11 to 46 lakh units in FY 2013–14.

In 2013, HMSI launched its second Dream series mass motorcycle, Dream Neo. Differentiating Dream Neo from the existing crop of mass motorcycles was the key to driving sales.

In a category first, Honda brought advanced technology to the traditional 100–110cc 'bread-and-butter' motorcycle segment. Dream Neo was the first Honda motorcycle with revolutionary Honda Eco Technology or HET.

The HET advantage

With HET, Honda's engineers had achieved what until then had been deemed impossible for the segment—to increase power while boosting fuel efficiency. By working on the trio in engine technology—reducing friction, improving combustion and optimizing transmission—Honda had given Indian customers what they truly wanted, a super mileage. Customers visiting dealerships were overwhelmed by the fact that despite a new technology, which made Dream Neo the most fuel-efficient offering from Honda, it was also Honda's most affordable two-wheeler.

At the designing stage itself, Honda's engineers ensured that Dream Neo had a longer and wider seat, higher ground clearance and other features which made the model most suited for rural conditions.

On the positioning front too, Dream Neo was pitched as an expression of individual identity for those who strongly believed in themselves and wanted a motorcycle that stood out from the crowd. New India's new dreams were larger than life, much like Bollywood films. And each Indian was the hero of his own life, effortlessly overcoming obstacles in pursuit of his dreams. The tagline '*Apni film ka superstar*' (The superstar of one's own film) essentially reinforced the idea that every Dream Neo customer was the real superstar of his life. With Dream Neo, Honda rewrote the equation for commuter mass motorcycles in India.

With the Dream series (Dream Neo and Dream Yuga), Honda posted stellar growth of 196 per cent and almost quadrupled its market share in the mass motorcycle segment to 11 per cent (between 2011 and 2014).

The series brought in Honda's impressive legacy of reliability and durability into its Indian products.

On the motorcycle front, new products from the Dream series have now made Honda more relevant for semi-urban and rural India. Expanding brand reach into larger parts of India was paramount for both customer and network success.

All this while, ATSC success continued

- The ATSC segment's contribution to total two-wheeler sales grew exponentially from 14 per cent in 2010 to 25 per cent in 2014–15, indicating robust demand continuing in this segment.
- With an overwhelming 55 per cent market share, HMSI continues as the unchallenged market leader in this segment.
- Honda launched the new Activa-i, its most affordable ATSC in India, tapping new growth from the personal compact ATSC category which contributed almost 25 per cent of ATSC sales.

Honda's portfolio now covered all four broad ATSC categories—moto scooter (dio), family scooter (Activa 3G, Activa 125), premium scooter (Aviator) and personal compact scooter (Activa-i).

Scaling new heights

The Honda CB Shine meanwhile has overtaken many competing models in its segment to become India's all-time highest selling 125cc motorcycle. It is also the first ever 125cc motorcycle to touch the 30 lakh units sold mark. On the global platform too, CB Shine has raced ahead to become Honda Motor Company, Japan's No. 1 selling motorcycle across Honda's two-wheeler operations worldwide for the first time ending FY 2013–14.

HMSI is today the second-largest two-wheeler company in India. Its cumulative investment in India has crossed ₹6,000 crore and the tight core team has grown to a 20,000-strong Dream family! For the first time in the history of the Indian two-wheeler industry, an automatic scooter—Honda Activa—has overtaken the long-ruling motorcycle models to become the top two-wheeler seller in India with monthly sales crossing 2 lakh units. What Honda's unabated ascent demonstrates is its deep understanding of the Indian market and the ability to leverage changing market dynamics.

Honda 2.0—The four Es strategy to reach the hinterlands

After raising the bar high, by closing FY 2014 as its most successful year since inception and grabbing a 28 per cent market share, Honda's next challenge was to redefine excellence for itself. Entering a new and empowered phase from 1 July 2014, Honda has developed its Wave 2.0

CB Shine

master plan which shows how the brand can fully exploit the potential of India's hinterlands. Honda is now seeking to reach deeper into the hinterlands by concentrating on four Es—experience, extend, engage and expand brand Honda in India's rural markets and increase the rural share of the business from the current 25 per cent to 30 per cent. As part of the Wave 2.0 strategy, a new rural vertical was set up with focus on strategy, communication and implementation to increase the share of rural markets.

» Connecting the dots with last-mile initiatives—mobile service van, service on wheels

» Retail finance partnerships with national banks, gramin banks, cooperative banks and non-banking financial companies (NBFC) across India.

» Engaging with customers innovatively from kanwar melas to mandis, and roping in opinion leaders at panchayats as well as engaging directly with women in rural homes.

» Add 1,000 new touch points at a scorching three outlets a day to triple its network from 1,200 outlets in FY 2010–11 to 4,600 outlets by the end of FY 2015–16.

» From the product perspective, Honda made the Dream series most its affordable value offering with the launch of its entry commuter offering, CD 110 Dream.

» Reinforcing its differentiated brand imagery with 'Honda is Honda' (symbolized by the wing mark for its two-wheeler operations globally). The message is clear—the 'wings' of Honda stand for its time-tested reliability, technology and legacy of excellence, quality and innovation.

Sustaining the dream run

Honda understands that as long as there are people, there will always be the desire to move ahead. As a global leader with a rich legacy, Honda is ensuring that it doesn't merely fulfil customer demands of today with hurried unpreparedness. Instead, it is working on influencing future customer demand by creating experiences that lead every customer to truly believe that Honda equals reliability, reputation, innovation, safety, trust and transparency.

Honda is strengthening its 'Make in India' resolve through steady and strategic investments with a long-term objective of creating 39 per cent additional capacity within the three and a half years.

Foreseeing future increase in customer demand for automatic scooters, Honda is constructing its fourth plant in India at Ahmedabad, Gujarat. Once operational in early 2016, this plant will be the world's largest scooter-only plant of 12 lakh units annual capacity. Additionally, Honda will invest to build a new production line at its existing third plant in Karnataka before the end of 2016.

Overall, this will take Honda's cumulative production capacity to 6.4 million units—1.6 million units (first plant), 1.2 million units (second plant), 2.4 million units (third plant with upcoming new line) and 1.2 million units (upcoming fourth plant).

The year 2015 is set to create new records for the company. Under its 'Bigger, Better & Bolder' roadmap for FY 2015–16, Keita Muramatsu—president and CEO, HMSI and Honda Motor India—has announced a massive product blitzkrieg of 15 new models including 7 brand new models. Staying true to its commitment, Honda had already launched 10 models in just 7 months. One of these, CB Unicorn 160, marks Honda's entry into the new 150–200cc segment and has fast climbed to garner 30 per cent market share in this segment.

Taking the connect with fun-loving youth to new highs, Honda is set to unlock a 'New era of revolutionary fun-biking in India' with Honda REVFEST—Unleash the Power, India's grandest launch ever across eight cities on the same day! This will start the revolution of fun biking with CBR 650F—Honda's first in-line four-cylinder 650cc motorcycle to be made in India.

At stake is the world's biggest two-wheeler market. And every day, Honda is racing ahead while giving wings to millions of Indians and their dreams to soar to dizzy heights. Today, Honda can say with well-deserved confidence that it is well on its way to firmly entrenching the wing mark in the hearts and minds of its Indian customers.

CB Unicorn 160

Trailblazing success

2001   Honda Activa launched
2002   Dio—moto scooter
2003   Eterno—geared scooter
2004   150 cc CB Unicorn—performance motorcycle
2006   125 cc CB Shine—mainstream motorcycle
2008   125 cc CBF Stunner—sportz motorcycle
2010   110 cc CB Twister—stylish 110 cc motorcycle
        End of JV partnership with Hero
2012   Dream Yuga—first 110 cc mass motorcycle
2013   HET technology introduced in all Honda automatic scooters
        Dream Neo—second mass motorcycle
2014   New era as Only Honda begins
        CD 110 Dream—Honda's most affordable motorcycle in India
        Activa 125—Honda's most powerful automatic scooter
        Goldwing—Honda's iconic tourer lands in India
2015   CB Unicorn 160—Honda's stylish performance bike with HET
        Livo—fusion of modern design with practicality for first-time
        aspirational buyer in 110 cc segment
        CBR 650F—Honda's first 'Made in India' in-line four-cylinder engine
        motorcycle

SENSODYNE

CHANGING THE ORAL-CARE LANDSCAPE IN INDIA

*One great insight is worth
a thousand good ideas*
—Phil Dusenberry

B rand Sensodyne was not created on a mere idea because ideas, valuable as they may be, are dime a dozen, but an insight is rarer, deeper and, therefore, much more precious. Sensodyne's success clearly demonstrates the power of a strong insight. Like most iconic brands, Sensodyne has been a true game changer in its area of operation— the oral-care market in India. There are few brands that can boast a compelling story like that of Sensodyne in India, rooted in a simple yet powerful insight.

Sensodyne's big challenge

We would accomplish many more things if we did not think of them as impossible.

In the year 2011, when GlaxoSmithKline (GSK) decided to launch the Sensodyne brand in India, it knew that odds were heavily stacked against its success. Sensodyne was GSK Consumer Healthcare's No. 1 brand globally and was successfully positioned as an effective sensitivity-relief toothpaste, enjoying the tailwinds of a highly evolved international oral-care market. In developed markets, consumers understood dental health very well and specialized oral-care products and oral-care regimes were popular.

The Indian dental-care market had made a recent transition from tooth powder and neem sticks. The Indian branded toothpaste market was at a basic-benefit level where brands were mainly focusing on three benefits: freshness, cavity and germ-kill (80 per cent of the market). Numerous researches showed that consumers were happy with their current toothpastes and there was almost no need gap in the market, people being habituated to consuming basic-benefit toothpastes. Consumers did not have awareness of or did not care how different types of toothpastes addressed different oral problems; price was the typical deciding factor and the entire family used a single brand of toothpaste. There was fierce competition from heavyweight players who dominated the oral-care market in India. Local home remedies were the typical treatment for common dental problems.

It was a big challenge to successfully launch a global flagship brand in a market where the concept of specialized oral-care products did not exist. The consumer was not aware of tooth sensitivity as a problem and, therefore, did not see the need for a product with sensitivity-relief benefits. What made the task more uphill was the fact that *Sensodyne was a premium offering in this highly price-sensitive market (six times economy toothpastes)* coupled with low brand awareness levels among consumers. To create a market for a specialist toothpaste in the middle of all this appeared to be an insurmountable challenge.

Going glocal

The first step in dealing with any business problem is research. Data is collected so as to approach the problem with knowledge. As the data, analysis, numbers and opinions are reviewed, some outliers stick out. Intelligent analysis can bring these to the fore and that should lead to insights about the brand.

The Sensodyne team understood the importance of listening to consumers upfront and mounted comprehensive research to study the usage and attitudes of Indians towards dental hygiene. The research revealed some significant gaps in consumers' understanding:

» The sensitivity-awareness index in India stood at a low of 17 per cent versus 33 per cent globally.
» Although people suffered from sensitivity, they were unable to articulate the problem and were largely unaware that there existed a solution.
» Only 4 per cent of Indians visited dentists and most Indians did not follow proper oral-care hygiene practices (like brushing twice daily).

Sensodyne was the first to identify the gap between the existence of tooth sensitivity and awareness about the condition and its solution, and to realize the large business opportunity it presented.

The larger insight was the fact that consumers with sensitivity problems were not able to enjoy their favourite food and drinks.

The journey ahead was now clear and Sensodyne's innovative strategy for solving this consumer problem turned out to be the recipe behind the brand's success. The important idea was to build awareness and drive trials among the sensitivity sufferers to place the brand in their consideration set. Instead of gaining category share from other brands, the task clearly was to build the category from scratch and then make Sensodyne synonymous with the category in the long run.

The brand identified a clear task in building awareness around the condition of sensitivity and offering a simple, clinically proven effective solution in the form of Sensodyne.

Colgate had started advertising its desensitizing toothpaste Colgate Sensitive from 2007. Sensodyne became the first brand in its category to identify a gap in awareness around the condition called 'sensitivity' and created a comprehensive success story that is a clear example of how market leaders must be game changers to achieve success, combining the best of global knowledge with local insights.

Sensodyne was about five years behind its biggest competitor in launching a brand in the sensitivity-benefit segment. There were multiple local pharma players selling sensitivity toothpastes in India. However, these were sold on dentist recommendation only, and did not advertise. It was only from 2011, with Sensodyne's entry, that there was aggressive advertising, with both Colgate and Sensodyne investing behind media. Sensodyne adopted an educational approach to advertising, teaching consumers to identify the condition and then presenting the recommendation of the expert, the dentist in this case.

Building a go-to-market strategy with an edge

Given the high competition and the spends required to create a market, Sensodyne charted a very systematic and structured course for its India strategy. Its multi-pronged strategy involved intensive product development to get this essential building block in place, a comprehensive test marketing initiative and rigorous consumer and clinical research lasting over two-three years.

Refining the product to suit the Indian palate

Sensodyne's R&D team tweaked the product to suit the Indian palate and the local regulatory environment. Extensive research, conducted over two years, showed that Indians have very distinct product expectations as compared to global consumers. *Elements such as foaming and taste were the driving factors in making buying decision,* so the brand tested different levels of foaming and decided upon a mid-appropriate 'foaming' level for the Indian market. Given that the Indian taste palate is dramatically different from the western palate of GSK's other markets, the brand adopted a very rigorous process of testing different flavours with consumers. The flavour option that it finally went ahead with was a localized fresh mint flavour that appealed to the Indian palate and eventually became very popular with consumers.

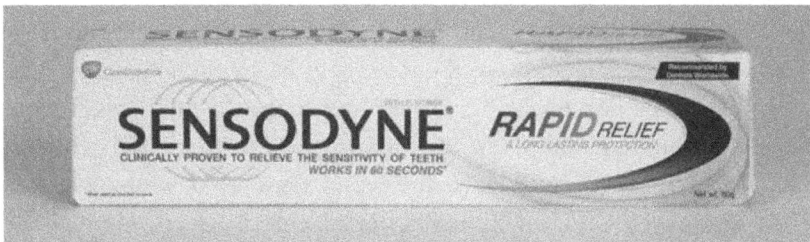

Proofing the go-to-market strategy in a comprehensive test market environment

Sensodyne's journey in India began with a test market in the south. Sensodyne chose south India owing to several factors that gave it an edge over other markets—media isolation, high literacy rate combined with it being a high-revenue-generation market for GSK.

The brand adopted a unique four-way matrix for the test marketing initiative with different operating levels in each of the markets, keeping in mind consumer preferences. The four-way matrix was based on metrics such as media share of voice, expert marketing, visibility and activation. The right mix of all these elements was necessary for the launch. This strategy allowed the brand to be nimble, proactive and responsive, and ensure course corrections based on real time consumer and market feedback.

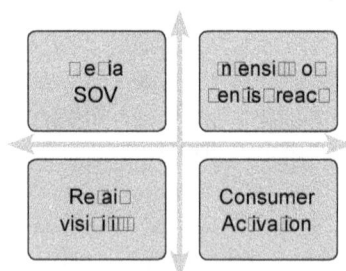

To illustrate, in a market like Tamil Nadu, the brand focused on high media share of voice (SOV), high expert marketing and low activation, whereas in Andhra Pradesh, it focused on high media SOV, low expert marketing but high activation. This was backed by rigorous research for almost a year. The test market gave numerous insights into consumers' psychographics. It revealed that consumers were seeking specialist products but would prefer listening to an 'expert' on their problems, however, they were hesitant in reaching out to them for help. Many such learnings, heavy investments in clinical research powered by a simple scientific visualization of the solution, have been instrumental in making the brand what it is today. This test marketing helped the brand draw up a winning strategy, paving the way for its launch across the country.

Innovative and extensive consumer activation: The winning stroke

The entire focus was on educating the consumer around the sensitivity condition and, therefore, Sensodyne invested heavily in taking the sensitivity challenge to the consumer's doorstep. The rationale was simple—consumers weren't aware of the problem called sensitivity and that there was a simple solution to the problem. Over the next three years, Sensodyne invested heavily in building awareness and educating the consumers about sensitivity through its extensive consumer outreach programme—chill tests at various high footfall areas, asking people to drink cold water. The simple yet effective tests made people realize that they unknowingly suffered from teeth sensitivity which was preventing them from enjoying foods and drinks which they could easily have done. When engaged in a conversation with the brand promoters, people recalled that they had experienced short sharp sensations earlier too, but had never taken them seriously. Once their curiosity was piqued, the brand promoters explained the benefits of Sensodyne to the sufferers. The 'Winning with a glass of chilled water' campaign for Sensodyne was extremely successful and fetched GSK the coveted Effie gold medal for the most innovative/best activation campaign in 2013.

Sensodyne's magic recipe: Deeper engagement with the dentist community

Building on the insight that consumers want to listen to experts, Sensodyne, in another significant outreach programme, redefined 'engagement' with the dentist community in India. Although competition had been engaging with the dentist community for a very long time, Sensodyne adopted a significantly different and more comprehensive approach.

Being a scientifically proven product, it was important for Sensodyne that experts in the category, that is dentists, have a strong understanding of the product's composition and benefits. As a global sensitivity expert, Sensodyne worked closely with dentists across the world and the success of this relationship lay in the credibility and trust it enjoyed amongst dental-care professionals. Globally, Sensodyne engaged with the dental community on a regular basis to update it on the latest developments in the area of teeth sensitivity.

As an extension of this critical aspect, Sensodyne launched the Dentist Outreach programme in India. It invested heavily in establishing a world-class medical detailing field force to strengthen the professional relationship and drive product education with the dentists on a long-term and consistent basis. Its medical representative teams interacted with dentists, meeting them frequently, educating them about the condition as well as the product. Sensodyne also invested in dentist camps to build salience around the condition. In a first of its kind initiative, Sensodyne partnered with leading experts of the dental-care community to create a 'sensitivity guideline' document to help dental experts and professionals make informed decisions on sensitivity and build awareness around the condition.

The outcomes were heartening. *As per research conducted among dentists by TNS (Taylor Nelson Sofres)—an independent market-research firm—in early 2014, Sensodyne emerged as the clear leader in the sensitive toothpaste category and was voted 'most recommended' brand by dentists surveyed across the country. Eight out of ten dentists recommended Sensodyne to their patients suffering from sensitivity, helping Sensodyne become the No. 1 brand in the category.*

Marketing campaigns designed to project authenticity

Unlike western markets, only 4 per cent of Indians visit dentists, the key influencers for this category. To overcome this challenge, Sensodyne got the dentists into the drawing room instead. Unlike other players in the Indian market, Sensodyne did not follow the oft-repeated formula using models, celebrities or catchy jingles in its advertisements. Instead, the brand chose to go with its 'authentic, professional and understated' brand promise and used real dentists practising in the UK and other parts of the world in its communication, without scripting their message. This worked wonders for the brand and helped establish Sensodyne as a dentist-recommended brand in India.

The media strategy matched this step for step. Given the high levels of competitiveness and clutter in the Indian market, with maintenance GRP (gross rating points) levels being 1.5 times higher than global averages, Sensodyne chose to run a unique media outreach programme through various innovations and associations, making it seem larger that it was to the audience. The brand broke through the so-called 'lifestyle or beauty products' domain and introduced a product-integration concept with Sensodyne integrations in ongoing popular daily soaps, a category first. It was a strategy that clearly helped the brand garner market share rapidly.

SENSODYNE

35% of adults complain of a sharp sensation in their teeth when having hot, cold or sugary food.

Are you one of them?

Dr. Anuksha Khanna
Dentist, Practising in the UK

Solving for the crucial 'P': Placement

The other big challenge for the brand lay in retail outreach. So far, toothpaste brands were seen as 'just another item on the grocery list' and were stacked way behind on the shelf—almost to a point of no visibility. To solve this challenge of product visibility, Sensodyne introduced shelf highlighters and shelf-in-shelf concepts, and used bay flags extensively to enhance salience at the point of sale.

Till the launch of Sensodyne, specialist toothpaste brands had been sold only through pharmacies. Sensodyne was the first in its category to tie up with Big Bazaar in an exclusive ten-day preview. In those days, Big Bazaar, being the largest modern retail chain, provided the brand with a perfect opportunity and platform to drive activation and generate buzz. Sensodyne's unique retail strategies have not only benefited the brand but also encouraged retailers to provide it prime placement in their outlets.

Shaping a portfolio strategy

Over the next two years, Sensodyne strengthened its sensitivity portfolio to four segmented offerings:

1. **Sensodyne** (fresh mint and gel)
2. **Sensodyne Rapid Relief**, which is clinically proven to instantly relieve pain of sensitive teeth.
3. **Sensodyne Repair and Protect** that contains patented NovaMin® technology, which finds vulnerable areas of the tooth where dentine is exposed and forms a tooth-like layer over them.

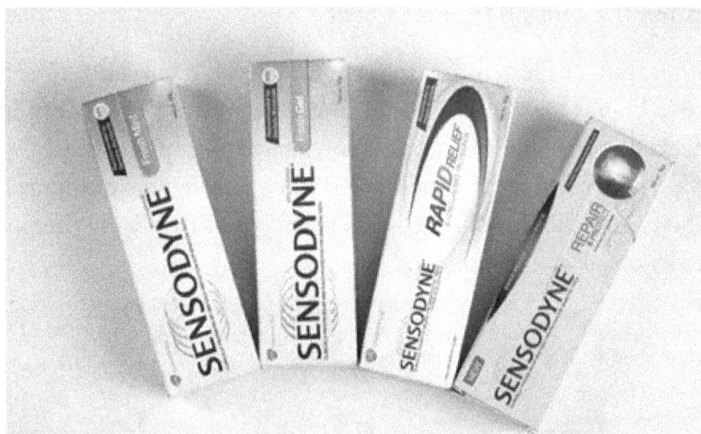

4. **Sensodyne Toothbrush**, designed for sensitive teeth, available in Soft and Extra Soft variants and gentle on sensitive teeth for better care.

Sensodyne's offerings cater to specific conditions that people suffer from and provide them with expert solutions and specialist benefits. This helps the brand strengthen its sensitivity expert positioning and leadership in the market.

Scripting an inspirational success story: From an entrant to an iconic brand in just three years

Three years into its launch, Sensodyne was an inspirational success story. Within this short span, the brand was already a market leader in its segment, having overtaken a major brand by a huge margin.

» The brand has crossed numerous milestones in its journey, achieving business of ₹150+ crore in year three of launch. At retail prices, this category was worth over ₹600 crore (FY 2014).
» It commands over 27 per cent market share in the sensitivity category, boasts a market position 160 per cent of its nearest competitor and has a 3 per cent share of the total toothpaste market in India.
» Sensodyne became the No. 1 brand retailed by chemists.[1]
» In 2013, *The Economic Times* described Sensodyne as the most successful personal-care launch in recent decades.
» A key success indicator was the significant rise in India's sensitivity awareness index to global levels, moving from 17 per cent (2010) to 32 per cent (2013).[2]
» Sensodyne's success continued with it being ranked as the No. 1 sensitive toothpaste brand recommended by dentists across India.[3]

For Sensodyne, this was just the beginning of the road. There is still a vast population suffering from sensitivity and doing nothing about the condition. Going forward, the brand aims to grow the category by touching more lives through consistent education. Sensodyne's vision is focused and simple: to create a future where every life is sensitivity free.

[1]Nielsen.
[2]TNS Sensitivity Research, 2013.
[3]TNS, January 2014.

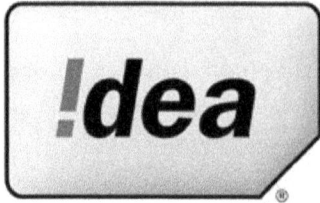

THE IDEA STORY

*Our vision is simple. We want to be the
number one Telecom Operator in the minds
of the customers, the most Trusted Brand and
number one Employer in the minds of our
employees. We keep challenging ourselves to
continuously reinvent, in order to meet the
evolving needs of the growing Indian population
and employee aspirations.*
—Himanshu Kapania,
managing director, Idea Cellular

I t is often said that nothing succeeds like
success. In the context of brands, this
aphorism assumes a certain predictable
momentum in the course of a brand's journey
that not only helps it gain acceptability in the
market but also translates the growth in terms
of financial strength. But the most optimistic
and extravagant interpretation of success can't
even begin to capture the kind of exponential,
and almost stratospheric growth that brand
Idea has experienced in less than a decade.

Behind Idea's success was its audacious
belief that it existed to empower India and
change the lives of people. It was the cause

of action. It is this 'sense of purpose' that has made Idea India's fastest-growing telecom company.

Numbers that spell a success story

To highlight just a few parameters, the customer base has grown 10.7 times, from 14 million across eleven circles in March 2007 to a mind-boggling 150 million across twenty-two circles by December 2014. In terms of infrastructure too, 29,000 cell sites in March 2007 have increased to over 133,000 sites in December 2014. Consequently, the revenue is estimated to leap 6.9 times, from US$730 million in FY 2007 to over US$5,000 million in FY 2015. Consequently, the earnings before interest, taxes, depreciation and amortization (EBITDA) will witness a similar 6.7 times jump, from US$196 million in FY 2007 to over US$1,660 million in FY 2015. As a result of this stupendous growth, Idea's customer market share rank has leapfrogged from a shared No. 6 to a clear No. 3. Idea's journey has taken it from the position of India's No. 6 telecom operator to that of the world's No. 6 telecom service provider in terms of subscribers and minutes traffic.

But the story of brand Idea is not just about market success. It's a story of the proverbial underdog that overcomes the odds, the story of David, slaying quite a few Goliaths along the way. As Idea's managing director (MD) Himanshu Kapania puts it:

Our success can be attributed to a transformed mind-set. One could have gone around like a timid bit player, but we held our head high and had the courage and conviction to act like a leader.

We have transitioned from a marginal, regional player to the fastest growing telecom operator, now one among the top three, from a privately held company to a publicly traded one at multiple times our EBITDA and also one that has seen a structural shift in business from Mobile Voice to Data. But all through these changes, two fundamental cultural tenets have remained the same—*Customer Centricity and Employee Orientation.*

History of Idea

Idea's journey in India dates back to 1995, when the Aditya Birla Group and AT&T (through Birla AT&T in Maharashtra and Gujarat) and the Tata Group (through Tata Cellular in Andhra Pradesh) were among the pioneering operators to set up cellular networks. In the year 2000, the three players increased their range of operations. A merger and the subsequent acquisition of RPG Cellular, Madhya Pradesh circle, led to the formation of Birla Tata AT&T Limited.

Till 2002, it was part of a consortium under the umbrella brand of BATATA (Birla, AT&T, Tata). With the mobile landscape dominated by a few big players (Airtel and Vodafone), it was operating in Maharashtra, Gujarat, Andhra Pradesh and Madhya Pradesh. In Maharashtra it operated under the brand name AT&T, in Madhya Pradesh under the brand name RPG and in Andhra Pradesh under the name Tata Cellular. This was also the time the company obtained a licence for Delhi. It was now important to introduce a common identity across all its circle of operations and leverage the benefit of a common brand name. *On 1 May 2002, the company changed its brand name from Birla Tata AT&T Limited to Idea Cellular Limited.*

In 2004, Idea Cellular concluded the largest-ever acquisition in the Indian mobile industry with the acquisition of Escotel, enhancing Idea's network to about 60 per cent of India's population. However, Idea Cellular was still not a national player and it was only in 2007—eleven years into its existence—that it shed its complex parentage and found its identity as an Aditya Birla Group company.

Building a brand new Idea

By 2007, some of the world's leading telecom brands had entered India with huge advantages in terms of scale, technology, process and financial muscle. Idea, on the other hand, was ranked a lowly No. 7, with even its own investors and employees sceptical about its success.

With five existing players becoming pan-India GSM (global system for mobile communication) operators and three new players entering the market, the battle for urban India became extremely intense. Idea decided to pursue a contrarian path and explore the market that constituted 'Bharat'.

The hinterland in any case comprised fifteen of Idea's established markets. Today, these markets deliver a whopping 95 per cent of Idea's revenues and 100 per cent of its EBITDA. *As the result of single-minded pursuit, Idea today has 55 per cent of India's rural subscribers.* More significantly, mobile penetration in rural areas is still just 41 per cent of the 860 million rural population, pointing to huge unmet demand for basic voice-based mobile services.

Given the fact that Idea in 2007 was a small, marginal player targeting the hinterland with limited resources and up against the world's largest and most competitive brands, it decided to adopt a bold policy—think, talk and behave like a national brand.

Consciousness at one level is about understanding where we are in the play. At another level, it is about understanding our position in the play—top dog, underdog or somewhere in the middle. And consciousness at a third or an altogether different level is about stimulating the future.

Only visionary and path-breaking brands have the ability to see that far into the future. Idea chose to belong to that club. It needed to be that to stand out. And to do that, the brand also adopted three crucial norms—customer centricity, people orientation and the pursuit of excellence through execution.

To once again quote Himanshu Kapania:

> Despite our size now in 2014, we are still a ₹30,000 crore start-up. Our leaders behave like that—entrepreneurial, nimble, collaborative and agile. Our business model is to ensure that our Circle Heads are empowered to act like mini CEOs, with a customer focus, adaptable to change while pursuing growth and profitability goals.

The marketing Idea

The story of Idea is essentially that of a late-entrant, marginalized, challenger brand that joined the big league of the Indian mobile telecom market by the sheer strength of its ability as a brand to create a deeper meaning for people in their lives.

It's the engaging tale of a 'storied brand', one that delved deep into the power of story-telling with a sharp and insightful cultural context, to establish meaningful brand conversations.

It's the engrossing account of a brand that has consistently connected to its audience with relatable episodes that unfailingly prove that '*an idea can change your life*'.

At the time of its brand launch in 2002, as part of a consortium under the umbrella brand of BATATA, the mobile landscape was dominated by a few big players, brands that today go by the names of Airtel and Vodafone.

These brands were not only operating in a large number of telecom circles but also dominated the urban areas, especially the leading metros. Their extensive national presence as well as their intensive brand-led communication ensured that these market leaders had an enviable share of mind amongst the influential urban audiences.

As Himanshu Kapania says, 'In our brand positioning, we chose not to drumbeat tired attributes like network, product features, price or promotions. We are not the biggest, but that did not stop us from thinking like a champion. Our USP is our bold mind-set.'

Even in 2007, when the Aditya Birla Group decided to go it alone, the odds were definitely stacked against Idea. Operating in just a few service areas and no metros, Idea had to think different to even register its presence, let alone beat the competition. Every facet of the brand had to be nuanced just right to gain a far greater advantage than the brand's resources and presence would allow.

For instance, the brand name was originally conceived in 2002, after much deliberation to connote not just the power of the category but also the power to change cultures, and hence lives, through innovation. It was a simple word, very commonly used and understood. The two-syllable 'idea', with its good, positive association was perfect even for those with limited vocabulary. It is amongst the top 100 most commonly used words across the sixteen official languages in India, and, remarkably, it means the same thing in all of them.

Besides, once the point of view of the brand—*an idea can change your life*—was coined, it even enabled the brand name to be integrated seamlessly into a phrase. Even visual elements like the bright yellow brand colour, the connotation of a SIM card for the logo and the exclamation mark incorporated into the brand name had the synergistic effect of giving the brand a saliency and recall way beyond what the company's meagre resources could afford at that point.

To elaborate, all mass-cultural expressions—whether a film or retail store design or pack graphics—rely on elements for which the meaning has been well established historically in the culture or compose a new one. Cultural codes provide shorthand for consumers, allowing them to easily understand and experience the intended meanings.

In a telecom world dominated by red and blue, yellow is an uplifting and illuminating colour, offering hope, happiness, cheerfulness and fun. In the meaning of colours, yellow inspires original thought and inquisitiveness. Yellow is the colour of creativity, the colour of new ideas, helping find new ways of doing things. It is the colour of the practical thinker, not the dreamer. And above all, it is a colour sacred to Indians and Indian culture.

The exclamation mark means multiple things in multiple contexts. For Idea, it signifies the 'Aha!' moment—the instant at which the solution or idea to any problem becomes clear, the experiential moment of the brand when one had a sudden realization or an insight.

According to Sashi Shankar, the brand's chief marketing officer, 'Idea's vast management programmes are created to serve new markets for existing products. At Idea, our job is always to create new and difficult markets which competition identifies as unprofitable.'

The HR Idea

Up until 2006, Idea was not really big. As it was not yet an aspirational brand, it was tough to attract the right talent and to even be called for campus selections. But with the change in ownership in 2007, everything began to change.

Not only did Idea retain all 3,000 team members, it also invested heavily in them. It wanted to develop an egalitarian culture, one that was non-hierarchical and driven purely by the quality of ideas that people brought to the table.

With business expansion came new opportunities. Most of the demand for talent was met by organic growth, through training and promotions.

All companies access the same talent pool. What differentiates Idea from competition is the ownership of the people who work at Idea that is a shade higher than anywhere else. There is an emotional bond they share with the company and their peer group. This collaborative team spirit is a key driver in today's business context. Besides, the large base of cross-functional teams helps prepare leaders for the future.

People orientation was achieved with people satisfaction scores going up and people enjoying working with Idea. From a mere 3,000 people in 2006, Idea today has a staff of 25,000. Last year, Idea won the Best Employer award at the Asian Communications Forum. Yet, it believes in staying grounded in reality rather than becoming intoxicated by success. The Idea team likes to believe that they are ordinary people who deliver extraordinary results.

As Vinay Razdan, the company's chief human resource officer, says:

> There are varied leadership styles in our army of leaders. Some swear by strategy, some by their people, some by customer centricity and others by execution—but all of them are clear that they have growth at the centre of their agenda. These high growth gladiators have led the company with élan and vigour, despite a challenging economic environment.

The network Idea

For a telecom company, network is the equivalent of the factory in the manufacturing industry. Almost 95 per cent of the capital expenditure goes in developing the network. From 550 sites in 2006, Idea has grown to a staggering 133,000+ 2G and 3G sites today, the fastest-growing telecom infrastructure in the industry.

Idea became a pan-India network in 2G services only as late as in 2010, against national players who had registered their pan-India presence by 2002–4. Idea is the only telecom brand to build, operate and maintain its own network—a testimony to its comfort with technology. In an environment where leading brands outsourced technical services, Idea built its telecom infrastructure in-house and still maintained the lowest churn rate in terms of employee turnover owing to constant training and retraining programmes for its people.

A measure of Idea's equal attention to both customer service and network quality can be gauged from the fact that all the system upgrades at Idea are done only between 12.30 and 3.30 a.m. so as not to inconvenience customers. It is truly proud of its executional details as that has been the key to its success.

To quote Anil Tandon, Idea Cellular's chief technology officer, 'Telecom is an unforgiving sector. The room for error is small.'

The distribution Idea

Once a 'minutes factory' is set up at a location, where minutes are destroyed the moment they are manufactured if not consumed immediately, a sales force has to follow it to convert the minutes into consumer traffic. Idea recognized how crucial it was to get its sales model right and got cracking immediately. While leading the charge into rural India, it created probably India's first deep rural direct distribution model.

Till 2008–9, even the largest of fast-moving consumer goods (FMCG) companies in India serviced rural retailers and 'rural-stockists' through a larger distributor based out of the nearby big town. This was supplemented in some cases with 'van activities' or participation through stalls and kiosks in weekly or monthly melas and haats. Idea rejected all these models as secondary and made 'direct rural distribution' its primary model. It appointed distributors directly in small towns and villages as close together as 10–15 km and as far as 100–120 km away from the larger towns in a district. These distributors had direct access to Idea just like their urban counterparts and got their stock replenished by Idea as and when they needed without having to wait for a monthly or weekly trip by the 'super-stockist' from town. This model not only established distributors who took brand Idea and its flagship ₹10 paper voucher deep into surrounding villages but also built a corpus of loyal and rooted business partners who values Idea for reaching out directly to them.

The company followed up this by recruiting its last mile field sales force, which managed these rural distributors from the local area, under its pioneer 'son of the soil' scheme. Idea's territory sales executives came from within 20 km of its base location under this scheme so that local youth did not have to travel far from their homes to find gainful employment. This also supplied Idea with stable and dedicated employees who could work and stay near their homes while spreading business deep into the hinterland.

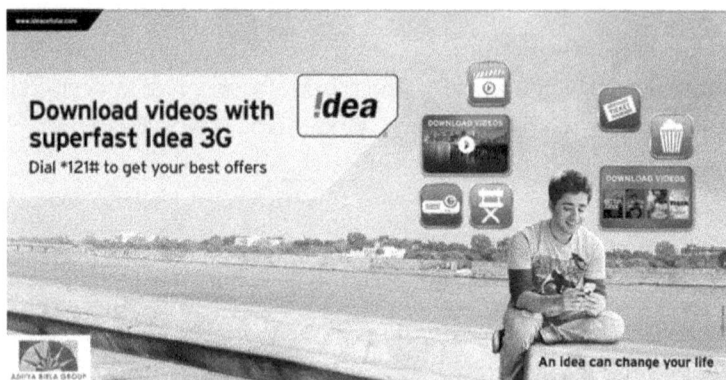

Idea's distributors in 2014 numbered over 30,000 across the length and breadth of the country, serving over 1.4 million outlets, reaching to within a stone's throw of its remotest customers. *This distribution network is till date one of the widest across any brand in any sector.*

The service Idea

When Idea embarked on a new journey in 2007, it had two crucial gaps to fill—world-class IT systems and customer-centric service. As the two were inter-linked, both had to happen or improve. Hence, the company had to transform and build scale capable of handling transactions manifold its volumes in 2007. Thus came into being 'One Idea. One service'. Idea was the first company in the world to launch the largest-ever integrated prepaid customer relationship management (CRM) and IT platform in

2007–8, providing unified information and ability to manage customer relationships. An Idea customer could therefore call any of its 15,000 strong contact centre team spread across India or walk into 6,000+ Idea service centres to learn, complain or upgrade their services.

At Idea call centres, customers have a choice of being responded to in seventeen different languages. To do this, it recruits people from towns and villages where people speak the same dialect, not just a major language. Idea has 25,000 people involved in 1.6 million interactions every single day, with a massive success rate.

In the last seven years, Idea has grown from 350 (own plus franchisee) outlets to a phenomenal 6,000 service centres across 4,400 towns. The larger Idea's network grows, the more intimate is its relationship with its customers, as the company has adopted the neighbourhood kirana store model—get as close to the customer as possible. For instance, as people in villages are apprehensive of taking support from 'telephonic' call centres, the company has stationed fully trained Idea representatives at the local service centres to assist and support customer needs in voice and emerging data business. These customer care officers, therefore, develop a close, personal understanding of the problems involved at the micro level.

This model is also being used in rolling out the latest mobile Internet services. With the complexity of different devices and multiplicity of operating systems and Apps, Idea is educating customers at contact centres handling over 5 million calls per day. All this has enabled Idea to steadily improve customer satisfaction, placing it at *No. 1 position for the last five quarters in a customer satisfaction survey conducted by IMRB*. Idea continues to innovate its services, like the recent launch of its super-specialist segmented Service Plus programme for premium customers that ensures one-touch access to services depending on the loyalty segment category of the customer.

Navanit Narayan, chief delivery officer of the company, believes, 'Set scary unrealistic goals to get employees to innovate and come up with breakthrough ideas. Mismatch between aspiration and resources is a necessary condition for any breakthrough thinking—and the key to a contrarian approach.'

Story-telling, by speaking a different language

The story of Idea is incomplete without its game-changing advertising. To reflect Idea's inspiring brand attributes, it was essential for the brand to develop communication that projected this larger-than-life yet down-to-earth persona of the brand, flagging social and cultural issues that had to be resolved, rather than communicating mundane, feature-led, tactical benefits.

Idea's communication was never inward looking. It was not about the products that needed to be sold. It was about how the use of Idea mobile services could impact the customer's life positively. Therefore, the brand followed them to address the issues close to their lives.

Idea believed that conventional branding is characterized by dog-eat-dog fights to outdo competitors on a conventional set of benefits—either rational or emotional, both of which are traps. Both the functional and emotional approaches imply that branding is about embedding associations between brand and valued benefits in consumers' minds. And as a property of mind, the brand and valued benefits are both assumed to be durable and context-less, often resulting in degrees of comparison between brands. In a parity world where there is hardly any difference between one brand and the other, they fall short of creating deeper meanings with people.

Idea wanted the brand to be based not just on a big idea, but on a big ideal. Vital as ideas are, Idea wanted to be built on the underpinning of an ideal that gives guidance to all aspects of the brand. It wanted the brand to project a certain point of view, its deeply held conviction on how the world, or some particular part of it, should be. In short, its point of view is the brand's declaration of what it believes in and why it behaves as it does.

'An idea can change your life' isn't just an idea but Idea's ideal (point of view) of creating telephony solutions to life issues.

Brand Idea's point of view was expressed as 'An Idea can change your life', while the brand promise was 'a simple telephony idea can solve a big problem'. Idea combined the above thoughts with its belief that a brand needed to have a cultural context, and developed a refreshing brand communication that teemed with innovative cultural expressions.

Idea wanted to be society's ultimate problem solver. Not with a missionary zeal but in an entertaining way. Each time the team asked 'what is the real big problem our brand can solve' and then found an innovative telephony idea to solve it.

As Sunita Bangard, president, marketing, puts it,

Our belief is that brands are a product of society, culture and politics. Therefore we adopted a cultural brand strategy to deliver a unique and innovative cultural expression that permeates society and provide people the building blocks with which to construct meaningful stories of their lives. We looked at Idea as a prime commercial vehicle for marketing cultural expressions, riding on opportunities for innovations created by cultural/historical changes in society.

Tackling social issues with an Idea

Through the years, the brand captured the culturally relevant issues of the country—caste wars, education, democracy, health, environment, language barriers and population control—in various memorable stories and demonstrated how a simple telephony idea can positively impact/ change the lives of people in any of these contexts. This approach, in the course of five plus years since it started, has given Idea cultural authority and not just brand authority.

In fact, the expression 'What an Idea Sirji' has now become part of popular culture, used liberally by the man on the street whenever someone has to be applauded for their out-of-the-box suggestions.

The first story was a television commercial (TVC) on caste wars, with the conflict resolution coming in the form of Idea phone numbers that would henceforth be the new identity of the masses. This was followed in quick succession by TVCs on democracy, where people are consulted by political leaders on important issues through the mobile phone; health, where people are urged to walk while they talk into their mobiles to aid health and fitness; education, where children in remote schools with a shortage of teachers are taught through mobile phones; environment, where a paperless society that uses mobile phones is promoted to counter the felling of trees; population, where engaging 3G content keeps young couples from indulging in procreation as recreation; language, where young

Indians overcome language barriers with the help of mobile phones; relationships, where a couple save their marriage as a mobile phone helps them appreciate each other's issues; and the latest series on the Internet, which tells people to '*Ullu mat bano*' by staying more informed with the help of mobile Internet. In each one of these stories, Idea was seen as the ultimate problem solver, not with a missionary zeal but in an entertaining way.

Idea also tackled the issue of a wider network reach in every corner of the country through the wildly popular 'Honey Bunny' executions that not only made the ring tone a favourite with millions but also conclusively established that Idea is now a major national player with a footprint to match its largest competitors.

Most of these ideas have later come to the fore in real life, emphasizing Idea's marketing practice of foresight over insight in everything it does.

Mobile Internet access, the new game

In business, as in sport, leadership, these is no permanent victory. Voice mobility has reached 886 million Indians. But the next big idea is the mobile data game. In 2013, 210 million Indians had access to the Internet,

while 188 million accessed the Internet on their mobile phones, and more than 600 million are waiting to be connected in the next four–five years. This is equally true of both Bharat and India. Clearly, Internet on mobile plays a central role in the transition to a digital lifestyle. And Idea is keen on transitioning to a balanced voice and data player in the near future.

Communicating better with a distinctive voice

The cultural coding of Idea's communication doesn't just connect with a wide cross-section of audiences for its relevance and creativity but has also given the brand a distinctly unique image and voice amongst the competition.

In today's context, even a high-technology product doesn't create the difference. The difference lies in the story, because the story is what drives the bond between the brand and the consumer. If anything, Idea's journey over the last decade has proved convincingly that a storied brand doesn't just connect better, and in a more relevant manner, with its varied audiences because of its engaging stories, but also has the ammunition to pull off a brilliant marketing success story.

It's no mean feat to stand at US$409 billion in just twelve years of existence and rival some of the big brands in history that have taken a good seventy-five years or more to reach that mark. While that is just the numerical data, all tracks of human data show that brand Idea to consumers is less like a service and more like a beloved friend and this affection is rooted in emotion, identity and personal philosophy.

Says Himanshu Kapania, 'During our seven-year journey, we have imbibed a number of powerful attributes. We have learned to think big, act fast but with honesty, integrity and transparency. We have imbibed a culture of meritocracy, nurtured an army of leaders and scaled up operations with legendary discipline.'

Our Idea of the future

Lastly, creativity in business is this amazing intersection between a company's imagination and the reality in which they exist. The problem is, many companies don't have great imagination, but their view of reality tells them that it's impossible to do what they imagine. For Idea, it's that consistent combination of creativity with effectiveness that continuously endows resources to create new and more wealth.

The fact that technology has been changing all of our lives at a breathtaking pace makes this a great time to be creative. Fortunately, the speed of change hasn't tempered humanity's fascination with an impulse towards creativity—it has actually fuelled it. So it's critical to have a spirit to solve as well as a spirit to create.

Idea's learnings in this epochal journey are immense. If one had to capture some, they would be:

Customer centricity: Base brand strategy with the customer at its heart.

Clarity of purpose: Define purpose, have conviction in it, and follow it consistently.

Innovation: It is not necessarily a product or a service, it can be a promise, process or proposition.

Differentiation: Create and convey a distinct proposition in both purpose and communication.

Relevance: Follow the consumer and continue to be relevant.

Ahead of the curve: Keep a finger on the pulse of the market and change before you are forced to.

Hopefully, this story of Idea opens a door. Maybe it has planted a seed that will enable your company/brand to start telling its own story. Opportunities abound and the door lies wide open.

Himanshu Kapania, the MD, sums up the company's future policy, 'Our future goal is not to be complacent about our growth leadership position. We will continue to be a contrarian brand, constantly challenging ourselves and annoying the competition, and ensure that we always lead, both on thoughts and practice in real and digital worlds.'

ECOSPORT
The making of a success story

Go Further

A market is never saturated with a good product.
—Henry Ford

Apopular automotive blog in India captured the frenzy around the Ford EcoSport launch in 2012 in these words, 'A local Ford showroom was holding a dealer launch, with snacks to welcome customers. I guess they would need a lot of samosas today because the number of people walking in a Ford dealership easily outnumbers the amount of walk-ins in a Hero showroom [two-wheeler showrooms have significantly higher footfall]. If you haven't met your friends lately, you are bound to clash into them at a Ford showroom near you, I know, I met a few childhood buddies who came to check out the EcoSport.'

Taken together, this real life situation and Henry Ford's quote are reason enough for the story of the great marketing success of Ford EcoSport to be recounted here.

The first-generation Ford EcoSport as a mini sport utility vehicle (SUV) was being built in Brazil by Ford Brazil since 2003 and it was the time for the second generation to be brought to India. Ford EcoSport was a perfect example of how Ford's global One Ford strategy works.

The Ford philosophy

The One Ford philosophy was initiated in September 2006, when Alan Mulally was appointed chief executive officer (CEO) of Ford Motor Company. The major component of the strategy was belonging to one team and having a single plan for a global enterprise.

Traditionally, while Ford's regional operations functioned as autonomous business units, the One Ford philosophy encapsulated the concept of a unified entity that knit together disparate operating units.

To describe One Ford in Alan Mulally's words,

At the heart of our culture is the One Ford plan, which is essentially our vision for the organization and its mission. And at the heart of the One Ford plan is the phrase "One Team." Those are more than just words. We really expect our colleagues to model certain behaviors. People here really are committed to the enterprise and to each other. They are working for more than themselves. We are a global company, so we really have to stay focused on the work. There are so many people around the world involved in our daily operations that it has to be about more than a single person—it truly has to be about the business. Some prefer to work in a different way. Ultimately, they will either adopt the Ford culture, or they will leave.

Under Alan Mulally, Ford has been following the One Ford plan, leveraging its global assets and building vehicles that people wanted and valued. The One Ford plan embodies Ford's global business strategy and it was time to bring it to India as a market where Ford had been present since 1995.

Tracing Fords' India journey

Ford started in India through a joint venture company with Mahindra and

Mahindra (M&M) with 50:50 equity participation. Mahindra Ford India Ltd was formed to assemble and distribute the company's first product, the Ford Escort. In February 1999, Ford Motors increased its stake to 85 per cent and the company was rechristened Ford India Ltd. In 2005, Ford India became a wholly owned subsidiary of Ford Motor Company, after divestment of its crossholding portfolio with M&M.

During this period, the company launched many products including Ford Escort, Ford Fusion, Ford Endeavour and, most importantly, a mid-size car specifically for the Indian market—the Ford Ikon. Ford Ikon was the first car which gave Ford a view of the attributes important to Indian buyers. There was overwhelming response in the Indian car market to the Ford Ikon, reflected in its excellent sales. It became the largest selling car in its category in the corresponding year. Ford Ikon proved that it is imperative to understand the special needs of the market in order to be successful.

With continued growth of core global platforms, the B segment was the most competitive for Ford to play a role in and ensure success in India. Ford remained committed to playing a pivotal role in the next phase of growth in India's automotive industry, which is expected to grow up to 7 million vehicles by 2020.

Ford was also not new to the segment which had been outpacing the industry for almost a decade to come. Ford Figo was the first product with which Ford marked its entry into the volume-driven small-car segment. The Figo was a distinct product, targeted squarely at first-time car buyers, enticing them with an unmatched value proposition packed with convenience features uncommon to its segment.

The Figo aided Ford in capturing new customers, with a whopping 60 per cent of them being first-time buyers. Till today, Ford Figo continues to take the B growth story forward along with the other products like the Ford Fiesta which targets the enthusiast consumer and demonstrates Ford's technological prowess.

Ford India had delivered a successful product in Figo but as the customers grew and aspired to move up the ladder, there was a need to grow along and elevate their experience by bringing a distinct product that stood out from the crowd and created a segment of its own.

The quest for differentiation

The challenges for Ford were diverse—continue to be a strong player in the B segment; spot voids in the already crowded segment; identify a product from its global portfolio without making it a force fit and, most importantly, understand the evolution of the quintessential 'smart and aspiring customers' from the B segment.

After copious amounts of coffee and numerous meetings spanning several months, Ford identified 'Sameer', a young, dynamic individual, more than thirty years of age, married with one child, living with parents in a very Indian set-up with an average monthly household income between ₹70,000 and ₹100,000.

Being a well-informed urban citizen who had benefitted from India's economic growth, Sameer seemed interested in a vehicle that was fresh off the shelf, a head-turner and a reflection of his young, confident outlook. Sameer owned a hatchback, probably a Swift, an i20 or a Figo, and aspired to upgrade to a bigger, bolder vehicle that matched his growing social stature. His ideal vehicle would give him the freedom to commute hassle-free within the city and also head out for those perfect weekend holidays.

The challenge was to find a differentiator as a marketer! In the exhaustive time spent on research, Ford found out that most of the customers like Sameer were upgrading to three-box sedans even though they actually aspired to own an SUV. *The research revealed that customers wanted a vehicle that offered the manoeuvrability and fuel economy of a compact car, with the practicality and robustness of an SUV.* However, in absence of any suitable choices to suit their pockets, they settled for sedans.

SUVs were notionally considered off-roaders and introducing an SUV in the B segment seemed a contradiction in terms!

For a company looking for a suitable answer, the stakes were high but so was the confidence. Everybody knew that the time to challenge the quintessential notion of SUV had come!

Venturing into an all-new category

Ford turned to the One Ford plan and worked with global teams to develop a vehicle that best suited the needs of the target customer in India.

The brand EcoSport was created a decade ago in South America, where an innovative new SUV, especially suited to the compact-car market, was first introduced. The name combines the economical value this product offers customers with lifestyle appeal and sporting spirit that make it inviting and ready for work or play.

Now, with the second generation, Ford Motor Company was harnessing the power of One Ford to create innovative new global products to meet customers' aspirations but not before they had been tested for safety, affordability and fuel efficiency.

But it could not be a force fit. As part of the product development process, Ford involved Indian engineers to conduct extensive tests and ensure that the vehicle was optimally customized to deliver on the aspirations of Indian customers.

Ford EcoSport was targeted at changing the definition of SUVs. As an essential SUV, Ford EcoSport had to enable drivers to discover new possibilities in busy urban lives. Its intuitiveness had to keep them connected without losing out on safety and convenience.

Positioning the Ford EcoSport: Capable, Contemporary and Compact

'EcoSport has a tough, robust attitude that says "I can play with the big boys",' said J. Mays, group vice president, Design, and chief creative officer, Ford Motor Company, about the car. 'But it also makes you want to play. EcoSport is perfect for crowded urban streets and it inspires you to seek adventure away from the city too.'

First introduced as a concept at the New Delhi Auto Show in 2012, Ford EcoSport took the world by storm. The new EcoSport had a completely modern look, shaped by Ford's new global design language, aerodynamic honing for fuel efficiency, a short, raked hood and distinctive profile. It combined the agility and practicality of a compact car with high ground clearance, a command driving position and integrated lower-body cladding for robustness.

The product: Leading on firsts

There were several firsts in the product introduction. The all-new Ford EcoSport was all set to make driving addictive and intuitive with an array of smart segment-first features. The urban SUV was going to be the first in its class to offer Ford SYNC, the voice-activated in-car connectivity system co-developed with Microsoft. SYNC was also going to feature emergency assistance, which helps occupants place a call to the emergency services operator directly in the event of an accident. The Ford EcoSport was set to be the first-ever vehicle in India in this category of automobiles to offer this extremely advanced and potentially life-saving feature.

Even though positioned in the burgeoning B-segment (comprising hatchbacks and compact sedans) which made up more than half of passenger vehicle sales in India, EcoSport's distinct styling, compelling design and a host of convenience features were seen as path-breaking by an audience spoilt for choice.

Taking fuel efficiency to a new high, the 1.0l 125 PS EcoBoost engine—which was 20 per cent more fuel efficient than a traditional 1.6l engine and low on emissions—was also introduced for the first time in India in EcoSport.

Meeting the urban road requirements such as ground clearance (200 mm), Ford was set to redefine what SUVs stood for and made people hold on to their next car purchase for 'the most awaited product of 2013'!

Promotion to manage the odds against

The Ford EcoSport was first unveiled at the 2012 Auto Expo and launched eighteen months later in June 2013. The EcoSport, given its compelling positioning and promise of great technology, mustered a lot of interest from potential consumers and industry experts throughout this period. The biggest challenge at the time was to keep the momentum and interest alive considering the long gestation period between the unveiling and introduction of EcoSport in India.

With the launch of EcoSport still far away, Ford had a huge task ahead of it of building aspiration among Indian customers known for their informed, value-conscious and tough-to-please mindsets. The answer to the challenge lay in Ford's marketing strategy which was closely guided by the media consumption habits of the Indian consumer.

'Took the one less travelled by...'

While the market was still dominated by traditional media, the order was changing at a fast clip.

Instead of devising separate campaigns for traditional media and then moving to a novel medium, in a first, Ford reversed the process and started the campaign with a thrust on digital with EcoSport Urban Discoveries.

In essence, the EcoSport Urban Discoveries campaign was an initiative that gave people a chance to discover their cities like never before by getting behind the wheel of the all-new Ford EcoSport before its official market launch in India. EcoSport Urban Discoveries was a 360-degree pre-launch campaign across twelve major cities in India that set the stage for Ford EcoSport's launch in mid-summer 2013.

The campaign went live on 1 March 2013, hosted online at www. ecosportdiscoveries.co.in. This website was the central content aggregation and dissemination platform—one that helped Ford capture all the consumer stories in a single place.

The platform allowed for rich interactions using maps, photos, videos, vote/follow and conversation features integrated with Facebook and Twitter. With this platform at its centre, the campaign to date has proved to be the largest socially led 'reality show' in the Indian automotive space.

The EcoSport Urban Discoveries roadshow kicked off with a unique domino topple installation on the theme of urban discoveries with 80,000 domino tiles toppling to create the EcoSport Urban Discoveries motif. The entire act was live streamed, further widening the scope of the audience.

Keeping it real!

Built around real people and their real experiences, the EcoSport Urban Discoveries campaign informed the audience that the Ford EcoSport was on its way and helped remove any negative sentiment around it.

Potential consumers were at the heart of the integrated campaign while building the narrative of the Ford EcoSport's positioning as a desirable urban SUV that customers would want and value. The campaign had one broad objective—to create extraordinary buzz around the soon-to-be launched Ford EcoSport.

In yet another industry first, the consumer took precedence and the EcoSport Urban Discoveries campaign gave nearly 100 consumers the opportunity of driving and experiencing the Ford EcoSport ahead of its market introduction. The long-term aim was to establish EcoSport as the most desirable compact-SUV

Ford used a three-pronged approach, with earned, owned and paid media in every leg of the EcoSport campaign, till the launch of the car. This also included extensive outreach to media influencers, key opinion leaders, Ford evangelists and analysts.

The campaign was supported by outreach across twelve cities—Delhi, Mumbai, Bangalore, Pune, Cochin, Hyderabad, Kolkata, Chandigarh, Kochi, Ludhiana, Jaipur and Ahmedabad—covering the length and breadth of the country.

Adding to the word

Ford installed EcoSport Urban Hub in malls across these cities where visitors could touch and feel the EcoSport in an environment for which it had been developed. It was an urban SUV and an EcoSport Urban Hub offered customers the right urban environment to experience this great vehicle. With this campaign, Ford achieved over 16 million impressions on Facebook and Twitter along with a reach to about 5.2 million people.

In yet another first of its kind, the digital and on-ground engagement was further supported by an international media drive, which not only helped create great and credible content for the Ford EcoSport but also set the stage for the vehicle's launch and subsequent *bookings of a record 30,000 units within just seventeen days of its launch.*

The international media drive had media representation from more than six countries. An engaging drive programme—Tech Deep Dive—gave Ford an opportunity to showcase the capabilities and technological prowess of its urban SUV.

The media shared its first-hand experience of driving the EcoSport through articles, tweets, Facebook statuses and videos. It worked like a charm!

The content created through the media engagement programmes helped Ford reach out to more than 270 million readers through articles and 82 minutes of broadcast time, resulting in 277,933,065 unique visitors on Ford India's social channels. With over 1,850 tweets since the start of Tech Deep Dive, Ford EcoSport gained consistent exposure of around 100,000 impressions daily.

Consumers were at the heart of the campaign and Ford engaged them consistently through digital platforms. Ford has, over the years, been successfully connecting with its consumers on social media. Carrying the legacy forward, Ford's faith in letting consumers drive the product through positive feedback worked wonders. Real people from every walk of life and their real experiences gave a new buzz to Ford EcoSport like none other. The strategy helped Ford generate conversations about the product. The interest and anticipation grew organically and was augmented in the traditional media to gain scale.

Appealing to the cost-conscious Indian

Apart from getting the product, promotion, positioning and target audience right, it was paramount for Ford to get the fifth 'P' of price also right for the EcoSport.

In a market like India, price might be the last stage but could prove to be the make or break. In addition to pricing, Ford had the arduous task of positioning EcoSport to target the heart of the market.

Starting late 2012, the differentiated tax structure made room for a unique category of compact sub-4 metre vehicles. The excise duty on sub-4 metre vehicles was reduced to 12 per cent, that is, half what was levied on large vehicles. The EcoSport perfectly fitted the sub-4 metre criteria and that gave the vehicle scope to be priced lower and compete at aggressive price points.

A lot was at stake from January 2012 till June 2013 when the final price was to be announced and Ford did not disappoint. With a commitment to delivering a great-looking product that packed in outstanding value, the Ford EcoSport India launch raised the bar in India's fast-growing compact utility segment with its compelling value-for-money proposition, giving customers in the sub-4 metre segment a refreshingly new option.

Launching the product at a highly competitive price, Vinay Piparsania, executive director, marketing, sales and service, Ford India said, 'EcoSport sets new standards in India's SUV industry classification.'

And he was right as the product had redefined the segment. One of the main reasons attributed to the success of Ford EcoSport in India is its aggressive price tag, owing to which the car has found many takers in India. With the EcoSport, Ford perfectly mastered the art of pricing its vehicle according to market expectations.

A sub-4 metre SUV, Ford EcoSport really baffled competition, courtesy its competitive price and an entry-level tag in India. *As a matter of fact, its launch pricing of ₹5.59 to ₹9 lakh (ex-showroom Delhi) perhaps gave all premium hatchbacks a run for their money!*

As one of the most anticipated launches, the live streaming of the launch event trended for over twenty hours on Twitter. With most number of tweets from Delhi and Mumbai, three out of the top ten Google trends from India were about the EcoSport launch. The price announcement for EcoSport received over 6,700 likes, more than 800 comments and close to 1,600 shares on photos posted on Facebook.

Ford EcoSport was the #1 hot search on 26 June 2013 on Google India and became the most engaged auto brand in India on Facebook. The announcement appeared in 400 media publications the day after, with 90 per cent of the news reports carrying pictures, and in twenty-five broadcast stories amounting to one hour of airtime.

No signs of slowing down!

Since its launch, the high interest rates and rising fuel prices have dealt a body blow to car sales in India and top car makers have failed to push volumes.

However, consumers continue to be in love with the value proposition being offered by Ford EcoSport, resulting in both bookings as well as the waiting period continuing to grow despite the overall slowdown. Over 100,000 EcoSports were being driven on Indian roads as of December 2014, and more are to reach customers in the near future. Besides, they are being exported to various growing and mature markets. Setting yet another benchmark of success, Ford India's most awarded urban SUV, the EcoSport, celebrated the 100,000 sales milestone in domestic wholesales and exports combined in August 2014 and is fast approaching 200,000—with 40 per cent market share and no discounts being offered since the India launch.

The recognition

Marketing successes are often celebrated through awards and recognition of which too Ford EcoSport has had more than a fair share. With over thirty awards and counting, Ford EcoSport has been one of India's most awarded vehicles ever in its debut year—allowing Ford to relive the success first created by Ford Figo. This most awarded vehicle added yet another laurel to its achievements when it emerged as the highest ranked SUV in the J.D. Power 2014 India Initial Quality Study (IQS). The initial quality study (IQS), is considered a benchmark in the industry that measures new-vehicle quality after the first ninety days of ownership. Ford EcoSport registered least problems per 100 vehicles—an unmatched performance in its segment.

Awards are an important criterion to evaluate success and the EcoSport has been crowned the most awarded car in India. It has also won the prestigious Bloomberg TV Autocar car of the year.

NO. 1 QUALITY. OUR TRIBUTE TO YOU.

India's most awarded vehicle ever is now the highest ranked SUV in the J.D. Power Award for Initial Quality. We thank Ford EcoSport customers for inspiring us to go further.

Go Further

Even more than awards is perception, as reflected in an editorial by Ishan Raghava, a renowned auto journalist,

> One of the resounding themes is the sudden interest in SUV's by manufacturers—correction, compact SUV's. A segment that was unheard of till a couple of years ago, suddenly has virtually every manufacturer displaying a concept or design study. Why is it? Thanks to the success of the likes of EcoSport as it was the only SUV's-compact SUV's specifically—that was able to show robust growth in a market with negative growth in almost every other segment.

Filling the void

For a marketer trying to taste success, 'differentiation' has been the foremost guiding principle to ensure that their product stands out from the crowd. It is a seed that a marketer continues to nurture with ideas until it transforms into an all-encompassing campaign to take the product's journey forward. The evolved mantra for success of brands that create a legacy today lies in their courage and conviction to push boundaries and carve out niches.

Differentiation is good but the ability to disrupt and challenge norms is what separates good marketers from great marketers. And with EcoSport, Ford managed to enter the latter category! Ford EcoSport not only filled the void in the segment but also introduced a new category for customers to choose from.

Doing the unthinkable at a time when the Indian automotive industry was going through its worst slowdown is an example of how a great product and the right marketing strategies work together to create market magic.

Fiama DI WILLS

CHALLENGER TO GAME CHANGER

If you want something new, you have to stop doing something old.
—Peter Drucker, management consultant and author

Poring over stacks of old marketing material and sifting through scattered sheets of formulae from the lab, Subhash Singh—divisional manager, personal wash, ITC Limited—tried to ignore a throbbing headache that had kicked in. Singh was at a loss. How does one shake up the market in something as ritualistic as a daily bath? What could be imparted to the tedious toilet soap tablet to transform the everyday bathing routine into an exotic sensorial experience that leaves the consumer humming all day?

The year was 2004. The entire ensemble at ITC's personal care products division, from the marketing team to the R&D personnel, had been working tirelessly for months to arrive at a formula that would change the game in the premium bathing category.

A soap is a soap is a soap. Even thinking

about product innovation as a strategic game changer in this highly functional category could be considered blasphemous.

But as they say, nothing ventured, nothing gained.

The search begins

The premium soap category consumer comprised primarily urban, young (under 45) women looking for skin-pampering from their soap as against a mere wash. In the premium bath space the growth opportunity lay not in market penetration or inter-brand movements but in garnering a sizable share of the consumer upgrade pie, from both mid and popular segments.

After much deliberation, the personal care team concurred that only a contrarian way could help redefine the terms of competition and move into the blue ocean where you had the water to yourself. But what *was* the contrarian way? So far, the only attempts at innovation in the soap industry were the transparent glycerine bath soaps or the cream bathing bars introduced much later.

In its pursuit of differentiation, the first cue for the ITC came from the Western world, where consumers had mostly switched to liquid soaps for both convenience and hygiene reasons. The ITC had developed shower gels in 2004 but they soon realized the product was actually ahead of its time, and that consumers were not ready to embrace the shower gel yet. *However, the product formulation containing suspended encapsulated beads filled with moisturizing oils was a potential winner in the stable.*

Traditionally, Indians prefer bathing with the bucket and mug and a soap bar in hand. Top showers are still considered a luxury driven primarily by scarcity of water. This was clearly not the best-case scenario for shower gels. Also awareness of the product was low with confusion over how and how much to apply, and the ubiquitous soap cake continued to monopolize bathroom racks by default, even in premium urban households.

However, in customer surveys undertaken to understand bathing habits of Indians, the quality perception of shower gels was very favourable. Most among those who had used shower gels at some point, felt it did nice things to their skin and left a lingering sense of freshness long after they had stepped out of the shower and dried themselves. So the problem with shower gels lay more in attitudes, habits and water constraints and not with the experience.

The challenge now was to harness this positive perception of shower gels and present the product to the customer in a format that would elicit greater acceptance. And the team figured it wouldn't really have to break the mould, well, not literally.

The insight that changed the game

If only all the natural goodness and sensorial appeal of the shower gel could be taken and transported to the convenient and familiar mould of a bathing bar...

So, while the objective for shower gels was to become the brand of choice when consumers evolved to using shower gels, the clear immediate agenda was sharp-focused on an innovative product which could deliver all the benefits of a shower gel in the ease of usage of a bathing bar format.

This was the big opportunity for crafting a unique shower gel soap and thus began the success story of the Fiama Di Wills gel bathing bars.

Serendipity

Subash and his team of scientists, researchers and marketers were in the midst of high decibel sessions debating buzzworthy innovative ideas. However, a worthwhile conclusion seemed to elude the team. One fine morning, a young scientist, from the R&D centre, simply froze shower gel in an ice tray to throw up a near-Eureka moment. However, this was just the beginning of the journey, and there was a mountain to climb to create a product that was unique but could be mass-produced and delivered to the consumer seamlessly.

Thus began the arduous five-year-long journey to craft and perfect the gel bathing bar that would go on to transform this age-old category.

Challenge No. 1: The first challenge was to achieve stability of form

The gel liquid upon freezing would change to solid state; but when exposed to normal ambient temperatures, would change back to liquid form. The aim was to bring about a stable change in the rheology[1] of the product so that even at ambient temperatures, it retained its solid form.

A plethora of experiments with solvents and processing technology were undertaken, before the R&D team hit upon a 'liquid crystal freezing technology', which changed the crystalline structure of the product, making it stable in solid state even at room temperatures.

Challenge No. 2: Aesthetic appeal

There was also the concern for aesthetics, since changing from liquid to solid state often affects the transparency of the product and leads to discolouration. So scientists needed to find the right cooling process to retain product transparency and colour stability for better aesthetic appeal.

Challenge No. 3: Wear rate

Wear rate was perhaps the biggest challenge as Indian consumers are culturally more inclined towards value-for-money products. So a gel bar which didn't last long enough was useless. Again, the trick was to strike the right balance of texture. An overdose of ingredients to make it last longer would make the gel bar harsh, while it would wear too fast if made too mild. Reaching this optimal level was an iterative process demanding significant research.

The cradle for all this experimentation was the ITC facility in Haridwar, where an entire floor was dedicated to developing gel bars. The years of diligent effort and sheer detailing that went into the creation of this unique bathing accessory are mind-boggling. No stone was left unturned in crafting a product that would cut through the clutter and create a unique proposition.

Challenge No. 4: Differentiation

A lot of thought was put into the shape of the gel bathing bar to make it a key differentiator. For ages, soap bars had been either oval or square in shape. ITC decided to break the mould and introduce the Fiama Di Wills gel bar in a unique dewdrop shape. A design house specializing

---

[1]The branch of physics that deals with the deformation and flow of matter, especially the non-Newtonian flow of liquids and the plastic flow of solids.

in ergonomics was appointed to create the novel shape that fit snugly into the palm and enhanced grip in water. The dewdrop shape has since become one of the strongest brand attributes of the Fiama Di Wills gel bar.

Challenge No. 5: Cue 'premium'

The entire bathing experience had to be luxurious and pampering. So for the first time, the concept of exotic ingredients and skin conditioners in a soap was introduced. From patchouli, Brazilian orange, ginseng, seaweed, peach and avocado to bearberry extracts, blackcurrant, lemongrass, macademia nut, oats and nutgrass, Fiama Di Wills gel bathing bars introduced exotic skincare ingredients from around the world in each of their variants. Till that point, only indigenous natural ingredients like commonly known fruits and flowers and traditional Indian naturals, milkcream, glycerine, etc. were being used in soaps by the competition.

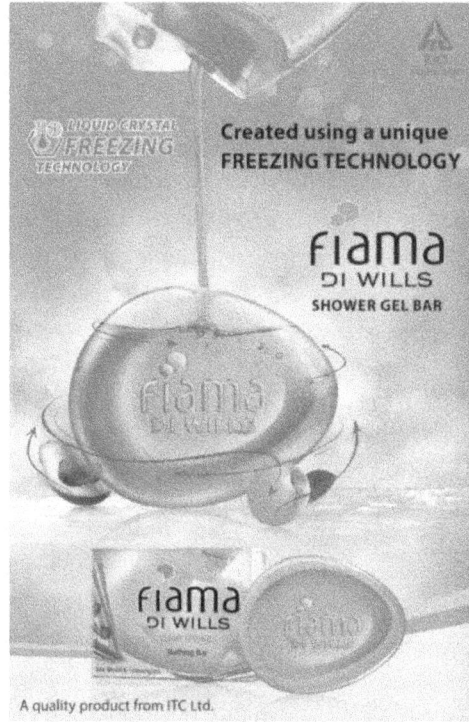

Challenge No. 6: Building the aroma advantage

The next, and perhaps most significant, task was to create a strong olfactory recall at every stage. From the first whiff on opening the product packaging to the actual in-use bathing experience and finally, the lingering fragrance long after one steps out of the shower, there had to be an olfactory wow at every moment. Some of the world's finest fragrance houses were approached to develop winning fragrances for the innovative gel bars.

In this exercise, it had to be kept in mind that the Indian environment is endowed with so much of strong natural aroma, that subtle western perfumes would be overpowered in these conditions. So customization of the fragrances was needed to arrive at the right balance between subtle and strong—a formulation that would wow users with distinctive notes.

Again, fragrance, like music, tends to be extremely personal and there can never be one winning formula which appeals to all. Leading fragrance houses were brought on board to create a wide array of scent leads to cater to diverse tastes—harmonized with the exotic ingredients used in the gel bars—Fruity (peach and avocado), Citrus Fresh (Brazilian orange), Green Fresh (seaweed and lemongrass), Floral Beauty (patchouli), Gourmand (bearberry). This blend significantly enhanced the premium appeal and a winning product was ready.

Challenge No. 7: Manufacturing technology: Borrowing from unconventional sources

Overcoming multiple challenges, systematically and relentlessly, the prototype was perfected after five years of intense R&D, trials and errors. The last hurdle was to put in place a mechanism for mass producing the gel bathing bar.

Getting the product right at lab-scale level is one thing, but commercial production to feed the market is a different ball game altogether. This challenge was far more daunting given the amount of innovation that went into creating the gel bar. There wasn't any existing soap manufacturing unit with the appropriate equipment available to handle its production. The conventional bar soap is usually manufactured by stamping all the ingredients together in the mould. That process wouldn't hold for the gel bar.

In search of an ideal solution, the company was forced to look at other domains. The study of manufacturing set-ups, mostly in the food segment, like confectionery and candies, served as an important learning, which again would require a lot of optimization to adjust to changing parameters, including the weather, besides ensuring all the special ingredients in the product retained their core qualities.

In the end, *the technology solution for gel bars production came from a completely unrelated industry—the manufacturing of hard-boiled candies where liquid is converted into candies.* Liquid shower gels were developed in large mixers and then poured into moulds and channelled through large freezing chambers to solidify the gel into a bathing bar format—a first of its kind in India and perhaps the world.

2009: A star is born

The journey of Fiama Di Wills Gel bar is one of relentless pursuit to innovate in an industry that, over many decades, had not experienced much novelty.

The dewdrop-shaped gel bathing bars thus came to stand for the young and contemporary in an age-old soap industry characterized over decades by formulaic routine bathing bars, either oval or square, thus creating a bravura wow moment in one of the largest FMCG segments.

To go with the unique story of shower gels frozen into gel bathing bars, the heady mix of exotic ingredients in a refreshing new range of bright colours and the assortment of intoxicating fragrances combined to make the product a consumer favourite, both for reasons of aspiration as well as curiosity to try out a whole new bathing experience.

A unique packaging solution added novelty to the product offering. Superior packaging, employing food-grade foil wrap, was used to keep the freshness alive in the gel bars over an extended period.

Telling the story

So how was communication to do justice to the task of telling the story of this dramatic product to the consumer? How did one articulate the positives of such a unique product, which was a first in so many respects, to drive home the message?

The launch communication in 2009–10 centred around 'Nature and

Science', an amalgamation of exotic ingredients depicting 'nature' and the advanced, patented liquid crystal freezing technology cueing 'science.' But the campaign impacted only a small set of consumers, with most not able to relate to the message.

Next, the Fiama Di Wills team tried the 'skin benefits' and the 'sensorial experience' route, which gave the brand a temporary boost before hitting a plateau again.

If it is unique and different, why not let it make headlines

Eventually, the marketing team realized that the best option was to cut the jargon and take the direct route by highlighting the unique product differentiation—the shower gel in a bathing bar format story—to consumers. This had the desired effect and the uniqueness of the product was finally conveyed, loud and clear.

'Shower Gel in a Bathing Bar' is what clicked with the consumers and the Fiama Di Wills gel bar saw a meteoric rise in demand, mindshare and consumer franchise.

The communication created exclusivity and an intrigue value for consumers to try the bathing bar.

A lot of innovation went into experiential marketing initiatives that emphasized gel skin conditioners as a special enhancing ingredient. Consumers were engaged through the application of gel skin conditioner, with a moisture test meter giving instant reading to highlight the increased moisture levels. A film showing the innovative 'liquid' to 'bar' journey accompanied the consumer engagement activities in modern retail, multiplexes and other target rendezvous where premium consumers could be accessed.

Result

The outcomes were a whopping 15–20 per cent share gain from the market leader and successful uptrading by the urban consumer into this new product segment.

Jewel in the crown

The many firsts Fiama Di Wills gel bar notched up—from its unique dewdrop shape to the first Indian patent in liquid crystal freezing technology to exotic ingredients and skin conditioners and even pure gold in it—earned it the 'Product of the Year' in 2010, within six months of its launch.

> 'Product of the Year' is a global consumer recognition standard that celebrates champions and rewards the best innovations in retail products done through an independent consumer survey across the country. The recognition standard has been awarding innovative retail products for the past twenty-nine years across twenty-eight countries. In 2009, 'Product of the Year' debuted in India with twenty-six product categories ranging from grooming and consumer durables to foods and beverages. Fiama Di Wills gel bar won the award in the soap category in 2010, based on a large independent survey conducted by AC Nielsen with 40,000 Indian consumers across thirty-six centres in India.

Soon after this, Fiama Di Wills extended its franchise to a premium range of personal care products comprising shampoos, conditioners and shower gels, designed for young, contemporary and confident consumers who sought to indulge themselves. The gel bathing bar, with its liquid shower gel in a bathing bar format, became the jewel in the line's crown, catapulting Fiama Di Wills into the orbit of an exclusive club, hitherto represented by only large imported brands. It created a new sub-category in soaps, enabling the company to own a unique space without the worry of 'sharks from the red ocean'.

2012: Introducing high fashion in this commoditized category

On the back of its initial success, Fiama Di Wills introduced the concept of designer series soaps in India, another first, collaborating with ace Indian fashion designer Wendell Rodricks, to create the first signature series of the couture spa range of gel bathing bars with pure gold. Launched with much fanfare in 2012, the signature

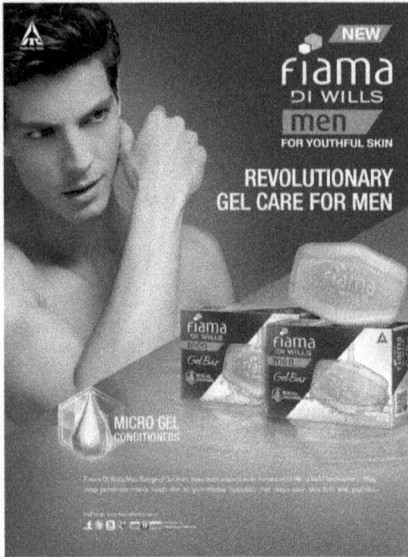

series was a roaring success, and served to accentuate the intrinsic ties with the fashion world Fiama Di Wills had from the outset.

To further cement the connection between beauty and fashion, Fiama Di Wills associated with the high-octane Wills Lifestyle India Fashion Week, a natural synergy with Wills Apparels—the lifestyle house brand of ITC. Fashion and lifestyle went hand in hand as aspiration markers in the personal grooming space, and this association helped integrate this as part of the brand's DNA.

Looking ahead

Having achieved a clutch of firsts with the game-changing 'liquid-to-soap' gel bathing bar—like the dewdrop shape, exciting colours, introduction

of skin conditioners and skincare emollients that would condition the skin to make it look younger—the next focus would be to carry the gel story forward and offer a range of gel products across the multiple categories in the wash and care segment. Gel is clearly the future and the Fiama Di Wills gel bar has simply delineated the path to the future.

It was a massive leap of faith that enabled a challenger brand to carve out a niche among well-entrenched toilet soap titans hogging market shares. The project was fuelled by the desire to create a unique brand proposition through smart product innovation. It was a fresh, bold approach with no cobwebs of the beaten path attached. And the end product not only stands out in a crowd, it gives a new direction to the bath soap segment.

Legacy

Cadbury HOW A FOREIGN CHOCOLATE WON INDIAN HEARTS

We have all savoured both the chocolate and its ground-breaking campaigns for many years. The remarkable story of the brand that was able to pull off the near-impossible challenge of integrating itself into the food habits of a nation strongly habituated to eating indigenous sweets is recounted here.

It is a behind-the-scenes look at the Cadbury Dairy Milk journey in India over the last six decades. It shows how strategy and perseverance can overcome prolonged periods of stagnation; warns that a large potential target group can turn into a roadblock to future business and that you can go only so far if brand codes are not in sync with culture and category codes; demonstrates how it is possible for a foreign brand to become part of the cultural fabric without localizing the taste; and finally conveys that improving market share is not the only path to growth.

It all started in 1948

Cadbury milk chocolate arrived on Indian shores exactly a year after the nation turned independent. In the early decades, the brand catered exclusively to westernized Indians but before long, it realized the need to look beyond this niche in order to grow. Efforts continued slowly and steadily until the year 1984 when a big turnaround took place. Operation Flood, a nationwide effort by the government to boost milk production and consumption in the country had become a spectacular success. Cadbury sought to leverage the easy availability of fresh milk by replacing powder-based milk chocolate with actual 'dairy milk' chocolate.

The product became more delicious, more natural and more of an indulgence than ever before. It wasn't enough to improve the product, this improvement had to be visible to the consumer. Thus the packaging underwent a makeover to reflect milk as a vital ingredient in chocolate making. Cadbury also revamped its distribution to boost product visibility by launching its first-ever open display unit, the sheet-metal dispenser that we now take for granted in retail counters. Advertising too took a new form. Colour television had just arrived in India. Advertisements took full advantage of this new medium in order to turn the message of 'fresh milk' into a powerful consumption motivator. Needless to say, these company-wide efforts paid off. The rather sedate growth of the past got turbo-charged, with sales trebling for the next six years.

Turbulent 1980s: When one segment jammed another

However, by the late 1980s, business began to stagnate again. The brand had focused its marketing efforts on children, thinking that it would be easier to develop a new taste with them than try to change habituated, tradition-bound adults. As a result, Cadbury chocolates were part of sweet childhood memories of millions of Indians; but this approach also created an unexpected roadblock to further growth. As children grew up, they outgrew the category. Even for kids, the brand was seen as an occasional 'foreign treat'. Efforts to up-age chocolate consumption naturally followed but it was not until the mid-1990s that any serious headway was made.

Halcyon 1990s: From 'just for kids' to 'the kid in all of us'

The revival of the brand's fortunes coincided with the rise of the Indian economy. In 1992, India made a shift from its socialist past and embraced a market economy. The liberalization of the economy had a transformational effect on the larger consumer culture. Until then, advertising in India suffered from an English hangover and, not surprisingly, lacked mass appeal. Cadbury recognized this and gave its creative agency Ogilvy a clear mandate to appeal to the masses by going beyond the English advertising prototype.

The result was some game-changing advertising that connected with mass Indian sensibility. Known as 'The real taste of life' (*Asli swad zindagi ka*), the campaign captured moments when people shook off convention and broke free, revealing their real selves, and demonstrating that Cadbury Dairy Milk (CDM) was not only for kids but for the kid in all of us. The brand soon became associated with spontaneity and happiness for people.

The most memorable in the series was the cricket advertisement where a girl jumps on to the cricket pitch and dances when her boyfriend scores a six. It was awarded India's advertising campaign of the century by Ad Club of India.

Further, aided by initiatives such as a cheaper ₹5 pack which made the brand more accessible to the masses, the launch of variants (ensuring consumer choice was 'which Cadbury' rather than 'Cadbury or something else') and an expanded sales coverage—over a million stores— the Cadbury India business trebled again between 1994 and 1999.

Trouble in chocolaty paradise: Circa 2004

While the 1990s were kind to Cadbury, by the early 2000s, growth began to dry up.

The brand's growth rate dropped by 78 per cent over the four-year period from 1996 to 2000 and sales flattened between 2000 and 2004.

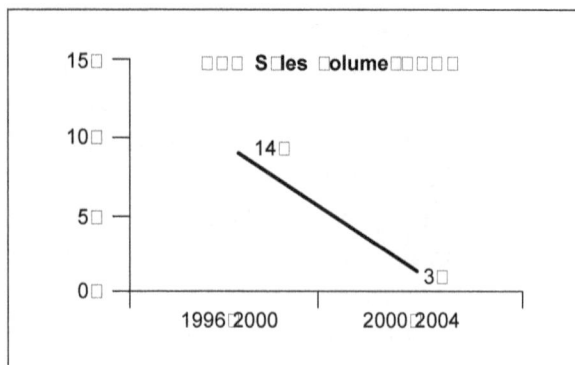

Dropping sales volumes

Clearly, the brand was running out of fuel. New triggers to fuel growth had to be found. However, given CDM's importance to the company's bottomline, this had to be managed without compromising profits.

Since the market share of all Cadbury brands put together was already 65 per cent, playing a market share game would inevitably entail cannibalizing one's own brands. On the other side, the brand's competition came from value-for-money offerings[1] (chocolate-coated wafer biscuits which had lower chocolate content or used chocolate substitute, which allowed them to offer more for less). These were discernibly bigger bars than what CDM offered at the same price. Clashing with them for share was bound to prove unprofitable.

The rising trend of commodity prices (cocoa) was only adding to the pressure on sales volumes and testing the brand's price elasticity. While prices had fluctuated, they had nearly doubled in four years.[2]

Possibility of share gain through promotions was bound to be expensive and unlikely to sustain long-term growth. Moreover, the inevitable competition response, compounded by price pressures, would further erode profitability. All these factors appeared to suggest that raising market share may not be the most profitable growth avenue for CDM.

---

[1]Nestle Munch, Nestle Kitkat, along with Cadbury Perk, accounted for 30 per cent of the chocolate category. These were all chocolate-coated wafer biscuits.
[2]World Bank statistics.

A new growth path: 2005 and beyond

Consumption among teens and adults was still very low when compared to global benchmarks. Understanding why was the key to growth.

As the world is now discovering, India is not one country but two countries in one.

Modernists, who are Indian in appearance but western in thought and lifestyle, dominated affluent India. Greater exposure to western (English) media and rising disposable income had meant that they were more open to experimentation and indulgence. Most of Cadbury's growth had come from this market.

However, it was in the other India that untapped potential resided.

Traditionalists, conservative in mindset and in lifestyle, constituted this other India—the largest chunk of the population. In comparison with the modernists they were tradition-bound and resistant to change. Their incomes too rose at a slow pace. Money was not exactly plentiful, so indulgence was limited. Though most of them were familiar with chocolate and had eaten it at least once, chocolate had little relevance in their lives and was seen at best as an occasional indulgence for kids. While they had made tea, potato and of course cricket their own, chocolate had got a cold shoulder from them.

But it was not as though they lacked a sweet tooth. *The size of the traditional meetha (sweets) market was more than nineteen times that of chocolate, valued at approximately US$4.2 billion, while chocolate was a merely US$215 million market.*[3]

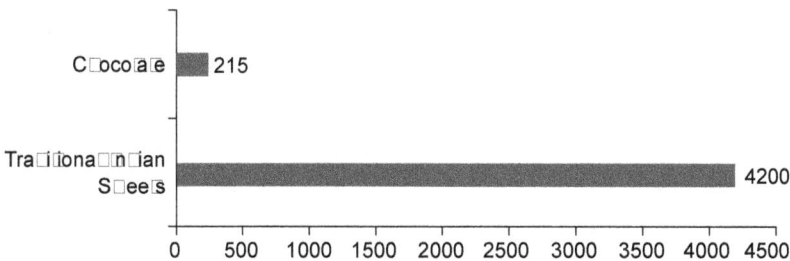

---

[3]Cadbury estimates, 2004.

The brand's growth strategy thus became to grow chocolate consumption by making it part of the Indian meetha consumption behaviour.

The transition from 'chocolate' to 'meetha'

In the case of India, a country with a vast, centuries-old indigenous sweet tradition, chocolate was a culturally antagonistic product. It was foreign sweet-treat trying to change age-old consumption habits.

The CDM team mounted an extensive ethnographic study to understand sweet consumption behaviours and how chocolate could enter this stronghold of traditional meetha occasions.

The team discovered that the answer lay in the *significant difference in the cultural perspective on happiness between East and West*. It was this difference that shaped the respective sweet consumption behaviours of these societies. And in this lay the strategic insight that shaped the brand's journey hereon.

Decoding the insight

The West has a strong belief in the independence and autonomy of the self (individualism). The self is believed to be the centre of thought, action and motivation; and happiness is to be found in personal striving and fulfilment of desires. Chocolate was mostly a private craving in the West, a means to individual gratification. A lot of chocolate advertising reflected this individualistic cultural perspective on happiness.

Sharply in contrast, happiness in India is 'collective'. In East Asian cultures, the self-in-relationship-with-others (collectivism) is the locus of thought, action and motivation. Consequently, happiness tends to be defined in terms of interpersonal connectedness and realization of social harmony.

This connects strongly to sweet consumption behaviour and occasions in India. Most happy occasions tend to be collective and are ritually accompanied by meetha consumption. Festivals, celebrations, and traditions or cultural markers of anticipated happiness (childbirth, success in exams, starting a new business, etc.) are never in short supply!

One could argue that it is not as if people in the West do not celebrate such happy occasions together, but the answer to that is that in the West there is no ritual mandating sweet consumption. Only in India does sweet consumption perform the role of a happiness ritual.

> Chocolate=self-indulgence
>
> Meetha=shared happiness ritual

In hindsight, the brand team realized that as a consequence of its western heritage, much of CDM's communication in India before 2004 reflected these western, individualistic happiness codes and was, hence, not considered on meetha-consumption occasions. This understanding of how 'meetha' was different from 'chocolate' was at the heart of its new strategy.

Repurposing 'chocolate' as 'meetha' to gain a share of India's abundant meetha occasions

How was this done? If CDM had to become synonymous with meetha, the word 'meetha' needed to become synonymous with the brand. Traditionally, people sweeten other people's mouths when something good happens to them or when they want to wish others happiness. This practice is popularly captured by the Indian/Hindi phrase '*muh meetha karna*'. The team made this more actionable by reinventing it. CDM advertising signed off with '*Kuch meetha ho jaaye!*'—a call to have something sweet.

Early slip-ups before hitting the sweet spot

But this did not happen without a few initial mis-steps that could have potentially derailed everything. The marketing team could well have come to the conclusion that the strategy wasn't working and abandoned it. But, thankfully, it persisted, understood what had gone wrong and course corrected.

One of the earliest '*Kuch meetha*' campaigns focused on small joys. Joys that should, but do not often, get celebrated. The thinking was these were occasions where Cadbury wouldn't have to compete with traditional sweets, occasions that it could own.

The small joys campaign, however, did not work. In hindsight, it became obvious that 'small joys' were often too personal or not worthy of sharing, hence not actionable. People did not share and celebrate them with others hence the role of meetha was not strong enough on these occasions.

The transition from small joys to big joys (occasions on which meetha was inevitably consumed) proved to be the game changer.

Over the years, CDM communication has spanned all traditional meetha occasions: celebrations, shubh aarambh (new beginnings of all kinds—journeys, new jobs, new purchases, forming new relationships); all typically Indian collective sweet-consumption occasions. The meetha consumption ritual is an inevitable part of these occasions.

Remaining loyal to the *Kuch meetha ho jaaye* (KMHJ) positioning over the last seven years has helped CDM become 'meetha'.

Summing up the strategic communication shifts that reinvented CDM

- From 'for kids' to 'the kid in all of us'
- From modernists to traditionalists
- From chocolate to meetha
- From 'individual' to 'collective' moments of happiness
- From 'occasional treat' to 'casual' consumption to 'ritualistic meetha' moment

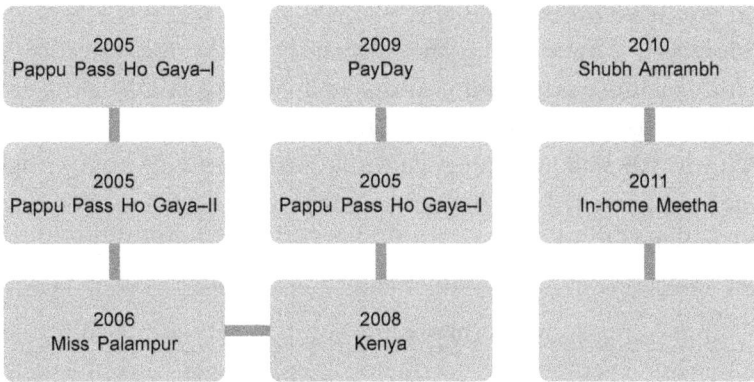

2005 Pappu Pass Ho Gaya–I	2009 PayDay	2010 Shubh Amrambh
2005 Pappu Pass Ho Gaya–II	2005 Pappu Pass Ho Gaya–I	2011 In-home Meetha
2006 Miss Palampur	2008 Kenya	

Brand learnings:

Look beyond the existing category users to grow both width and depth of consumption.

- Width: Price point and distribution
- Depth: Target both habitual and impulse consumers from five to sixty years

Do not re-engineer the product for the local palate. Position the product in a locally relevant way that reinvents the very essence of the product and anchor it in existing sweet consumption occasions.

- Consumers were subliminally given the message that it's best to substitute an Indian sweet with a Cadbury chocolate at an auspicious consumption moment
- Gifting and stocking of chocolate took over traditional 'sweet' occasions

Maintain image leadership by striking a deep emotional chord and smart marketing mix.

CDM growth[4] zoomed

This innovative strategy popularized the brand as meetha and chocolate started being considered on occasions when indigenous meetha was the traditional choice.

And the impact showed up in the tracking studies too. By 2011, penetration of chocolate increased by over 50 percentage points for both the teens and adult segments.[5]

CDM became the biggest brand to capitalize on this explosive growth in the chocolate category.

Moreover, despite being the biggest brand in the category (and therefore having a larger base compared to others), CDM managed to grow faster than every competitor brand.[6]

Clearly, the shift in strategy and the *Kuch meetha ho jaaye* campaign had not only reversed the flattening growth rate, but also super-charged CDM growth!

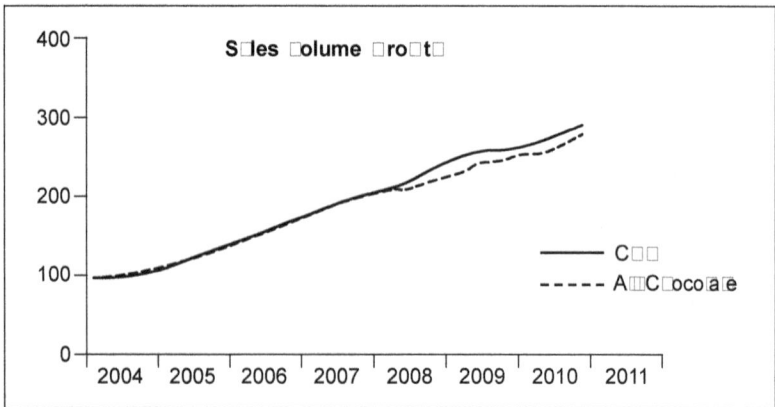

Note: Figures indexed at 100 for 2004 sales volume figures respectively.

---

[4]AC Nielsen sales data.
[5]Listing studies, 1995, 2002, 2011.
[6]AC Nielsen sales data.

Cover all bases: Driving occasion-led consumption brand extensions

CDM still had a long way to go, as the mass meetha market in India was and will remain humongous. But a solid start had been made and to build on this momentum, three new initiatives were launched in recent years.

Home Stocking of CDM

While chocolate had begun to find its way into many meetha consumption occasions from celebrations to Shubh Aarambh, the frequency of chocolate consumption was still eclipsed by that of meetha and the reason was chocolate consumption was still occasion centric, while meetha was part of habit. *Mithai was stocked at home; chocolate was not!*

So the objective became to get consumers to stock chocolate (CDM) at home.

Having something sweet after a meal (dessert) is common to many cultures. But to most Indians, it is inconceivable to end a meal without meetha! Research showed it is the single most frequent meetha-consumption occasion. From this came the idea of making every meal better, sweeter, happier, complete; and the '*meethe mein kuch meetha ho jaaye*' campaign was born. It has provided the elusive regular/frequent consumption occasion for chocolate that the brand has, for nearly two decades, been looking for. The initial results of this initiative have been hugely encouraging.

CDM Silk

This is the other big initiative. In chasing the large cappuccino opportunity in India, the brand hasn't forgotten the coconut Indian. As India is developing, more and more coconut Indians are getting minted. They are a growing young breed. These consumers are giving in to indulgence a lot more often and they have the means to indulge. To cover this segment, CDM Silk has been introduced. CDM Silk takes the taste of CDM that India has grown to love, but makes it more special and premium. The result is a fine, silky, creamy chocolate experience, suited to a discerning palate. CDM Silk is positioned as an intimate indulgence and the results so far have been nothing short of dramatic.

CDM Shots

Last but not the least, CDM Shots have been developed to make chocolate consumption more frequent and accessible to the cappuccinos. Price after all continues to be a barrier in an economy like India and the results for this initiative too have been hugely encouraging. In fact the Shots success story has been exported to other markets internationally and is featured in Professor Philip Kotler's latest edition of his seminal *Marketing Management*.

As a result of these three efforts, together with the cultural anchoring done in all CDM work, the brand is poised to grow in popularity and in business for many more years to come.

A little story sums it up:

About 300 years ago, the Parsis fled Persia (today's Iran) fearing religious persecution and arrived in India seeking asylum. The king of the land, however, told them that his family (subjects) was already very big and its members may not accept foreigners in their midst and feared a culture clash. The leader of the Parsis responded by taking some sugar and putting it in a glass full of milk and gently stirring it. The milk did not overflow, but became sweet. He pleaded with the king that their presence would be like sugar in milk. It would only sweeten their land.

Cadbury Dairy Milk and India have come together like milk and sugar.

Valuable Lessons from Cadbury's Meetha Journey

The difference between the East and West is much debated in many forums. Arguable proof abounds on the difference between cultures and their worldview and most of us agree there are indeed such differences. Clearly their significance for marketing is huge; yet often, despite all the literature and understanding on the subject, it goes unrecognized and un-utilized in practice.

When large global brands look at new geographies to conquer, they habitually try to change local tastes and behaviour and are usually unsuccessful. Others undertake expensive product engineering to make it culturally acceptable in the new market but that is both time and capital consuming and hence risky.

The CDM team's experience shows there could be a midway between these two extremes that is easier to implement. The 'meetha' positioning reinvented the very essence of the product, so it became something different, and by doing so, unlocked brand growth for CDM. It did this by transposing culture codes that got a target audience to view a familiar brand in a new light, making it a new product that generated a desire for purchase.

So instead of taking on tradition and culture and trying to create behaviour change, brands may do well to align with local culture and tradition to make gaining acceptance easier. Aligning with local culture may not need a new product but merely positioning the product in a locally relevant way.

GOING BEYOND FOOD

*We do not have to win at the expense of others
to be successful. Winning alone is not enough,
it's about winning with purpose.*
—Paul Polman, CEO, Unilever

Paul Polman's words may well hold true for Kissan, a popular Unilever brand in India. In its nearly sixty-seven-year-old history, Kissan as a food brand has made long strides by constantly reinventing itself to stand tall in the Indian market.

Kissan is a home-grown brand that is synonymous with jams, ketchup and squashes. In many ways it is more than just a range of food products. It is a brand that has come to be associated with the endeavour of mothers to make the growing up years of their children healthy and joyful.

Humble beginnings

The origins of Kissan go as far back as 1935 to Punjab. Trains that passed through Punjab made a stop close to a processing unit where farmers sold their freshly produced fruits and vegetables. The spot thus came to be called Kissan by locals. In 1947, UK-based Mitchell Brothers, who wanted to set up a food-processing unit in India, decided to move Kissan down south to Bangalore.

They, however, retained the name 'Kissan' and thus was born India's first food-processing unit in the year of India's independence. Based in Bangalore, this unit caught the attention of twenty-nine-year-old Vittal Mallya (the father of liquor baron Vijay Mallya) who had just been elected the first Indian director of United Breweries (UB). A year later, he was to replace R.G.N. Price as the chairman of the UB group. A big believer in inorganic growth, Mallya not only expanded by acquiring other breweries, but strategically moved into agro-based industries, thus acquiring Kissan from the Mitchell Brothers in 1950.

Joining the 'Hindustan Unilever' fold

Mallya Senior's vision of diversification paid off and the UB Group did fairly well in agro-based businesses. The processed foods company that Mallya owned operated under two brand names, Kissan and Dippy's. Jams and ketchup were sold under the Kissan brand and juices and squash under Dippy's. The company also set up a manufacturing plant in Nepal. However, when Vijay Mallya inherited the business in 1983 at the age of twenty-eight, after his father's untimely demise, he found that there was a rather eclectic mix of companies in the conglomerate.

With the turn of the decade, Mallya decided it was time for him to focus on his core business of breweries and distilleries and sold off Kissan and Dippy's to Brooke Bond India which was partly owned by the erstwhile Hindustan Lever (now known as Hindustan Unilever or HUL). Brooke Bond India on its part retained the brand name Kissan and dropped Dippy's; its juices and squashes were also now sold under the Kissan brand name.

The metamorphosis of Kissan into a food brand of stature: 1990s

In the early 1990s, when Brooke Bond India acquired Kissan, the food category formed a minuscule portion of HUL's overall product portfolio and comprised only cooking oils and fat. However, the entry of Kissan into its product portfolio in the year 1994, brought about a realization that this category was a huge untapped opportunity. With Kissan under its fold, HUL wanted to crack the food industry and it adopted the motto that good food should be 'loved'.

Accordingly, Kissan deployed an array of measures that shaped its successes over the next two decades.

The first and the most important challenge for Kissan was that of *differentiation* in a category with intense local competition. What really differentiated Kissan from its competition was the fact that it is made 100 per cent of real fruits and vegetables. Every bottle of Kissan products is packed with the goodness of real fruits and vegetables along with other best-quality ingredients.

Ketchup, which was another stronghold of the brand, too was given a facelift. A variant strategy was deployed to cater to local palates. A chilli-flavoured ketchup called 'Kissan Tomchi' was introduced in May 1997, and a tamarind variant in December, christened 'Kissan Tom-Imli'.

True to its proposition, Kissan also forayed into the squash category with the tagline '*Sachche phalon ki praapti*' as a refreshing summer drink.

Roping in Rahul Dravid, who was at the peak of his form at the time, to lend his nickname 'Jammy' to the advertising campaign was a strategy that worked well for Kissan Jam.

All these efforts paid off, and HUL recorded a 40 per cent growth in sales between 1997 and 1998. By the year 2000, Kissan was doing rather well with a market value of ₹400 crore and was leading in the jam market. In addition to its success in jams, Kissan was catching up with its nearest competitor in the ketchup market—Nestle's Maggi—as well. It was also fast replacing the likes of local squash brands like Mala and Druk.

Unveiling the 'Power Brand' strategy: Bold moves and ensuing lessons—2001–2005

HUL unveiled its 'Power Brand' strategy in 2001, which essentially meant that it would concentrate its resources and energies on the growth of some core brands that had potential to grab a higher market share, while pruning its exposure to others. As a result, the Kissan brand, which had tremendous brand equity in the 1990s and the early 2000s, was rebranded Kissan Annapurna. Under this repositioned brand, HUL planned to sell not just jams, ketchup and squash, but staples such as flour and salt as well.

Between the years 2001 and 2005, Kissan struggled to retain its brand equity. Although it managed to retain its leadership position in the jam market, it faced challenges across the entire remaining spectrum of product categories.

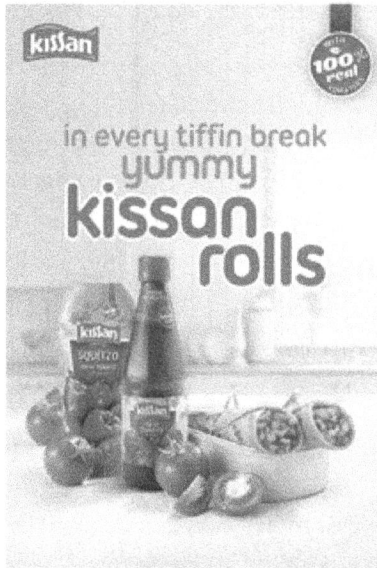

Threat from ITC: A new entrant in the staple foods category

Cigarette maker ITC entered the staple food market with its Ashirvaad brand of wheat flour (atta), which posed a threat to Kissan Annapurna. HUL at this time was eager to grab a greater share of the food market. Given its success in creating national mass market brands, HUL felt it could leverage its national distribution network to rapidly scale up Annapurna. However, the plan did not work and the company split into two brands, with Kissan concentrating on processed foods and Annapurna on staples. These decisions, however, took a toll on the Kissan brand.

Taking on Nestle Maggi in ketchups

Nestle was making aggressive moves in the ketchup category through its advertising campaigns, with popular actors of the day such as Javed Jaffrey and Pankaj Kapur endorsing its catchy tagline 'It's different!' Kissan rolled out a campaign in 2006 claiming that Kissan ketchup made samosas tastier but this did not make much of a dent in Maggi's market share.

Relegated to the back of the shelf in the squash market

In the squash category, too, players such as Rasna and cola makers made Kissan irrelevant. The challenge from Rasna had been in the making for a few years. Rasna, another homegrown product, was giving tough competition to Kissan squash as it targeted the great Indian middle class by releasing commercials that drove home its 'value for money' aspect as compared to popular squashes and syrups of the day.

Key learnings

While home and personal care had always been a stronghold for HUL, it was continuously experimenting to capture a wider share of the food market in India.

HUL's ambitions in the food market needed to be matched by the perseverance required to create sustainable success in this category—new products were withdrawn too quickly.

» In 2009, Kissan launched Amaze in the malted food drinks category. Amaze claimed it provided 33 per cent of the brain nutrients that growing children required daily. However, since the product did not pick up as per the market expectation, the company discontinued it.

» In more recent times, soya-based fruit juices were launched under the label Kissan Nutrismart, but these were also discontinued because they did not meet the desired expectations.

» Earlier, at the turn of the decade, Kissan had explored some other adjacent categories such as spices which it tried to introduce along with the staples of flour and salt.

» Kissan also made forays in the biscuits segment in December 2002 by launching the first indigenous fruit-cream biscuit brand under the Kissan franchise. Bistix was a unique offering of biscuit sticks with fruity dips. This again was withdrawn quickly based on initial results.

What is significant during this period is that Kissan kept innovating and each of these innovations brought in learnings for the brand. All these learnings were effective for the company to reinvent the brand and emerge as a strong player in the foods category.

Life comes full circle: 2012

Every limit is a beginning as well as an ending.
—George Eliot

HUL decided to focus on growing its core business. Low penetration levels of under 20 per cent left enough room for market development in the ketchup and jam categories in India. One of the unique challenges of these categories was that they were highly fragmented with a plethora of local players. Most regional players operated on discounts with highly optimized supply chain costs and no investments on advertising and promotion. Minimal perceived product differentiation, especially in the ketchup category, was another key challenge. For a consumer 'a sauce was a sauce' as long as it fit her monthly budget.

Hence the key tasks ahead of Kissan were:

» Get more and more consumers to start using Kissan jams and ketchup along with their regular food, thereby increasing consumption and penetration and leading the task of market development.
» Differentiate Kissan from the competition.

Back to the basics: Nurturing love for nature

In a bid to reposition the brand, Kissan first sought to differentiate itself from other branded competitors and local players. In a quest for a proposition, Kissan came back to something it had started out with—the power of 100 per cent real fruits and vegetables.

Every bottle of a Kissan product is packed with the goodness of real fruits and vegetables along with other best-quality ingredients.

Kissan carried out extensive consumer studies to find a compelling insight which it could use to build a connect and credibility with consumers while being differentiated from its competition.

This insight eventually led to the start of the now famous 'Kissanpur' journey that began on 15 February 2012. It all began with a 'positive response' in one of the first consumer studies that amazed the team at Kissan. Subsequent consumer interactions kept throwing up similar replies from children. When asked, 'Where do tomatoes come from?' children came up with a variety of innocent responses like they grow on trees or they grow under the ground, with a few kids even believing that they were manufactured in shopping malls!

These responses which showed that kids in India were quite distanced from nature gave Kissan its big idea. The idea was that if it gave its consumers a chance to experience nature and fall in love with it, they would always come back to Kissan. With this was born the 'Kissanpur' campaign asking kids to turn into farmers and get their hands dirty to grow tomatoes—tomatoes as red and juicy as the ones used for making Kissan ketchup

The building blocks of Kissanpur

Inspire

This phase was all about inspiring and inviting kids to grow real tomatoes and live the journey from 'seed to fruit'. One fine day in February 2012, parents and kids woke up to a sachet of tomato seeds in their morning newspapers. Kissan ran a campaign urging kids to plant these seeds and post pictures of their plants with tomatoes on Kissan's Facebook page (that was aptly named 'Kissanpur'). It came with a promise of launching a hundred new faces on their ketchup bottle soon. These would be of kids who had successfully grown tomatoes. The idea was to introduce children to the joys of growing a plant and nurturing it.

Engage

The second phase of the campaign was the most challenging and critical one, where the kids had to be captivated by the idea and motivated enough to complete the journey of growing tomato plants in their houses over the next five months. Digital media was used as a platform to share tips about growing tomatoes with mothers and kids and also for them to share their pictures, stories and experiences of growing tomatoes.

The campaign received further thrust with exciting SMS alerts, micro contests and other interesting apps. Interactive communication remained at the heart of this campaign, and a 109 per cent improvement was noticed in brand awareness through its Facebook page. These online efforts blended seamlessly with an offline event in which 7,000 tomato plants were seeded in a makeshift 'tomato farm' in the heart of Mumbai city in a popular mall.

Reward

The last phase was about recognizing and rewarding the top growers of tomato plants and establishing Kissan's 'real' credentials by demonstrating its 'real ingredients'. Top growers were identified and their tomatoes were taken to make 'real Kissan ketchup'. A flash-based application was also developed where kids were allowed to create their own Kissan ketchup bottle label and share their stories about their journey as little farmers. The stress was on 'real' experiences and it had the desired results.

The campaign closed successfully with over 2 lakh hits on the official website www.kissanpur.co.in, over 30,000 fans garnered through social media and more than 51,000 registrations on the website during the last phase of the campaign.

The seeds sown in Kissanpur are yielding a good 'crop'

Kissanpur not only helped mothers and kids engage together in 'real experiences' by transforming the way they lived their lives for five months, but also firmly imprinted itself in the hearts of mothers and kids in India.

The campaign has helped differentiate Kissan ketchup from its competition on the basic claim that it is made 100 per cent of real tomatoes. The campaign is in its third consecutive year and is still exciting kids across the country simply because it has enabled them to experience something different from their day-to-day lives; it has helped them to experience nature. It has also helped parents and kids bond while living the journey of Kissanpur.

Unlocking the growth potential of the Kissan portfolio

The year 2012 brought in great lessons for Kissan through Kissanpur. It gave it new-found confidence and also made it feel that it was playing too small a game by looking only to gain share. In order to unlock the true growth potential, the onus was on it to grow the reach of processed foods like ketchup and jams.

While looking around for inspiration from global Unilever brands, it came across Hellmann's (a mayonnaise brand) which was faced with a similar challenge in the past. The learning it took on board from the Hellmann's case was that to grow penetration or consumption for a category, it is imperative to build association of the product with the most commonly used food item. In India the dishes identified were paratha/ roti for the north and dosa for the south. Through extensive consumer research, Kissan found that packing the lunch box is one of the highest stress points in the life of a mother.

While she has limited time to prepare this lunch box, she needs to ensure that the lunch is tasty enough for the kid to come back home with an empty lunch box. Mothers were apt to treat this lunch box, or 'dabba' or 'tiffin' as it is popularly called, as a barometer of their success. If the child came back home beaming that not only had she loved her lunch, but her friends were envious of her too, the mom had indeed passed the 'tiffin test' with flying colours! Thus an advertising campaign targeted at mothers was launched with the tagline '*ungli ghuma ke bol*'. The campaign was aimed at giving mothers a quick solution to getting their children to eat nutritious food. Thus the 'boring' roti or paratha with sabzi could be transformed into an interesting 'roll' with just a dollop of ketchup.

After identifying this powerful idea, Kissan used different mediums like audiovisual, print and digital to communicate the idea. It also set up a helpline to provide new tiffin roll recipes to mothers every day.

This campaign has already started yielding fantastic results. It has not only helped grow consumption and penetration of the category and of Kissan, it has helped the brand grow to double digits in 2013.

Results

Today, in 2015, Kissan is the market leader in jams and ketchup with a 62 per cent and 25 per cent share respectively. It has steadily grown brand equity and penetration by leaps and bounds and is seen as a happy brand and a champion of happy growth. It offers health and functional benefits besides being fun and tasty and is a trusted partner of the modern mother. Motherhood is an exciting challenge in today's changing times, and the modern mom takes immense pride in her child's upbringing, as she views it as an opportunity to show her mettle. She is extremely involved in her kid's life and is always trying to maintain a balance between work and home. She strongly believes that the future is important but not at the cost of a happy childhood. She constantly needs to balance her roles of friend and parent. She recognizes the role that food plays in the upbringing of her kids. She believes that food should be loved and not shoved. Thus she constantly experiments and tries to come up with solutions which either makes healthy food exciting or exciting food healthy.

Tapping into this insight, Kissan offers the magic wand; with Kissan every mother can create magic with food.

KEY LEARNINGS

- Pick and choose adjacent businesses wisely: Strength in one category doesn't guarantee success in adjacent ones.
- Innovations warrant perseverance: Give enough time for innovations to succeed in the marketplace. Gestation period in the food category is long, owing to localization requirements, monitoring changing tastes and to sit out the time needed for changing food habits, ultimately building scale.
- Preserve the core: While experimenting with new innovations, at no cost dilute the equity of the core brand.
- Size of the prize: Gun for size and scale only in categories where differentiation is possible.

THE STORY OF A
LEGENDARY BRAND

To understand any great brand, one must first understand its legacy and the only way to do so is to go back in time to its first generation of innovators.

The journey of MTR is nearly a century long, over the course of which it has witnessed momentous events from wars to the independence of the country, changing governments and a rapidly developing nation, growing with each era and reinventing itself to stay at the top of its game. From a family-run business to becoming part of a global organization, MTR's story is one that is distinguished by its ability to survive against all odds.

The brand innovated even before innovation became a touted value in business.

MTR or the Mavalli Tiffin Room has its origins in Brahmin Coffee House, a small restaurant serving Udipi cuisine that was started by Parampalli Yajnanarayana Maiya and Ganappayya Maiya in 1924. Yajnanarayana Maiya assumed full control of the business in 1936 and moved to a larger space. Maiya was a man of limited education but his entrepreneurial vision embedded innovation in the DNA of the company.

Embracing innovation and quality as core values

During World War II it became difficult for the restaurant to procure rice for idlis. It was at this time that Yajnarayana Maiya came up with the idea of using semolina to substitute rice and thus was born the rava idli. This rava idli, both as a fresh item in the restaurant and later, a breakfast mix and packaged food, became an integral part of MTR's identity. This helped it survive the War as well as emerge as a player that was able to innovate when necessary. No other company or brand has created a dish that has gone on to become a ubiquitous part of the menus of south Indian restaurants as well as south Indian cuisine.

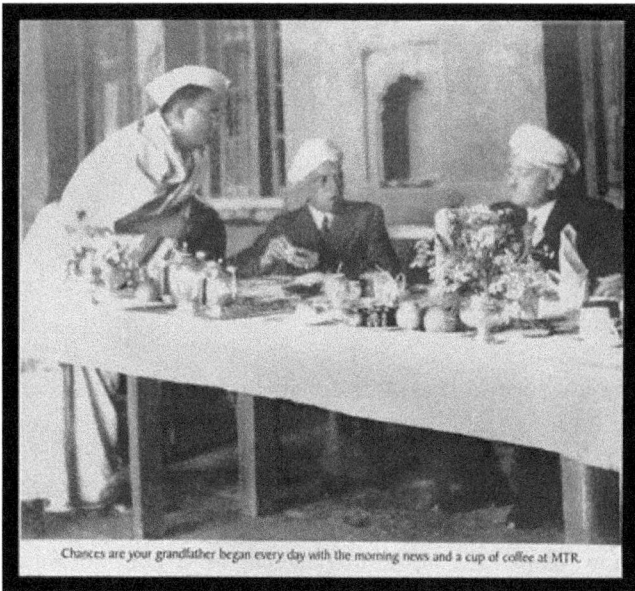

Chances are your grandfather began every day with the morning news and a cup of coffee at MTR.

In 1976, Emergency was declared in India and the government dictated that top restaurants in the country (which included MTR) slash their prices and make them affordable for everyone. While many in the business cut corners and compromised on quality, MTR continued to maintain its high quality standards and its only response was putting up a board which reported the daily losses. This emphasis on quality is of one of the brand's core values that has only strengthened over time.

Converting adversity into advantage

However, after two weeks of running at a loss during this period, MTR was forced to shut down its operations. Instead of being a low point in its history, this ended up being a turning point for the business. The employees were engaged to prepare the dishes that were hallmark of the restaurant menu, like rava idlis and gulab jamun as packaged foods in a factory space near the restaurant. Whether it was serendipity or deliberate planning that was taking MTR in a new direction, this new direction turned out to be extremely profitable, especially with the success of the gulab jamun mix which began flying off the shelves faster than it could be produced. In the 1980s, to handle the explosive growth of the packaged foods business and to manage the changing aspirations of the owners, the restaurant business was hived off from the packaged foods division, though both continued operating under the MTR brand. The MTR packaged foods business was ready to fly solo under the aegis of Sadanand and Harishchandra Maiya.

Reinventing the business: From a local restaurant to a fast-moving consumer goods company

Spotting new opportunities and converting them into a competitive advantage

Masalas and pure spices were making a slow but steady entry into the Indian market. Thanks to its expertise in the restaurant business, MTR had the knowhow of making authentic masalas on a commercial scale. With the increasing fame and near iconic status of the restaurant, packaging masalas/blended spices and pure spices and selling them under the MTR brand name was a natural step. Quality and authentic taste remained at the core of this offering. MTR's spices and mixes were made with the best-quality ingredients, sourced from the regions famous for them, and then made to undergo stringent quality control tests.

Traditionally, whole masalas were always pounded by the housewife to retain aroma and freshness. Pounded masalas helped retain flavours better than the commonly used grinding process. Pledged as it was to offering only authentic and best-quality products, MTR innovated to develop industrial machines that could pound masalas. MTR pounded masalas retained flavours better than the branded masalas using the grinding process. This innovation became a part of the brand's unique selling proposition in masalas and beyond.

The turning point

The launch of RTE (ready to eat) was a watershed moment for MTR and with it the brand moved beyond its south Indian to a pan-Indian presence. RTE was a turning point in the history of the packaged foods business in India. It was created with the latest technology bought from the Defence Food Research Laboratory (DFRL) and used to retort food and make it shelf stable for up to twelve months. The insight for this category came from Mr Maiya's own experience of not finding tasty vegetarian food when travelling abroad and trying to carry food items that were easily perishable. MTR introduced thirty-five different RTE products which included delicacies from the northern, western and southern parts of India, including dishes like paneer tikka masala, chana masala, bisebele bhaath and vegetable biryani. RTE was a great innovation that helped propel MTR to a dominant position in the nascent category, which it continues to occupy.

Over the years, the company has gone from selling traditional products like vermicelli, papads, ready mixes, spices and masalas to modern and new-age products in the RTE range and badam drink cans, while retaining quality and authenticity across its entire range. Innovations like introducing badam drink in cans have been in keeping with the traditional–modern outlook of the brand, with an authentic Indian drink marketed in a modern format as an alternative to western beverages. The idea was to identify products and categories that could grow exponentially. The company managed to taste success in all its forays and became synonymous with quality and authentic taste in Karnataka and, in a limited way, even beyond.

Going global: Positioning the brand for the international Indian

With the launch of RTE, MTR became a household name beyond Karnataka as the product became a blessing for travellers, students and working women. To target this segment, the brand positioned itself as 'the taste of home away from home'. Armed with this proposition, the RTE business led MTR's global expansion. Today, MTR is present in twenty-three countries from the USA to New Zealand and one can safely assume that MTR can be found wherever Indians have grown roots.

The transformation from a family-run business to a multinational

MTR had grown at a rapid pace in India and had expanded into foreign markets as well. Global private equity firms and angel funds had invested in this company believing in its potential. However, by 2007, the company needed more capital to expand and Mr Maiya decided to bow out and look for investors who would take over the company in its entirety and expand the MTR empire. While many Indian and international companies showed interest, the final bid was taken forward by a Norwegian conglomerate, Orkla.

For Orkla, MTR was a perfect fit as it preferred to acquire companies with strong local heritage and a dominant market position. Unlike other multinational companies (MNC), Orkla has a unique multi–local model of operations. It believes that strong brands and powerful innovations are a fundamental pre–requisite for growth in a long–term outlook of sales and profitability. This synergy in philosophy and value systems was pivotal in Orkla's acquisition of MTR.

About Orkla

Orkla is one of Norway's oldest business conglomerates whose history dates back 350 years. It started out as a mining company extracting the rich ore deposits at Løkken Verk in Sør-Trøndelag County. Today, Orkla is a leading producer of branded consumer goods and provider of concept solutions to grocery and out-of-home channels in the Nordic and Baltic regions. In addition, the group holds strong positions in certain product categories in the Czech Republic, Austria, Poland and Russia. The company is also a major supplier to the European bakery market. Orkla's vision is to improve everyday life with healthier and more enjoyable local brands.

After the 2007 takeover by Orkla, MTR invested over ₹100 crore in large-scale upgradation of infrastructure, IT, factories and other resources. There was renewed focus on brand building and marketing innovations. The brand architecture was redefined along formal categories and sub-categories to ensure appropriate focus on innovation and accelerating growth. This acquisition opened up new opportunities in international products for MTR. However, staying true to its core equity as an Indian food brand, it was decided to maintain focus on the brand's offering in this space and not dilute the equity by introducing western products.

In 2011, MTR acquired Rasoi Magic, a specialist in ready-to-cook meal mixes. This further broadened its already diverse product range as well as gave it a strong entry point into western and northern India, allowing it to take its pan-India plans to the next level.

Rasoi Magic was a boutique company operating from 2000 out of Pune, largely in the west Indian markets of Maharashtra and Gujarat. While MTR was operating in the breakfast/dessert mixes market, there was a gap in its portfolio with regard to meal mixes which was filled with the acquisition of Rasoi Magic.

A deep human insight that defined the brand's essence

Post the Orkla acquisition, MTR started the process of reinventing itself. So after upgrading and modernizing infrastructure and professionalizing management, the next obvious step was to accelerate growth.

MTR was a multi-category brand with a presence in eight-nine categories as diverse as spices and masalas at one end and ice creams at the other. But before new plans could be drawn up, it was important to take stock of brand MTR's perception with its consumer. Research revealed that while the brand had extremely positive associations like innovation, quality and authenticity, it was also seen as a tad traditional. The young consumer had different aspirations that the brand was not in tune with. *A revealing insight was that today's homemaker does not wish to spend more time than absolutely necessary in cooking as she is juggling more responsibilities than her mother ever did.*

This new Indian woman is now actively looking for help to cut down on cooking time. However, at the same time she does not want to completely outsource cooking as she believes she is the custodian of her family's health and well-being. She plays different roles—that of a nurturer who makes sure that every family member is equipped to do their best; that of a mood uplifter, who makes their worries vanish with delicious surprises; and that of an infuser of enthusiasm who breaks the monotony and predictability of life by making the family try out newer tastes.

Based on these insights, MTR's role was articulated. MTR would be the friend in every kitchen by providing solutions to cut down the homemaker's non-value adding effort (like soaking ingredients overnight or blending spices together). At the same time there would be ample scope for the housewife to add her own touches. In a way, the brand allowed her to cut down on the drudgery and concentrate on delighting her family.

The brand essence 'Modern Crust, Authentic Core' was coined and the new vision drawn up was: 'To be an indispensable companion in every kitchen to help create authentic and delicious Indian food'. MTR's brand strategy was to protect and preserve authentic Indian food while presenting it in a relatable modern format.

A portfolio strategy aligned to geographical preferences

Once there was clarity on the role of the brand in its consumer life, there was a need to have a portfolio strategy in place that would guide future product launches and innovation. In 2010, armed with a new marketing plan, MTR refreshed its proposition and packaging, and created what it named the three pillars of its category growth strategy. It was decided to focus on three categories: Spices and Masalas, Mixes and a whole new category, South Indian Snacks.

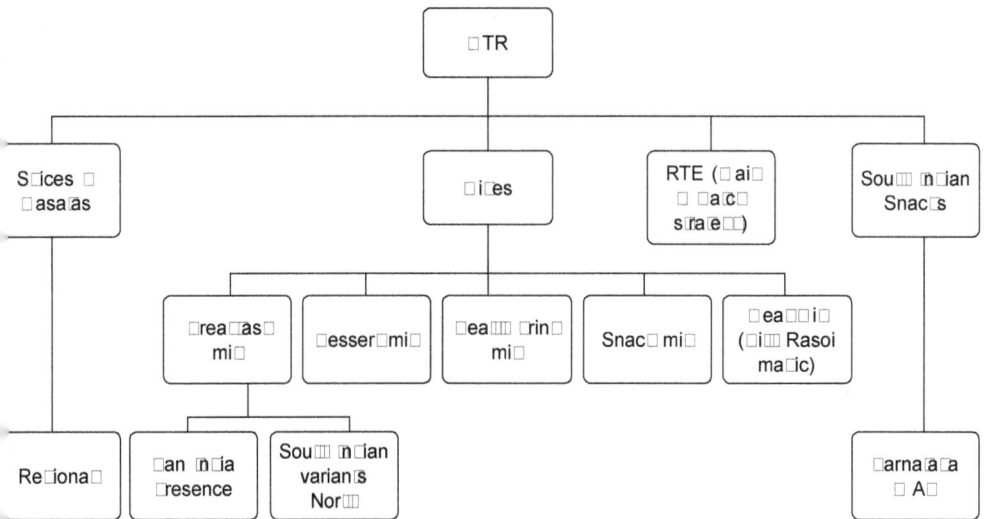

Basundi | Kulfi Kesar Pista | Kulfi Kesar Badam | Besan Laddoo | Gulab Jamun
Zero Preservatives - Easily Served

The portfolio strategy envisaged a clear role for each category. MTR's rich experience in the foods business pointed to this truth that while tastes could travel, very deep investments would be required for them to become mainstream. At this stage, MTR preferred to dominate the categories and markets they entered. With breakfast mixes tastes would travel outside of their local strongholds and in spices, masalas they would stay with a regional strategy.

» Mixes were an interesting category. From the consumer's point of view there was no category called 'mixes' and hence the range was broken up into four sub-categories: Breakfast Mix, Sweet Mix, Health Drink Mix and Snacks Mix. Breakfast and sweet mixes were identified as the areas with most potential. Once Rasoi Magic was acquired, Meal Mix was added to this category.

» The packaged breakfast revolution was starting in India with western breakfast options like cornflakes and oats gaining traction. It was seen that Indian consumers were looking for packaged solutions for breakfast and the only options available were western which were not a part of the traditional Indian food culture. Identifying this gap, MTR jumped in to provide an Indian alternative in packaged form for consumers who loved Indian breakfast options like idli, dosa and upma. Thus MTR aggressively marketed its breakfast options in places like the north and west of India which did not make the typical south Indian breakfast at home. *Mixes, especially breakfast mixes were to be the pan-Indian face of MTR.*

» Masalas' role would be in adding value and, with its superior pounded masalas, the brand's dominant position in Karnataka and Andhra Pradesh could be reinforced.

» Both spices and south Indian snacks were very regional in terms of the product promise (taste and range) and hence competing at regional level was a prudent strategy. As their presence was limited to the southern markets, activating the categories was easier as media strategy could be localized.

» It is also important to mention that RTE, which was an early success for MTR, was no longer seen as strategic. The RTE market in India had not developed with time and even after a whole decade was worth only ₹25 crore. From a consumer's point of view it made little sense as the Indian homemaker was looking for intermediate help and not a replacement or a final solution for her cooking. Hence this category had become a special-use category for occasions when a consumer travelled to places where Indian food was not readily available. It was decided to keep the category ticking till such time as Indian consumers were ready to outsource their meals.

It is at this interesting cusp of tradition and modernity that MTR stands today, straddling worlds of yesterday, today and tomorrow with equal ease.

The path to success

There are many lessons MTR has learned on its journey. There is a constant need to reinvent and recalibrate to cater to the ever-changing needs of the consumer. Today, MTR is a leader in terms of market share in breakfast mixes, sweet mixes, RTE and meal mixes nationally; and masalas and spices in Karnataka, with a very strong No. 2 position in Andhra Pradesh. MTR is already gearing up for future needs of its audience, at the same time looking to grow the size of the constituency.

Riding the packages revolution wave, powered by sharp insights into the Indian consumer.

When MTR classified its mixes as Breakfast Mixes, the category saw a huge jump. In the Indian breakfast options, MTR is the largest player. In fact, the brand found traction in households in the north and west where south Indian breakfast options were loved but not regularly prepared as the method of preparation was not known.

The results from this marketing strategy have been impressive. Company growth, which had been around 12–15 per cent for a decade or so started to grow at an impressive rate of 20 per cent plus year-on-year since the relaunch in 2010. The category strategy paid off handsomely. Earlier a flat growth category, breakfast mixes have been growing at 30–35 per cent year-on-year over the last four years. South Indian snacks, currently being tested in Karnataka, have been a success and the Masalas category continues to deliver a strong performance consistently.

Reinventing for the health-conscious Indian

Consumer health studies that were undertaken revealed that Indians are far more health conscious than most of their global counterparts. They think diet and nutrition are key to creating a feeling of well-being. With the rise in offerings like multigrains and oats in various product formats, MTR launched the innovation of blending different grains and oats in its south Indian breakfast mixes to create products like oats idli, ragi dosa and multigrain dosas.

In addition to these breakfast innovations, MTR decided to extend its expertise in the spice mix category and fill the gaps in the biggest masala market in south India—Tamil Nadu. The rich authentic cuisine of Tamil Nadu seemed to be losing out to products which were cheaper and used low-cost ingredients. Hence a range of superior masalas especially formulated to revive the authentic Tamil Nadu taste was launched. MTR has learned from its past successes that while some new launches will become runaway successes others are a medium- to long-term investment. As the company continues to modernize yet hold on to its authentic core, such new offerings will build aspiration around the brand in a manner that MTR desires, and consolidate the brand's shares across categories and markets.

The secret ingredient in MTR's success

What does brand MTR stand for? All legacy brands boast of some timeless values. There is *trust* that brands can earn only through longevity. And then there are other values that were once the founder's philosophy and then became a part of the brand's DNA. *Quality* and *authenticity* are two such values. But for a brand to survive fickle consumer preferences, changing lifestyles and competitive challenges, '*innovation*' is key. In keeping with this, innovation has been part of brand MTR's DNA from its very birth as Brahmin Coffee House. However, while the identity and perception of the brand may have changed to keep pace with the times, the soul of the brand—its authenticity, purity and culinary expertise—remains unchanged, making it every family's favourite kitchen helpmate for different occasions.

It remains the only brand that occupies the authentic Indian food space and every new product that is launched builds on this idea. MTR sees itself as a guardian of authentic Indian food. The brand's strategy is to promote authentic Indian food by making it an easy solution for the modern Indian consumer. Staying loyal to this vision has reaped rich dividends for MTR. Finally MTR's genuine appreciation and understanding of the needs of the Indian homemaker and career woman is one of the reasons the brand tastes success in every category it is present in.

To sum up, MTR's core operating principles to differentiate itself as a company are based on three key factors:

1. Staying true to its Indian roots and core of authenticity.
2. Local and regional approach towards developing and marketing food products.
3. Reinventing to meet ever-changing consumer needs.

It is also important to add that in MTR's great strides as a brand, the secret ingredient has been the development of the organization behind the brand. MTR's transformation into a modern brand has been backed by infrastructure development, up-skilling and training of its employees and defining a clear vision.

A Series of Milestones:

1924	Started as a small restaurant in Bangalore.
1939–1945	Invented rava idli by substituting rice with semolina.
1976	Entry into packaged food category
1995	Entry into spices and masala category
2000	Moved from being a regional south Indian brand to national brand with the thirty-five new RTE mixes with regional specialties from all across the country

2002	Quality certification with ISO 9002 and HACCP certification
2007	Bought over by Orkla, a 350-year-old Norwegian conglomerate.
2010	Launched a new brand essence 'Modern Crust, Authentic Core'.
2012	Ac☐uire☐ Rasoi ☐a☐ic ☐o s☐en☐☐en i☐s ☐oo☐rin☐in ☐☐e nor☐☐ an☐ ☐es☐

The MTR of tomorrow: *Growth by befriending the housewife during all meal occasions*

As Indian households shrink, disposable incomes expand and exposure increases, the needs of the consumers also change. In order to stay at the top of its game, MTR constantly adapts to the new challenges and competition. For this it taps into its in-depth knowledge of food trends as well as access to the latest technology.

Consolidate stature as national brand

MTR is looking to transform from a south Indian entity into a national player which provides modern yet authentic food solutions covering cuisines from different parts of India.

Adoption of digital

MTR continues to evolve along with its ever changing consumer needs and is looking at newer ways of communicating with them and satisfying their kitchen needs. The latest initiative of the brand is on the digital platform. MTR has recently set up a food-knowledge and recipe-sharing platform called Dishcovery (www.dishcovery.in) which it plans to use to talk about authentic Indian food.

Centre of excellence

As an addition to the new product development initiatives, a new department called Centre of Excellence for Indian Cuisine has been created. Manned by chefs, the objective of this department is to study and revive authentic foods from different parts of India and help funnel new ideas for innovation.

'All meals occasion' strategy

MTR wants to be omnipresent in the authentic Indian foods category and focus on the same. It also plans to strengthen its position in each category by expanding and adding sub-categories as well as having aggressive marketing campaigns to create strong awareness among consumers about all its product lines. Covering key mealtimes apart from breakfast, in which it is already a leader, MTR plans to grow in all meal occasions and be a friend to the housewife through lunch, dinner and breakfast.

India is firmly set on the path to growth; it is a nation that is rapidly changing. The second largest country in the world by population, India is also a relatively young country with 45 per cent of the population below thirty years. This new generation requires new answers and MTR continues to evolve along with its ever-changing consumer base, looking at newer ways of communicating with them and satisfying all their culinary requirements and presenting itself as one-stop food solution for authentic Indian food.

The Complete Man

Raymond

SINCE 1925

THE STORY OF A COMPLETE BRAND

From a small muted beginning in a tiny mill, this story has gone on to attain epic proportions. Over the decades, the company has grown in leaps and bounds, straddling changing political and economic scenarios in the country, to metamorphose into one of India's textile conglomerates and the world's leading producers of worsted fabrics.

When you think fashion you think anorexic models, unwearable-in-real-life garments, catwalks, aspirational but unachievable good looks and bodies.

Not so when you think of India's leading men's fashion brand, Raymond. In fact, Raymond is so real, so much a part of Indian life and legend that many people in this country would not think of it as a 'brand'. Over the years, Raymond has ingrained itself into modern Indian culture to become India's leading men's fashion brand. Such wide acceptance by consumers across diverse socio-economic groups is a rare phenomenon, and reveals how Raymond has, for many people, become a standard part of life.

The origins

At the turn of the century, in 1925, a gentleman named Wadia, prompted by the demand of the Indian Defence Forces for clothing for soldiers, decided to build a small woollen mill in the wilds of Thane, 40 km away from Bombay. Perhaps the spot was selected on a whim, or else he was gifted with prescience, for Thane was to become a prime industrial area over the course of time. However, Wadia Mills was not destined to remain with Mr Wadia for long; it found a new owner in E.D. Sassoon & Co., a prominent industrial family of the time. The mill acquired a new name too: The Raymond Woollen Mills. The next twenty years went by with a steady rhythm. The little mill turned out a modest quantity of woollen blankets and fabrics, the greater quantity of which was supplied to the armed forces; and its future seemed secure, if unremarkable.

Meanwhile, in a different part of the country, another entrepreneurial family, the Singhanias, riding the industrialization wave, was making rapid strides in multiple fields. It set up the J.K. Cotton Spinning & Weaving Mills Co. Ltd that supplied high quality cotton cloth and yarn to clothing manufacturers throughout India to meet the tremendous demand from the defence forces. Even in those early years, the Singhanias realized that industrialization was the path to self-reliance, the only means of bringing about economic stability in the future. This inherent pioneering spirit of the family propelled it into multiple ambitious ventures in fields as diverse as cotton, jute, sugar, steel and oil, with splendid successes in each new venture—the J.K. Oil Mills (1924), J.K. Jute Mills (1931), J.K. Cotton Manufacturers Ltd (1933) and J.K. Iron & Steel Co. Ltd (1934).

The Singhanias, focused on expanding their empire, entered into negotiations with the Sassoons convinced that Raymond Woollen Mills held and had the potential of becoming something infinitely larger. This turned out to be one of those decisive moments in the history of this company. Three years before India became independent, in the winter of 1944, the J.K. Group became the proud owners of Raymond Woollen Mills. Lala Kailashpat Singhania (one of the three Singhania brothers) took charge of this fledgling enterprise, and thus began the Raymond saga.

Product perfect

No brand can dream of achieving Raymond-like stature without an impeccable product to begin with. In the eight-plus decades of its existence Raymond has consistently stayed ahead of the curve by modernizing its manufacturing technology.

Continuously striving for loftier standards, Raymond is a company that has come a long way, from a mill manufacturing coarse woollen blankets to becoming the creator of the world's finest worsted suiting fabric ever (the Super 250, which is made of wool approximately one-fiftieth the diameter of human hair). This transformation is testimony to Raymond's globally acclaimed textile manufacturing strengths. Over the decades, Raymond has taken its place among the few companies in the world who can deliver a complete solution right from fibre to garment and has become the largest integrated manufacturer of worsted fabric in the world.

Adapting to the times

Raymond has always prided itself on staying ahead of the curve and being quicker than its competitors when it came to spotting fabric and fashion trends, consistently delivering contemporary blends and cutting-edge design.

» As early as 1958, Raymond launched India's first new wool-blended yarn 'terool' which turned out to be a breakthrough in the wool industry, providing a lightweight fabric that made for cool and comfortable wear.

» Raymond went on to develop Merino wool of extraordinary quality, produced indigenously by rearing Merino sheep from Australia, an initial batch of which was gifted by the Prime Minister of Australia, who was impressed by the exceptional effort in this venture.

» When synthetics became a more practical choice for the working individual in the late 1980s, Raymond responded by making forays into commercial production of polyester filament yarn (PFY) with a composite woollen division set up with the latest equipment and sophisticated processes and international technological expertise.

» With the economy opening up in the 1990s and the Indian consumer being exposed to fine fabrics from major Italian brands, Raymond countered the challenge with its Lineage Line collection of fine, all-wool fabrics using premium fibres like cashmere, angora and camel hair (Super 100s to Super 140s), to which there was overwhelming response.

» Soon after, with denims becoming a rage, Raymond added a new dimension to its textile-manufacturing capabilities with the launch of its denim division to fuel the escalating global demand for the fabric. The company was a pioneer in launching speciality ring denim in India, and is amongst the top producers of denim fabric and jeans in the subcontinent today. It has become the preferred source for global premium brands, producing 20 lakh pairs of jeans a year.

Today, the Raymond Group is vertically and horizontally integrated to provide customers with total textile solutions. Few companies globally have such a diverse product range of nearly 20,000 varieties of worsted suiting to cater to customers across age groups, occasions and styles.

> Raymond's product positioning can be summed up as 'premium at every price'. This is an assurance that every consumer will receive a quality product, regardless of the price he pays (from `200 a metre to `5 lakh for a suit piece). It is the result of investment in product development, which is evident in the number of 'firsts' Raymond has in the Indian textile industry.

RETAIL: A CORNERSTONE OF THE RAYMOND SUCCESS STORY

Raymond, not content with simply making the finest fabrics in the world, also wanted to take them directly to consumers. Hence retail assumed paramount importance, and great thought was given to establishing a wide network of Raymond shops all over the country and beyond. The management ensured that the franchisees were given appropriate training, so that the brand value remained undiluted. At a time when most businesses were run on practical learning and gut instinct, Raymond looked ahead by investing time and effort into training staff at each level. There were product-oriented programmes for Raymond dealers and retail shop managers, macro- and micro-level training modules for the sales staff as well as management development programmes at Harvard for departmental heads and managers.

Building enduring bonds

The Raymond distributor-dealer-agent-franchisee meet at regular intervals every year, and the brand and the network discuss trends, on-the-ground market intelligence and consumer insights. Some of the retailers have worked with Raymond for four generations. This smoothly running, interconnected system has stood the test of time and of competition from other brands, and will continue to do so.

> All successful relationships are two way, and that's exactly what Raymond invested in. On one hand it trained and built a strong consumer-facing front-end retail experience and on the other hand it used the same front end to gather consumer and market intelligence.

Made to Measure: Another innovation by Raymond

Raymond has introduced a unique garmenting service that gives a perfect fit with an impeccable finish. Tailored outfits often lose out on the finish of machine-made clothes. The Made to Measure service allows a discerning customer the opportunity to style a personalized garment while at the same time getting a factory-finished, customized fit. It understands the consumer's need for perfection as well as the desire to express one's own personal sense of style. The detailed process includes advice from experts on choosing the right fabric, the appropriate style and matching embellishments and a measurement process that is unique to each person.

Today, there are over 700 Raymond stores in 350 locations across India, from bustling cities to Tier-V towns, and 40 in overseas locations, and its products are available in over 20,000 multi-brand outlets. This ensures the brand reaches more people, before the competition, and in a way allows Raymond to advise consumers on fashion.

The Raymond Brand

Having built the perfect product backed by state-of-the-art manufacturing and an enviable distribution footprint, Raymond, over its long history, never compromised on its deliverables, the foremost of which is the quality and performance of its products and services, not only to its customers but also to its stakeholders. This image as the provider of the best quality product in the market is what has made the Raymond brand consistently stand out. Raymond enjoys the trust of all its stakeholders—customers, shareholders, suppliers, trade partners and employees.

Raymond's heritage value is indeed compelling. Few brands, not just in India but across the globe, have existed and flourished over such a long period. The Raymond brand—with trust, excellence, quality and leadership as its hallmarks—has always been the most important asset of the organization, with its preservation at the core of a lot of its decision making.

The greatest strength of Raymond is that it is a heritage brand that is still fresh, and the advertising is targeted towards maintaining that.

With eighty-five years of experience, Raymond is one of the only brands that could be considered to be in a position of authority to share its knowledge on fabric, style, colours and accessories with the consumer. The Raymond customer has an emotional connect with the brand. It can straddle different segments with ease—a 22-year-old and a 55-year-old can both relate to it. The customer actually owns the brand and it is this sense of ownership that makes Raymond such a powerful brand.

Raymond campaigns through the years

In India, western wear signified stature and sophistication. The brand too had to espouse these codes and appeal to the elite. So the first logo featured a chess king, which symbolized the brand's emphasis on a sharp and sophisticated attitude, and helped the brand win over a certain segment of society. The first two decades of the advertising featured this symbol as a motif and represented the brand's focus on a premium and upwardly mobile mindset.

In the 1970s India began to undergo a cultural shift which was best depicted by Bollywood. Popular culture started to rally around the 'angry young man' and, realizing this huge shift, Raymond moved its product and advertising away from the elite, sophisticated man to focus on the common man.

The 1980s saw the launch of the '*Guide to the Well-dressed Man*' campaign that moved beyond the mood of the 'angry young man' stereotype. In 1980, Raymond decided to add another dimension to the Raymond Man's personality by celebrating achievers in various fields. One ad even featured a ten-year-old football wizard, with a tongue-in-cheek message: You don't have to be a Raymond *man* to be a Raymond man.

This 1980s theme gradually changed to '*Celebrating Life's Moments*', where the communication was fine-tuned to connect people's celebration of certain moments in their lives to the brand experience. Following this was another set of ads which suggested: '*Never Say No to Life*'.

The first three decades had thus created a foundation of aspiration, connectedness and leadership to make the leap into the 1990s with '*The Complete Man*.'

The Complete Man

By the 1990s India was changing again; liberalization had set in, the economy had opened up and there was an upbeat sentiment. People, in their hearts, felt something good was around the corner, but not many were vocal about it. They were still conditioned by the tough environment of the 1970s and 1980s where the 'angry young man' dominated people's imagination. In the 1990s, Raymond decided to break away from the past and launched 'The Complete Man' campaign.

The portrayal of 'The Complete Man' not only broke the conventions of fashion advertising, it also went against the definition of masculinity— because 'The Complete Man' was not your classical knight in shining armour. He was real—With emotions, a sense of humour, sensitivity and even a hint of vulnerability. In an era when the 'angry young man' still ruled the silver screen and men's imagination, it was labelled by most as a risk.

But this leap was not into the unknown.

Research had indicated that men do not really aspire to be fashion models or testosterone-charged supermen. Social trends had pointed out that the Indian male was evolving or, at the very least, aspiring to evolve. 'The Complete Man' was built on these insights and hence was real and credible and not a unidimensional figure that was the reigning standard. And, hence, the daring step ahead was taken and the insights were translated into advertising strategy. It was still the angry young man era. But the Raymond man was softer, and every communication created showed the changes happening around the alpha male. Within no time, the stand was vindicated. In the years to come, even the Bollywood hero moved away from being 'angry'; and romance and family drama became success formulas for Hindi movies.

Owning this persona helped Raymond to 'own' a multitude of real-life occasions and situations for its product range—from a job interview to a day at work, a reunion of friends and a wedding.

Raymond's advertising themes display a strong continuity, with each new theme representing another step forward. Raymond, in essence, has always been linked with the discerning male, who cares about looking good, and who sets his own personal standards of conduct. At the same time, over the years, there has been consistent effort to ensure that the brand stays contemporary and fresh in the minds of consumers.

India has gone through many moods and, over the years, the brand has remained relevant by evolving with the consumer through its investment in consumer understanding, which leads the way for product development and consistent, yet fresh, marketing strategy, year after year.

The core theme for the communication strategy continues to build on this concept. *'The Complete Man' wears his success with grace, but, above all, is someone who has found a holistic approach to life.* Raymond's advertising celebrates family values, relationships and cultural values. The Raymond man has time to spare for others—it comes naturally to him; he doesn't have to 'make time' for his kids. The Raymond man is a warm, generous and compassionate being, who is greatly admired by peers and subordinates alike, and who cares for his family, friends, society and the environment.

Complete in every sense

Being complete is never linear, which means you have to continuously evolve along several fronts and it's by doing just that that Raymond became India's largest suiting brand. The company's 'complete' approach to business—investment in product development, manufacturing technology, distribution and consumer understanding—will ensure that it continues to lead fashion for Indian men.

In the nine decades of its existence, Raymond has tirelessly invested in the development of its products, manufacturing technology, distribution and workforce to remain at the top, not just in the market place, but in the Indian male's mind, because very early on in its journey, the company realized that it had to mould the Indian male, rather than espouse his current state of mind.

Raymond's dream for the future is to become an international brand by establishing its presence in mega cities around the globe, while remaining firmly rooted in India. Raymond plans to continue building on its rich legacy, be bigger and stronger and the face of emerging India.

LOOKING BACK: KEY PILLARS OF RAYMOND'S SUCCESS

1. **Premium at every price point:** Indians are value conscious; to succeed brands must come across as premium on imagery and product, yet accessible in monetary terms.
2. **Constant Innovation:** Use of progressive and cutting-edge manufacturing technology helps deliver innovative products that win in the marketplace.
3. **Evolve ahead of the times:** Culture evolves, and brands must be at the forefront of this evolution through product design, utility and imagery, to remain relevant.
4. **Build Relationships:** Indians bank on relationships, from how we buy to who we buy from. It's also the assurance of the retailer that a consumer buys into, and brands must leverage the power of the retailer to the point it becomes a competitive tool.
5. **Extensive consumer understanding:** The consumer remains the same, but what he wants changes, and brands that have stood the test of time ensure design, marketing and retail strategy flow from understanding the consumer.

Saffola *life*   THE BRAVEHEART BRAND

Saffola from Marico Industries Limited is the fascinating case of a brand that carved a niche for itself in a commodity market that was low on differentiation and branding. This meant standing up to strong and entrenched products like Postman and Dalda. Today, Saffola stands out as a brand that robustly accepted and dismissed challenges from local and global companies in its half-century-long journey.

A pioneer's vision: A brand not a commodity

Marico has made a name for itself by developing several strong Indian brands and the man who has been the principal architect of most of these iconic brands is Harsh Mariwala.

Harsh joined the family business in 1971, back when the company was called Bombay Oil Industries Ltd (BOIL). In 1983, BOIL formed three divisions: the consumer products division, the fatty acids and chemicals division and the spice extracts division. Harsh developed the consumer products business in BOIL and functioned as executive director from 1983 to 1990. In April 1990, BOIL was restructured and the consumer products division became a separate company that was named Marico Industries Limited (Marico).

Harsh Mariwala took over as managing director (MD) of Marico in 1990 and, under his stewardship, Marico developed marketing skills and transformed itself from a family-owned business into a company that created high quality consumer brands like Parachute and Saffola. Now chairman of Marico Industries Limited, Harsh says: 'With Saffola we were very clear from the beginning that we wanted to build a niche brand, offer a superior product to the consumer, charge a premium and not run after every single consumer available. We wanted everyone to recognize and remember us.'

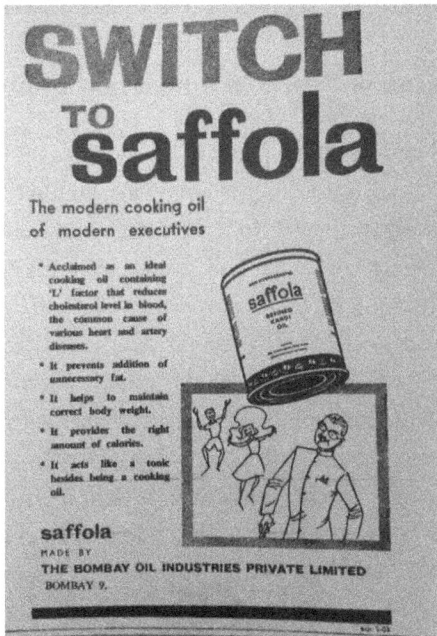

Investing in brand from very early days.

And remember they did, because Saffola spoke a different language at a time when most edible oils were about food and taste. This new language spoke directly to the nation's heart. Saffola urged the nation to move from traditional oils to a healthier oil as part of a new heart-healthy lifestyle.

India was epitomized by a distinct lack of a culture of exercise and fitness, combined with a palate known for its fondness for rich, spicy and oily food. The average Indian was thus a ripe target for heart trouble. With a new media environment of heightened awareness of modern-day lifestyles leading to increased risk to the heart and the impact of edible oils on the same, the arrival of Saffola with its unique ingredients which differentiated it from others in the market was unanimously hailed.

Saffola, however, was not just a timely coincidence. It was the brainchild of a keen sense of branding and differentiation: one of the sharpest brands in India showing decades-long consistency in its positioning of 'heart health'. And above all else Saffola was the result of a genuine mission to bring a great product into consumers' lives. Ever since, Saffola has worked diligently on the product side of the mix, offering new innovations and updating the oil on the lines of new scientific discoveries about heart health.

Behind every successful brand is a high quality product

According to Dr Lewis, former head of product development at Marico, 'Traditionally in the commodity market, you couldn't hide the truth of the product...There was no way to camouflage the colour or the texture. Consumers knew their oils well and would not accept a product that looked radically different from their existing choices.'

Despite this, Saffola was the first to innovate by creating a blend of edible oils (rice bran and kardi) in a market where the traditional perception was that blends were adulterated or inferior. But when Saffola offered a blend, the same market opened up and accepted it without question. Much of this success had to do with the credibility of Saffola. But it was also about the performance of a high quality product in the kitchen.

The fact that an oil company could create a blend that was superior and could satisfy consumers is a testimony to the product development genius at work in Marico over the years. Even today Saffola is a pioneer in creating new blends and adding much-needed innovations like antioxidants to their oil. The consumer clearly recognizes Saffola as a brand that brings great benefits into their lives.

Saugata Gupta, the MD and chief executive officer (CEO) of Marico smiles when he recounts that market conditions also played a not-so-small role in the innovations culture that Marico is now known for. 'At Marico we learnt how to convert every adversity into an opportunity', he says. 'Interestingly enough, quite a few of the innovations on Saffola have happened as a result of scarcity of raw materials, or perhaps a challenge from new competition. We were always ready with a new answer or solution. We would refuse to be passive observers.'

The turning point: Telling the tough truth

To the outsider, a key memory of Saffola was the hard-hitting ambulance ad released by Saffola in the early 1990s. Living rooms resonated with the sharp warning sounds of the arrival of an ambulance to take away the husband suffering from what seemed to be a heart attack—the wife distraught, the husband helpless, the children lost. If you were a woman, a wife, a mother, watching this film amidst the sounds of an electrocardiogram monitor, this wasn't just an advertisement but a mirror to the frightening reality of impending heart attacks. The message to the Indian woman was brutal but powerful—if you're not using Saffola, you are actually inviting heart trouble.

A Bold Strategy

Saffola has always had a clear vision and strategy, choosing to offer a daring proposition with premium pricing.
The Saffola Vision: Four Indians die every minute due to cardio-vascular disease. The brand's mission is to reduce this statistic.
Positioning: A premium heart-healthy edible oil in a category driven by taste and seed type.
Target Group: Urban consumers who face the impending threat of a heart problem due to a busy and unhealthy lifestyle.

And Saffola was not being unnecessarily alarmist. India is a nation where four people die every minute of a heart-related ailment. Saffola's mission has always been clear—to keep this staggering number under check.

This has meant that over the decades Saffola has never borrowed from the edible-oil category codes. In Saffola communication, there have never been women cooking wholesome food as sunlight speckles the kitchen; there have been no cherubic boys digging into fried samosas or doing cartwheels over just-cooked hot, fluffy, appetizing food items. The creative idea has always been to make the target audience face the hard truth.

The brand's greatest ally: An honest voice

What Saffola doesn't promise is a miracle cure or a quick fix. It is an honest, insightful, accurate and authentic brand that looks to change your perspective on heart health. Saffola does not encourage a lazy approach to exercise and diet, knowing well that using the right cooking oil is only a small but relevant part of a lifestyle change. Saffola has never been crafted like an oil by Marico, but as a heart-health solution.

A large part of this honest voice is an ongoing engagement with consumers. Nothing motivates all the teams that work on the brand like meeting consumers and hearing their stories. Knowing that you are positively contributing to life enhancement when working on Saffola is great encouragement. Adding Saffola to her shopping cart is an act of quiet self-assurance for an Indian homemaker. 'I know that if Saffola is here in my kitchen, my husband is here in my life,' says a twinkly-eyed fifty-something lady from a Mumbai suburb. There are enough instances of households that find Saffola outside their budgets but believe that it is the oil for their hearts. So strong is the brand equity, so strong the belief that, given a chance, at any time there are fence-sitters who are ready to be part of the Saffola universe.

So much so that back in the 1980s, rumours of shortage would spread panic among Saffola buyers, many of them queuing up in serpentine rows outside the Marico marketing office in Bandra Reclamation.

Millennium move: The pioneer accepts a new challenge

After a couple of decades of slow but steady growth, Saffola had, as planned, carved a niche for itself. But by the late 1990s Marico also recognized that there was larger potential for growth in the edible-oil category and potential for exploring other, newer categories. Accordingly, it drew up a strategic plan to develop the Saffola brand.

Strategic shift: From fear to care

The challenge for the marketing team was twofold: one, to move Saffola's image from that of a therapeutic brand to a more holistic heart-health brand and, two, continue to bring Saffola out of the confines of the edible-oil category.

Strategic Shift in Positioning

Move from a curative to preventive heart-care brand
This move impacted product packaging: Shift from old to new packaging.
Communication: Shift in tone from 'fear' to 'care'.
Move from impending heart attack as a trigger of realization to daily signs of an ageing heart.

Having been a pioneer in more ways than one, the challenge was wholeheartedly accepted by the company and, as time would tell, without ever compromising on its core values.

Sameer Satpathy, executive vice president and business head (Marico India) explains that the lens through which Marico viewed Saffola did eventually change. 'The ambulance film may have worked wonders in the short term, but in the long term we needed a warmer, friendlier image. The life-truth, but given out in a milder avatar.'

Knowledge about Saffola's powerful equity pushed Marico into working to change the association of the brand with 'fear' to 'care'.

Every element of the marketing mix was relooked at. The packaging of the oil underwent multiple innovations and improvements in form, function and aesthetics. Subtle and strong cues of care were designed into the packaging. Today, the yellow heart-shaped container is the most visible reminder of the care and heart-health association of the brand as it sits on the kitchen shelf. Saffola communication reflects the same journey.

Was *Kal Se* the shot in the arm that Saffola needed? Could this be the new philosophy, a new way of looking at life—not with fear, but with joy and understanding? *Kal Se* (starting tomorrow) was a film about procrastination, about men who postpone exercise and diet efforts until tomorrow. The brand entered with a simple statement: *'Dil ki hifazat zaroori hai aaj se'* (Your heart needs care starting today).

What this film did was to create a new character—a loveable quirky man who would be seen across all Saffola films. This was the picture of the real Indian man—slightly overweight, who pays the gym fees but never sets foot in the gym and eats back all the calories he's lost after a walk by gorging on jalebies and samosas. The weight he carries is a burden on his heart and reflects in his ability or inability to stride up a flight of stairs or chase down a thief. What this film (and the series that followed) brought to the brand was a refreshing charm that didn't exist before.

Huffing and puffing his way through a TV commercial, the Saffola man carried more than his weight; he carried a unique truth into Indian homes, a truth packaged in comic relief and not in fear. A subtle balance of anxiety and humour has ever since been key to the charm of Saffola's creative work.

Standing right behind her out-of-breath husband was the Saffola woman, no longer helpless, but now the alert, observant wife, ready to intervene, ready to take charge early. It's fair to say that as a brand Saffola has never guaranteed heart health, but it does prod the 'CEO housewife' into taking action earlier, rather than later. The brand asks her to take a few steps and, in turn, promises to help bring changes and interventions in her husband's life.

An Iconic brand looking for better visibility

In addition to having play only in the edible-oil category, Saffola was also held back by another unique reality. Edible oils are an invisible brand for the rest of the household. The homemaker engages with it, the others don't—because we don't eat oil, we eat food cooked in oil.

As much as it made the transition from commodity to brand, Saffola soon undertook the transition from being invisible to being visible to the rest of the family members. This continues to be the key thrust in the marketing plan at Marico.

As a result, the next decade saw product innovations and brave moves in the company to gain visibility.

Stretching the portfolio: To shrink waistlines

It was time now for Saffola to begin leveraging its massive equity and enter into newer categories. Research and studies pointed to the gigantic snacks market, a key culprit in mindless calorie consumption. Saffola Zest (baked snacks) was aimed at bringing a choice to discerning consumers who were aware of the need for a four o'clock snack without feeling guilty or needing to cook up a small meal for their children and families. 'A great idea, but perhaps not executed to its best potential,' says Satpathy. 'But failures are a great learning in disguise. With Zest we focused too much on health and not enough on taste. That was a mistake we learnt from.'

Saffola oats: Morning start for the heart

Learning from the Zest experience, Saffola identified a super-grain that consumers were beginning to appreciate and adopt for its health benefits— oats. With fast-increasing awareness around gyms and fitness, consumers were open to new but safe food products that helped in controlling their body weight. But their poor taste on the plate did not make oats the snack of choice for households. Marico could count on its learnings to know that for the first time it would have to introduce the 'taste' factor to the Saffola portfolio. The time was right for Indian households to accept a breakfast intervention like oats, repackaged to suit the Indian palate.

With the launch of Saffola Oats and Masala Oats, both sweet and savoury variants, Saffola moved out of the kitchen closet right on to the breakfast table.

'Today consumers have firmly accepted Saffola's health credentials', says Sanjay Gupta, head marketing (wellness and youth). 'We no longer need to put effort into that. We are here to work on giving a great "taste" to consumers now. In a healthy and convenient form.' For the busy household, a pair of scissors seems to be the only kitchen tool needed for a nutritious breakfast. A ₹15 pack of Saffola Masala Oats is opened and an appetizing breakfast follows, without sweat and toil in the kitchen.

In just a few years, Saffola Oats is finally the crowning achievement for the brand teams after a decade-long experiment in the food category.

'Sweatless results' is what the Indian man really wants, says Govind Pandey, president, McCann Erickson India, the company that handles Saffola's promotion. 'Not that we endorse this, but we understand this. This is a man like you and me—we all are in the same boat. Watching our waistlines, eating carefully through the week, celebrating cheat-days on the weekend, worrying, stressing, procrastinating and occasionally *actually visiting the gym.'*

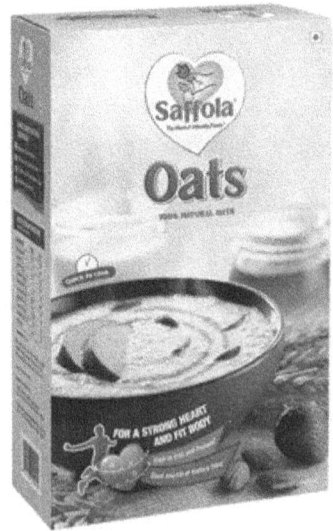

Saffolalife: Giving a higher purpose to the idea of care

The Indian man is unique—he does not think much of heart care unless he has been diagnosed with a problem. But equally unique is Saffola's approach to this mission, reminding the Indian family in many small and big ways about the need to be proactive about heart health. Saffola's methodology defies all known practices. The brand has always kept social consciousness firmly above profits and heart health above all corporate machinations. In 1991, Saffola created The Healthy Heart Foundation and in 2006 the non-profit artery of Saffolalife.

Interestingly, Saffola offers expensive cholesterol tests and 'know-your-heart's-age' tests instead of discounts and coupons, not just to users but also to non-users. This is a brand that engages selflessly with consumers living in denial about their heart health on occasions such as World Heart Day. This is a brand that expects nothing in return except a greater awareness of heart disease. It is this culture of giving to the consumers that accounts for the luminous halo around brand

High Science protects everything your heart beats for.

Saffola

Dil Ka High Science

Saffola. 'Saffola has always had an aura that is much larger than the size of the brand,' says MD and CEO Saugata Gupta. 'It will never behave like a brand looking for short-term rewards or cashing in on any trends.'

Creating Heart Awareness

One big step, selflessly executed, has been the appropriation of World Heart Day by Saffola. Free cholesterol and heart-age tests have been designed to bring in the consumers who are in denial about how their lifestyle affects their heart health. When someone takes a free test to check their heart age, they take the first step into the world of Saffola, not by spending money, but by availing of an expensive test for free.

This unique culture also stems from the way things are done at Marico. It's never been a trader company at heart or a commodity supplier. The company has been built by creating brands that offered clear value to the consumer. 'Saffola, Parachute and Kaya are the three great brands that we have built,' says Harsh Mariwala. 'And not just Saffola but each brand has been given a focus, a niche that rewards the consumer and rewards us.'

The rewards have come—slowly but steadily. If in the 1970s and 1980s heart health was a tiny niche, in 2014 the heart business is more than booming. The new generations are keenly aware of the repercussions of a sedentary life, desk-bound careers, obesity and diabetes. In this environment, Saffola has reached out to the newly conscious consumers with quiet dignity.

Jumping on to the bandwagon, competitors have feebly tried to muscle in to the heart space and challenge Saffola. But no one has lasted in the race so far. Govind Pandey of McCann Erickson says: 'Unlike the competition, we are here for a larger purpose and our products are intelligent interventions in the service of the larger purpose. We will never digress from that.' It is this larger purpose that has firmly kept doctors and medical experts believing in the brand, vouching for it and recommending it. This is the core equity of the brand that can never be usurped by competitors without the patience and tenacity to build up such a support network.

'We welcome competition though,' says Sanjay Gupta. 'Competitors claiming a share of the heart market will only bring more choice to the consumers. Because when faced with competition, we only reach higher and figure out better solutions for our consumers.'

What Saffola wants perhaps is to replace the traditionally known red heart in people's minds with the Saffola heart—a heart that's much more visible today, with a heartbeat that can be heard across the country. It's a unique heart that speaks honestly and urgently, a heart that celebrates life in all its failings and triumphs. Saffola is a brand which made strategic shifts that have transformed it without ever compromising on the core, a brand that has moved from fear to care, from heart health to heart health and convenience, from a kitchen shelf brand to a dining table brand, from proposition to purpose—encouraging a new, aware and awakened way of life.

'We want more people to be aware and awake—heart trouble is not something you should take lightly,' says Mr Mariwala. 'Whatever happens, Saffola will always be there to nudge more people into caring for their heart, and not ignoring its beat.'

All of Saffola's hard work has hardly been wasted on the consumer as awareness of heart health has dramatically improved over the past few decades. It is not a rare sight to see a vendor selling the Gujarati staple 'thepla' cooked in Saffola oil or even a chikki in Lonavla made of Saffola oil, a health guarantee of sorts.

Saffola trivia

Curiously enough, even though Saffola was launched around 1965, an avid collector of old magazines discovered possibly one of the first print advertisements of Saffola in a 1962 issue of *Femina* magazine. Conflicting history aside, the ad is relevant for one key reason. The essence of the communication message hasn't changed till 2014.

□□rd	nstituted B□	□e□r
Sa□o□a □or□□ □ear□□a□ cam□ai□n □ins si□ver in the Best Ongoing campaign for its campaign in □□e □ears 2009–12	Effies	2012
T□e Sa□o□a □ourne□ is □u□□is□e□ as a case s□u□□ □□ □arvar□ □usiness Sc□oo□ an□ □ar□o□ course curriculum a□□ea□in□ □usiness sc□oo□	□arvar□ □usiness Sc□oo□	2012
Grand Emvie for Best Ongoing Media campaign	Emvies	2012
Saffolalife 'Happy Birthday Dear Heart' wins gold □or □es□□e□ra□e□ □ar□e□in□ cam□ai□n	Emvies	2012
Saffolalife Heart Age finder wins gold in the Lea□ □enera□ion□Conversion ca□e□or□	□nau□ura□□o□i□ □ar□e□in□ Associa□ion A□ar□	2012
Sa□o□a □or□□ □ear□□a□□ Times o□□n□ia □nnova□ion cam□ai□n a□ar□e□ si□ver a□□□e S□□es Asia A□ar□ 2011 in □□e □es□ Use o□ □e□ia (□a□a□ines□Ne□s□a□ers) ca□e□or□	Cannes Lions □n□erna□iona□ Fes□iva□ o□ Crea□ivi□□ an□ Haymarket Media, □u□□is□ers o□ Cam□ai□n Asia	2011
Sa□o□a a□ar□e□ □ar□e□in□ Cam□ai□n □o□□ □or 'Saffolalife: Young at Heart' at APPIES 2011— Asia Pacific Marketing Congress	□ns□i□u□e o□A□ver□isin□ Sin□a□ore (□AS)	2011
Sa□o□a □ins □e□ia A□□□□ □o□□ □or □□e □or□□ Heart Day radio entry—'Radio Goes Silent'	AAA□□oa Fes□2009	2009
Sa□o□a □ins an Emvie si□ver □or □es□□□e□ia □nnova□ion in Ra□io □or □Sa□o□a□i□e□Lis□en □o Your Heart Beat' (Radio Goes Silent)	E□V□E	2009

Sa□o□a □ins □ree Emvie a□ar□s □or Sa□o□a □or□ □ear□□a□ ra□io cam□ai□n□ 1. Cri□cs C□oice A□ar□ 2. □o□ Emvie–Ra□io Ca□e□or□ 3. □ran□ Emvie	Emvie Fes□iva□ □um□ai	2008
□oaFes□□e□ia □o□ □or □es□Use o□Ra□io□ Sa□o□a □or□ □ear□□a□ cam□ai□n	AAA□□oa Fes□2008	2008
Adjudged one of India's Ten Best Marketers	□usiness To□a□	2006
Effie gold for advertising effectiveness of communica□ion □one on Sa□o□a □o□	Ne□ Yor□ American □ar□e□in□ Associa□ion □ A□ver□isin□ C□u□	2005
Grand Effie—Brand of the Year	Ne□ Yor□ American □ar□e□in□ Associa□ion □ A□ver□isin□ C□u□	2005

CHANGING INDIA, CHANGING 'TIMES'

' I f the world would only stop for us, so that we could all grow old together, what a pleasant state of things might ensue, but it refuses to halt for a moment: it declines to accept age and idleness in lieu of vigour and industry.'

These words appeared in *The Times of India* on 25 May 1857 in the context of the Mutiny. In the century and a half between that time and the present, while much water has flown down the Ganges, the paper has continued to reflect the essence of these words.

India has changed in this time, not once but many times over, with the Mughal Empire and the British Raj both passing from glittering acmes into history's dusty pages. During this tumultuous period, *The Times of India* has acted as the chronicler and harbinger of change and in recent times, as its enabler.

A slice of history

The newspaper came into being on 3 November 1838 with an early focus on mercantile news.

In keeping with the dynamic environment of its readers, the paper too has changed. Beginning with its name. When the passage quoted earlier appeared in the paper in 1857, it was called *The Bombay Times and Journal of Commerce*. In its journey, it absorbed other publications such as *The Bombay Standard* and *The Daily Telegraph and Courier*. In 1861, the paper was renamed *The Times of India* (TOI).

Over the next eight decades, the paper expanded its coverage dramatically. As India changed hands, so did the TOI, passing from its British owners into Indian hands in 1946. For a period of over thirty years, beginning with the 1950s, the brand continued to deepen its relationship with readers. New editions of the paper came into being in Delhi, Ahmedabad, Bangalore, Lucknow and Patna. The focus was on political coverage and keeping the reader informed on national developments. The tone was conservative, in line with the mood of the country.

Infusion of new thought

The next phase of changes, and major ones at that, came in the 1980s with India beginning to take its first, somewhat tentative steps towards liberalization. Thrift began to give way to a new wave of consumerism and the youth got their share of political space. The TOI was the first media brand to gauge the changing mood of advertisers, who began looking for channels to give significant pan-India exposure to their products and services, especially in key urban centres.

The brand began to change the rules of the game in a series of actions that would transform the Indian newspaper industry. Up to this point in time, the entire strategy of newspapers had been focused on increasing circulation and then pitching the higher numbers to advertisers as the sole reason for them to pay more. However, given that the cover price of one copy of a newspaper was less than the cost of producing it, this strategy ensured that any increase in circulation would eventually burden the system. Moving away from this hidebound practice, the TOI began focusing the attention of the advertiser on the value it gave him, by way of the *quality* of readership more than numbers. The thrust was on presenting an advertiser with the most relevant audience for his brand. For example, for a car brand it was important to target an upwardly mobile middle class family and the TOI's promise was to deliver just that. The thought faced initial resistance from advertisers and media agencies who were comfortable with the time-honoured strategy based on circulation numbers, which they perceived as tangible, as compared to the concept of value. The innovative strategy was tested in 1986–7, when the TOI announced a massive increase in advertising rates, ranging from 25 to 50 per cent. Based on a clear understanding of the market's potential to pay, the rate hikes survived the initial storm and over time were accepted by industry. This acceptance was because the new pricing was based on a clear rationale which also offered value to advertisers. The result: this was the first in a series of steps that were aimed at eventually enhancing profitability.

Mastermind: The game changer

The newspaper industry in India had been pricing advertising space in a manner that it merely covered costs with a small profit margin. The TOI objective in its new pricing strategy was to enhance profitability, while ensuring that the rate at which the advertiser paid was in correlation to the value he gained from the publication. The company took a hard look at its entire portfolio and based its strategy on its strengths across brands and markets.

This included other brands within the company such as *Navbharat Times* (NBT), *Maharashtra Times* and *The Economic Times* (ET). Seen in isolation, each brand had its strong and weak regions with no national pattern. Also, each brand was sold separately, with combo rates being the exception rather than the norm.

The new pricing strategy was based on the idea of presenting all these hitherto isolated brands in a single, more attractive matrix of rates to the advertiser—the Mastermind. It was not a mere rate card but India's first advertising-solutions package. Advertisers could choose from a variety of combinations. New editions were packaged with established ones and made available at irresistible prices. It was a win–win situation for both advertisers and the brand. The former could extend his reach at a nominal cost while new editions got a share of revenue and moved to profitability faster.

The result: *The Times Group was able to leverage its multiple brands across markets, much to the dismay of competitors that were strong in their regional citadels but had virtually no national presence.* This unique reach of the group gave an impetus to the TOI's Delhi edition, vis-a-vis *Hindustan Times* (HT). For an advertiser in Delhi, the prospect of having his ad also carried in the TOI's Mumbai edition at an attractive rate was a tremendous incentive. Advertising volumes shot skyward and soon a pattern was established, with competition hiking rates on the heels of any rate hike by the TOI, thus growing the industry itself.

More for less

In the early 1990s, rising literacy coupled with low newspaper penetration presented another opportunity. The plan was to reduce the cover price in a bid to grow circulation, with the reduced circulation revenue being offset by higher advertising revenue as a consequence of the brand delivering a larger number of readers. This contradicted the earlier trend, which had been to chase both circulation and advertising revenue. With this move, the TOI showed its willingness to sacrifice one for a big leap in the other.

Emboldened by a successful experiment with the ET, this strategy—termed Invitation Pricing—was tried out in Delhi in 1994. Both the TOI and HT were at ₹2.90, when the TOI decided to drop its cover price to ₹1.50. This was an immense risk because it was accompanied by an increase in supplements such as *Education Times* and *Ascent.* The brand was running the risk of potentially reducing its revenue and increasing cost simultaneously. The bold experiment of Invitation Pricing, coupled with product enhancement, saw the TOI's circulation move skyward. The result: *In circulation terms, the TOI in Delhi grow by 138 per cent between 1995 and 2000. The TOI's Bangalore and Pune editions attained leadership positions, the former's circulation growing by a dramatic 780 per cent.*

The contrarian thinking of the TOI was also reflected in the shift from the predecided advertising space measure of column centimetre to square centimetre. While the former varied from broadsheet to tabloid and from brand to brand, the latter made sure that the advertiser got precisely what he paid for.

June 2003 saw the TOI taking another giant leap with the introduction of the combo offer for readers. In a first, the TOI and NBT were offered at a special price of ₹75. This meant that the NBT reader could now get the TOI at a small additional sum, giving a family a complete package. Before the offer, the TOI and HT were neck-and-neck in Delhi at about 4.5 lakh copies while NBT was at 2 lakh copies. The result: *The combo offer saw the TOI increase circulation by 2 lakh copies, by selling to NBT households, while the latter's circulation also went up by a lakh copies*—all in a period of just one year. In July 2003, the combo offer was replicated, with the TOI and ET being offered at the same attractive price of ₹75. The response was overwhelming.

Enhancing reader experience

To justify the increase in advertising rates, the TOI had to deliver the most relevant audience, which meant reaching out to younger, more affluent readers with a higher inclination to spend. Consciously taking up the challenge in the early 1990s, the brand moved away from the earlier focus on politics and prioritized the task of giving the reader a sense of optimism each morning.

There was strong emphasis on local content with city editions reflecting the local character of their region while being true to the brand. Proximity to the reader increased with the brand now covering local cultural events, touching activities in schools, colleges, malls and market places and sprinkling useful news digests in different sections. Pages were added for sports, business and entertainment, infographics and fun-to-know news were introduced. Stories became short and crisp, typography and design also improved. With editions launched in Hyderabad, Pune and Kolkata, the TOI was truly a national paper in every sense of the word by the end of the millennium.

The process of product enhancement was continuous. Adding a new dimension were city-centric lifestyle supplements, such as the *Delhi Times* and *Bombay Times*, introduced in 1994. They had an uninhibited focus on the good life, celebrities and Bollywood, and also made space for fine dining, art and exciting happenings in the city. In May 2002, the TOI arrived in a slimmer form, in line with international newspaper formats. Early 2003 saw the brand's constant urge to innovate being manifested in another dramatic transformation—the TOI's Delhi edition became the first mainline daily in the world to go all colour. This was a path-breaking decision at the time as the investment in colour printing facilities was nearly thrice that of black and white. But the brand's logic was simple: why should a newspaper be dull and boring when the world around was so colourful? Beyond the paper, the colour theme of Krishna and his friends playing Holi, painted on the TOI's Bahadur Shah Zafar Marg office, became a symbol of the 165-year old brand's youthfulness.

The brand also became more irreverent. Political news became easier to access with innovations such as branding electoral news as 'Dance of Democracy'. Today, the paper offers between twenty and thirty-two pages of news, views, information, entertainment and more. Extensive use of cartoons and caricatures helps cheer up the reader. *The impact is seen in the numbers: the Indian Readership Survey (IRS 2012 Q4) gives the TOI over 7.6 million readers across India, making it India's leading English daily.*

Dance of Democracy

The activist brand

Over time, the focus of the brand evolved from merely informing the reader to empowering her. The mood of the country was buoyant, a vast middle-class was thrusting ahead, desiring to be unleashed towards the future and seeking its effort to be acknowledged.

The TOI, with its finger on the pulse of its readers, launched a series of city-centric campaigns. Each campaign was tailor-made to the city's needs and aspirations. While Chalo Dilli celebrated the capital's coming of age with symbols such as the Metro and the upcoming Commonwealth

Games; Mission Mumbai highlighted the angst of a city neglected by its policymakers. Similarly, Kolkata Rising, Now Lucknow, etc., captured the imagination of readers across cities. City-centric initiatives culminated in a festival, a veritable riot of music, art and theatre that had readers in raptures.

The brand took a strongly activist turn in 2007 with Lead India. Understanding the vacuum in the country's political leadership, the initiative urged public-spirited citizens to come forward and fill the gap. The thrust of the initiative was on inducting younger people from non-political background into the arena of governance. The initiative received over 35,000 entries and had citizens abuzz, culminating in a televized final selection round.

Another example was Teach India, which gave educated Indians an opportunity to dedicate a part of their time to teaching less privileged citizens, especially children. The idea was based on education being a great socio-economic leveller and the enabling tool for children from a modest economic background to attain career parity. The brand took a tremendous risk in the 2008 Aman ki Asha initiative which propagated friendship at grassroots level between India and Pakistan. The initiative tried to drive home the thought that friendship at citizen level could help overcome the frosty relations between the governments of the two nations.

In its 175th year, the brand took activism to a new high with a slew of campaigns under the I Lead India initiative. The Youth Brigade programme encouraged young people between eighteen and twenty-four years of age to take on a civic-related issue in their city. The idea was to demonstrate that a group of motivated young individuals, sans any official standing or authority, could make an impact on issues where the authorities had failed to deliver. Across twenty-seven cities of India, the Youth Brigades made their presence felt and many ensured sustainable change.

Going a step further, the I Lead India Organ Donation Day, on 6 August, drew the attention of citizens to a subject that had been the preserve of the medical profession. The initiative busted long-held myths on the subject, got support from a galaxy of celebrities and, within a fortnight, achieved over 60,000 pledges for the cause, higher than any NGO involved in the space achieved in an entire year.

THE TIMES OF INDIA

LOVE PAKISTAN

Feels odd to see those two words side by side doesn't it?

Terror, hatred and fanaticism somehow sit more comfortably in our minds when we think of the other side of the border.

Words that we've been fed in daily doses over the last six decades. And in greater doses over the last one year.

Shutting our minds to the undeniable truth that people across the border are, above all, people. Like us.

So here's the question. Is there any chance at all, that we could still raise a hand, not in anger but in greeting?

Depends on who raises his hand first, some of us would say. Also how, whisper a few others. But mostly, it all boils down to one simple question.

Why? Why must we do it? Why do we need them? Why don't they first say sorry for what they've done? And the answer is simple.

It's easier to say Hi than to say Sorry. It's shorter too. Besides, there is no rule that says a book has to be closed before a new one is opened. Not even if it's a history book.

So on the first day of this new year, we're going to make a start. Again.

With Aman Ki Asha. A brave, new people-to-people initiative by The Times of India and Pakistan's Jang Group to bring the people of two fine nations closer together. Culturally, emotionally and peacefully.

Starting with a series of cross-border cultural interactions, business seminars, music & literary festivals and citizens meets that will give the bonds of humanity a chance to survive outside the battlefields of politics, terrorism and fundamentalism.

In the hope that one day, words like Pakistan, India and Love will not seem impossible in the same sentence.

aman ki asha
AN INDO-PAK PEACE PROJECT
THE FIRST STEP

Ever-expanding footprint

The TOI currently has editions in fifty-three cities of India, with more in the pipeline. With a total print order of more than 4.8 million copies, the brand is the undisputed leader in key metros such as Mumbai, Bangalore, Ahmedabad and Pune, is neck-and-neck with HT in Delhi and a close second to *The Telegraph* in Kolkata. It continuously challenges incumbents in Chennai and Hyderabad.

The approach the TOI adopts for entering a new market is essentially to target the youth. The biggest example of a successful launch in recent times is that of Chennai, for long the bastion of a well-entrenched rival, *The Hindu*. The TOI realized that the youth of the city were open to a change, after years of consuming the conservative rival. A high-decibel launch which grabbed the city's eyeballs, superior local coverage together with the glitz of lifestyle supplements, accompanied by aggressive newspaper pricing and attractive package rates for advertisers saw TOI gain strong presence in the market, making the incumbent look over its shoulder in alarm.

What is also interesting is the brand's increasing focus on non-metro markets. From a scenario wherein the metros used to contribute 100 per cent of the turnover, today their share is 85 per cent and the day is not far when Tier-II cities will contribute 30 per cent. The idea is to capture the highest quality reader profile and target group in these cities. In line with this thought, TOI's leadership is also established in a slew of smaller cities such as Jaipur, Lucknow, Patna and Bhubaneswar. Recent months have witnessed the TOI being launched in markets such as Madurai, Trichy and Kolhapur.

Youthful at 175

Few brands in the world can boast of a legacy that goes back 175 years and appeal to the young even at this venerable age. The West has seen the newspaper industry decline due to the drop in young readers. So what is the magic potion that ensures the TOI is picked up by all ages from sixteen to sixty and seen as relevant for them?

The TOI makes a conscious attempt to target youth. This is based on two sound reasons. The first is that under-thirties make up 60 per cent of India's population, ensuring the average age of the Indian is twenty-six. The second is that this is a digital generation that can access news from several alternatives.

What the brand does is to empower the youth, giving them a forum to express themselves, celebrate achievements and voice angst. Instead of the traditional role of moulding public opinion, it tries to give young readers the choice of arriving at their own conclusions. Acknowledging

THE TIMES OF INDIA

A DAY IN THE life of INDIA

My husband works in the Amrika...

Oye ji, mine works out of Tihar jail only.

www.day.in
submit videos, photos,
cartoons, jokes

MAYAVI YANTRA

PRAADA

ChristianDire

Hey! Get me out of this aasan !!

That'll be another 500 bucks.

Honey, buy me a cricketer this b'day ...pleeeease

Namaste Bhabhiji... or am I wrong again, sir ji??

INCREDIBLE INDIA

Jai HO !!

Audition for a new reality show.

That's power to the people.

This Friday Munni Jawani

Rail reservation?

But I've already downloaded the movie....

Sob..!! I've no friends... in Facebook.

Next !!

My Engliss the goodest in India.

LURN ENGLISH FAST

Almighty, wash away all my old sins so that I can start making some fresh ones...

TIGER WOODS

Bizarre. Overloaded. Technicolo
Chaotic. Golmaal. Jugaad. Chalta

You'd run out of words long before you'd run out of an India that all those words describe. And in not just one language, but many. Including SMS.

India is not a contradiction in terms. It sets the terms for all contradiction. It's the world's biggest and most energetic democracy, where people chuck out governments as frequently as they chuck out their garbage. It's a byword for immense wealth and terrible poverty, a realm of billionaires and beggars, the Maha Kumbh mela and mega malls, tantrics and Twitter.

Have you ever seen a large 'Commit No Nuisance' sign and a line of men standing under it and peeing? A state-of-

the art expressway with cows roaming across it? A train with people sitting on the roofs of the es than passengers inside? A bo advertising 'Chilled Bear Served

As we celebrate the 61st year raucous and irrepressible Repub we invite you to share the sigh and the sounds, the scenes an surprises, that you feel make India. Join us in what we hop will be the biggest exercise ev collective story-telling: A Day Life of India. Hosted on www. Turn the page to find out mor

Jai Ho! And Ho Jaye

the irreverence of youth, TOI gives primacy to the individual over the establishment. View-Counter View, Speak Out and the I Lead India initiatives stand as prominent examples.

It acknowledges the passions of the youth, increasing coverage for cricket and Bollywood, to name but two aspects. Youth prefers brevity and this has seen the average length of a feature story drop from 700 to 400 words. Coverage of areas such as education, jobs and career and health has also increased. The TOI also stands for positivity, always viewing the glass as being half-full rather than half-empty. It offers readers a buffet of content spread over a diverse range of interests.

Possibly the greatest lesson for marketers from the dynamism of the TOI is to attain a balance between heritage and modernity. The only constant in the TOI's marketing plans is change, in accordance with the ever-changing needs of the reader and the advertiser. The brand has understood the danger of getting so enamoured of what has worked in the past that one could neglect what will appeal to the youth of today who are the future, the tomorrow.

Taking the brand ahead

In the current period and coming years, the digital medium will increasingly dominate information and entertainment for the most desired audience of advertisers, upwardly mobile youth. The challenge will be to remain relevant to them.

The Times Group has begun taking steps in this direction. The TOI's online version is already India's most popular news portal with its web, online and application versions together having a massive 57 million unique visitors (Google Analytics). Times Now, the English news channel launched in the previous decade, is a leader in its own segment. The recent introduction of Alive, an augmented reality application enabling readers to use their smartphones to access video content offers a new platform for advertisers. The group enjoys the advantage of being able to leverage multiple platforms, across radio, television, Internet and print. This gives it the strength of being able to cross-sell to advertisers across platforms.

At the heart of the future strategy will remain the newspaper—the soul of the brand. The thrust now will be on lightening the paper's content, simplifying writing styles to make the language more sharp and punchy, enhancing design to make it more contemporary and enabling readers to access news as it develops through the day using tech-enabled online links placed in the paper. User-generated content will find more space in the paper, adding another layer to reader engagement. The TOI will continue reflecting the changing India, tomorrow as it does today.

What you didn't know about *The Times of India*

- The TOI's earlier avatar, *The Bombay Times and Journal of Commerce*, was a bi-weekly, published on Wednesdays and Saturdays only. The paper turned daily in 1850.
- The sobriquet 'The Old Lady of Bori Bunder' was given to the paper by B.G. Horniman, editor of *The Bombay Chronicle*.
- On 7 July 2002, the TOI informed its readers that it was now the world's largest-selling English broadsheet daily with 21,44,842 copies, pushing *USA Today* to second place.
- The TOI's spectacular 150th anniversary celebrations included 'Timeless Art', an exhibition of outstanding contemporary canvases and sculptures at Victoria Terminus (now Chhatrapati Shivaji Terminus).
- TOI's campaigns have won global acclaim and advertising awards. Prominent among them were the Cannes Grand Prix 2008 won by Lead India, Cannes Gold Lions won by 'A Day in the life of Chennai' (2009) and the Farmer Suicide film (2013).
- Former President K.R. Narayanan worked for The TOI in 1945, during the course of which he interviewed Mahatma Gandhi. The interview was not published.
- Articles by a galaxy of guests have appeared in the TOI, including Mahatma Gandhi, Jawaharlal Nehru, Winston Churchill, Martin Luther King, Albert Einstein, Sachin Tendulkar and others.
- The TOI was only one of two newspapers in the world to grasp that the assassination of Archduke Ferdinand would trigger World War I.
- The activist intent of TOI was stark when the accused of the Jessica Lal murder case were set free and TOI's headline 'Nobody Killed Jessica' unleashed a public storm.
- The Adarsh Housing scam of the last decade came to light when TOI reported that the land was not meant for those it had been allotted to.

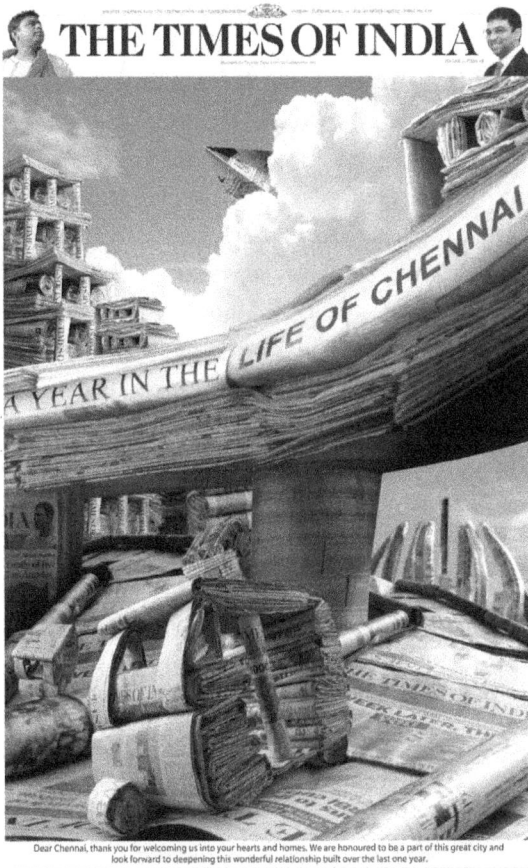

Capturing the essence of a city—TOI Chennai anniversary jacket

Strategic lessons for marketers:

» **Innovation and change as drivers**: At Bennet, Colemen & Company Limited, we have had a history of innovation. In fact we believe that if any new measure is legal and disruptive, we should try it. Even if it does not succeed, it invigorates the organization with a sense of having tried something new and fresh. Having said that, we are proud to say that many of our innovations have gone on to becoming outstanding success stories.

» **Positivity**: The TOI has also stood for positivity, always viewing the glass as being half-full rather than half-empty. We would like to define our role in terms of what the reader takes away from the newspaper rather than just what we put in—in terms of emotional feelings and not just the functional aspects. So, what do we see as our primary role? We believe it is getting our reader charged up early in the morning with a feeling of empowerment to face the challenges that lie in the day ahead. To give him an energizing start to the day.

» **Engagement and empowerment**: Traditionally newspaper journalism was defined by lofty editors preaching to the masses on what was good for them and the country. Post liberalization in the 1990s, attitudes began to change. Readers began to question the established order. And then the arrival of the Internet truly empowered them. The voice of the reader had to be recognized much more, and interactivity became vital for a newspaper in the changing milieu. TOI was a pioneer in this area.

» **Voice of the reader**: The TOI, in all its initiatives, is reader-centric in the sense that brand campaigns and communication is less about the brand itself and more about the reader's aspirations, hopes and concerns. It does not arrogate to itself the right to herd readers to a predefined point of view but seeks to empower them.

AFTERWORD

Market norms are stormed either by irreverent new entrants or by gutsy incumbents who have seen an opportunity they can't unsee. These storms tend to leave markets far more vibrant than they find them.

What does it take to storm a norm by design, and at will?

The twenty brands featured in this book belong to diverse industries that have their own unique challenges. Yet, they demonstrate an interesting ability that's common to all of them—the ability to shake up and transform stale, stagnant markets into fresh, vibrant ones.

This unique collection of stories proves beyond any doubt that market storms aren't purely accidental. There is a method to the magic, and they can be made to happen by design.

The method we discovered could be used by you as the framework to make better sense of the stories or to drive your own next big challenge.

The method to the magic

It all begins with staleness. A market that has stagnated is ripe for a storm. These markets don't necessarily have a felt need; just simmering, often indiscernible, tension of discontent below the surface.

> Look, for instance, at cinema exhibition space. In the past we have watched movies in cinema halls that looked and smelled, literally, stale. The business just trudged along through an extended period of sameness. Everyone cribbed a little but accepted it as a given.

Stale norms

Stale markets have norms that haven't changed for years, leading to commoditized offerings, mindless ritualized operations and wafer-thin margins. The market generates very little revenue and hardly any profits. The players seem to have grudgingly accepted it and become resigned to their fate.

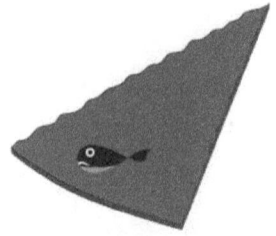

Every entity adapts itself to survive in a resigned-to-fate industry, until a stormer arrives.

> Cinema halls resented the apparent price sensitivity of the consumer. All value-chain entities accepted their fate. Scarcity made everyone risk-averse and unimaginative.

Spot the hidden suboptimal

The stormer has a unique perspective. He spots a potential change in norms that could cause disproportionate impact. One that makes the current norms seem suboptimal in comparison.

The realization is breathtakingly obvious in hindsight and is so surprisingly powerful in its promise that once the stormer sees it, he can't unsee it.

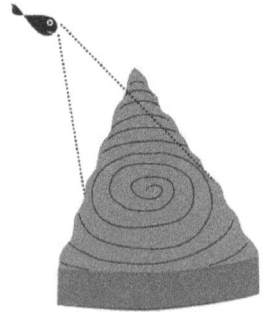

> Pioneers of the multiplex revolution realized that the cinema-watching experience that the consumers had accepted as a given was really a penalty. They endured it to watch their favourite movies. Undesirable spaces, rigid schedules, limited choices and unpleasant consumer engagement were suboptimals that were cramping the industry from achieving its true potential.

Conceive and iterate the breakthrough

The stormer conceives a breakthrough—a new product, process or business model. It's so compelling for him that he can't wait to build the first prototype, plays with it in the market and rapidly goes through multiple iterations to evolve it.

This leads to discarding many concepts before hitting the most powerful one. One that is elegantly simple, with the kind of simplicity that is found only on the other side of complexity.

Cinema was always about a break from the mundaneness of life. The large-screen audio visual experience allowed people to escape into the world of fantasy. But it took a lot for people to get to it.

Multiplexes offered a far more immersive experience thanks to technology; they also made it very seamless. You could catch a show almost any time, impulsively—a refreshing change from planned, appointment viewing of the past. As a bundled proposition, cinema + food + shopping is vastly more compelling than just cinema.

Pace to critical mass

A great concept must trigger a storm and for that it must hit the critical mass at a certain pace. Any slower, and the concept could join the large number of 'great ideas' that almost made it.

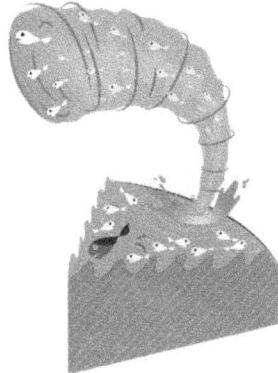

Lazy incumbents love failed upstarts. They reinforce their long-held view that nothing is possible beyond what they have been doing for years.

Concepts that have evolved rapidly through iterations in live markets are not just accepted but lapped up by the market that is surprised by their elegance. This leads to them hitting the critical mass at vigorous pace. The large-scale impact of newly unlocked value begins to show. Synergistic economies of scale and scope get triggered; and the bandwagon effect follows.

The price that the average cinema consumer is willing to pay today was absolutely unimaginable before the 'storm' arrived. More people watching more movies and willing to pay more for each, has been generating huge surplus that has altered the industry forever.

This has impacted not just the cinema exhibition space but cinema itself. The newly generated surplus is fuelling innovations—new genres of movies new breed of producers, directors, artists and actors. New entrepreneurial energies have been unleashed and the industry has turned truly vibrant.

Fresh norm

And before anyone realizes, the new concept has become the new norm and the lazy, cynical incumbents are anxiously playing catch-up.

It doesn't end here. It's a cycle. The fresh norm is after all a norm. And norms are usually the lull before the next storm arrives. The next stormer will spot the suboptimal in it and pursue unlocking of newer surplus that reinvigorates the market.

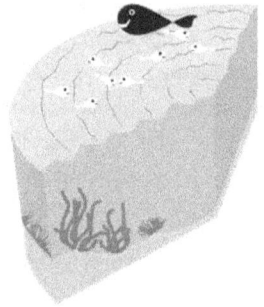

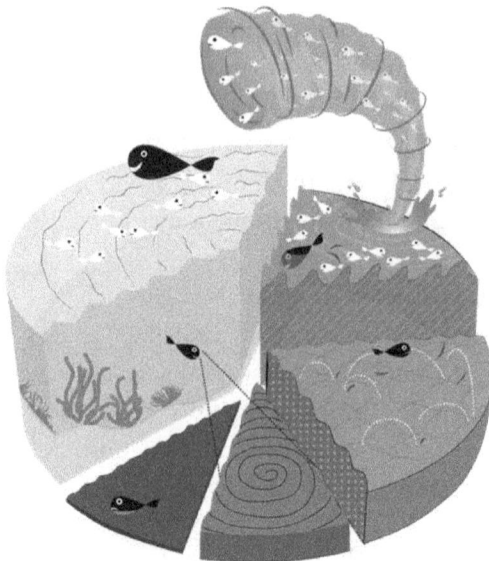

Movie watching is already experiencing the beginning of the
next storm—the Internet.

Decoding the method

A key effect of such a transformation is its impact on *total surplus*, which
is the sum of *consumer surplus* and *producer surplus*.

Consumer surplus is the maximum price the consumer is willing to
pay over the market price; and producer surplus is the minimum price
the producer is willing to accept below the market price.

Total Surplus

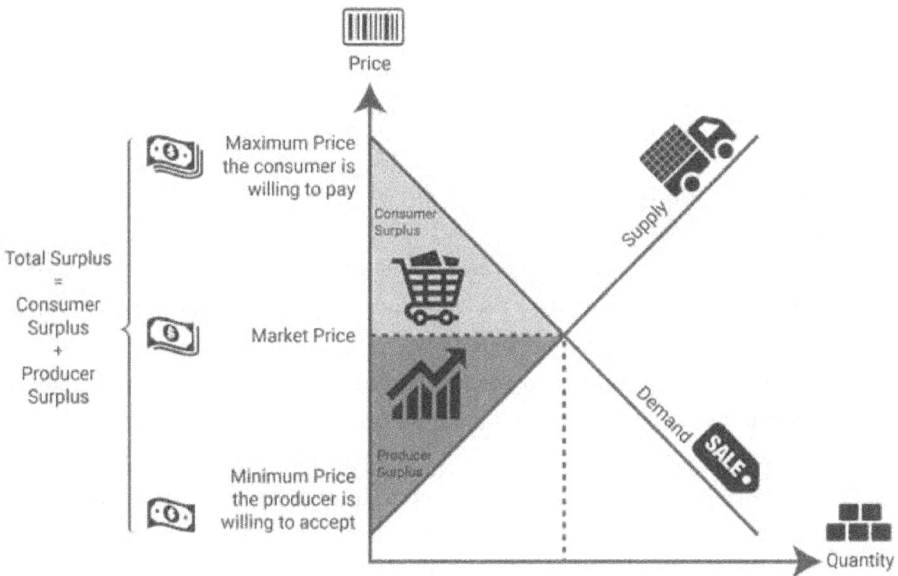

Notice how each brand in this book ended up unlocking new value
by triggering generation of disproportionately large surplus.

Stale, stagnant markets produce very little surplus. Consumers resent
price rise. Producers find it difficult to make profits that can be invested
in innovation that leads to better offerings. It's a vicious cycle.

A storm turns this into a virtuous cycle.

Stale, Stagnant Market   Fresh, Vibrant Market

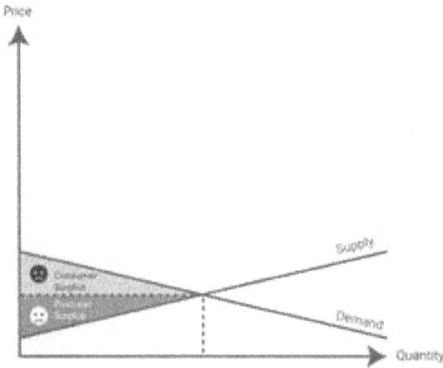

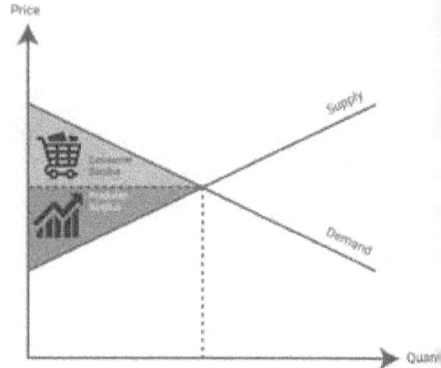

An insight that the stormer has, throws up a new value equation that points to the possibility of unlocking new surplus.

The insight leads to a breakthrough—and that could be a product, process, or a business model, or in some cases even a new ecosystem architecture.

A stale, stagnant market turns vibrant as the new value proposition surprises consumers who find the new offering very compelling and are willing to pay far more than before.

Producers have money to plough back into business leading to more innovation and even more demand. Economies of scale bring supply price down further.

This leads to a steep change in demand, more total surplus and more innovation—an almost magical upward spiral that causes the storm.

Any function in an organization can initiate a storm-the-norm strategy. Here's an example for you. The global financial meltdown in 2008 had an adverse impact on the life insurance sector. The market suddenly shrank and then stagnated.

Marketing function at Max Life initiated a mission aimed at a market step-change. Here's the storm-the-norm framework mapped by the team:

This is how the Max Life team stormed the norm

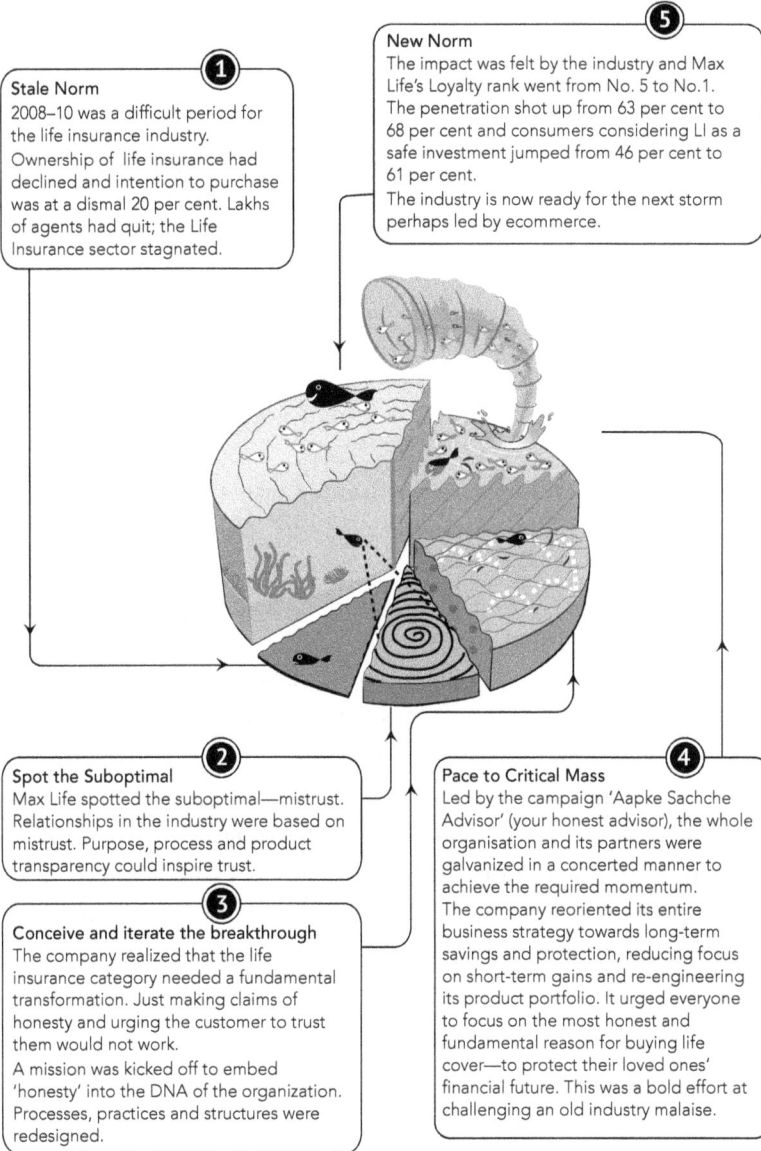

⑤ New Norm
The impact was felt by the industry and Max Life's Loyalty rank went from No. 5 to No.1. The penetration shot up from 63 per cent to 68 per cent and consumers considering LI as a safe investment jumped from 46 per cent to 61 per cent.
The industry is now ready for the next storm perhaps led by ecommerce.

① Stale Norm
2008–10 was a difficult period for the life insurance industry. Ownership of life insurance had declined and intention to purchase was at a dismal 20 per cent. Lakhs of agents had quit; the Life Insurance sector stagnated.

② Spot the Suboptimal
Max Life spotted the suboptimal—mistrust. Relationships in the industry were based on mistrust. Purpose, process and product transparency could inspire trust.

③ Conceive and iterate the breakthrough
The company realized that the life insurance category needed a fundamental transformation. Just making claims of honesty and urging the customer to trust them would not work.
A mission was kicked off to embed 'honesty' into the DNA of the organization. Processes, practices and structures were redesigned.

④ Pace to Critical Mass
Led by the campaign 'Aapke Sachche Advisor' (your honest advisor), the whole organisation and its partners were galvanized in a concerted manner to achieve the required momentum.
The company reoriented its entire business strategy towards long-term savings and protection, reducing focus on short-term gains and re-engineering its product portfolio. It urged everyone to focus on the most honest and fundamental reason for buying life cover—to protect their loved ones' financial future. This was a bold effort at challenging an old industry malaise.

Now browse through the stories again and see if you, too, see this pattern. Or a new one!

Ranjan Malik

Source of data: Syndicated Life Usage & Attitude Study, Nielsen 2012-15; Customer Relationship Assessment Syndicated Study, IMRB 2012-15.

ACKNOWLEDGEMENTS

I wish to personally thank the following people without whose contributions and support this book would not have come about in the form it has.

Mahinder Motwani, my life partner for over twenty-seven years, for his companionship and unconditional support in every decision of mine, right or wrong.

My lovely children, Prerna and Prithvi, who inspire me to live my dreams every single day.

Ranjan Malik, my thought partner, innovation speaker and facilitator, whose insights into innovation helped shape a unique 'Storm the Norm' framework to anchor the content of the book.

Pragya Khanna, my colleague and a branding expert who played a pivotal role from the very beginning in developing the master framework and selection of brands from amongst hundreds of choices.

Abhijit Bansod, founder Studio ABD, the most gentle and graceful person. His design help has been invaluable.

Special thanks to Santosh Desai, for setting the right context and laying out the scope of the book.

I would like to acknowledge the contributions of Knowledge Studio and Partner Index PR Pvt. Ltd. (a Ketchum Sampark subsidiary) for research and knowledge support in some of the cases.

Many thanks to Rupa Publications India for believing in me and enabling me to publish this book.

Above all, I would like to express my gratitude to the brand owners of all twenty organizations featured in the book for having generously given their time and wholeheartedly participating in the creation of this book.